PENGUIN BOOKS
IN SEARCH OF CONRAD

'What is so strikingly original about *In Search for Conrad* is that it is an essay in sustained affection and understanding ... It does not seek to nail Conrad down ... What we get instead is a sort of prolongation of Conrad, often dizzying in its piled-up memories, visits, citations, scenic details ... It is a very rare sort of book, quite unlike several recent "in the steps of" works, because Young himself is a confident and tactful enough writer to admit Conrad into his prose, without reductiveness or patronizing summary' – Edward Said in the *London Review of Books*

'Part journal and part historical and literary detection, it is above all a homage to the imaginative power of a great novelist, to a writer's ability to create and sustain his own world ... He is far too good a traveller to ignore what is in front of him, but it is a landscape that takes its imaginative colour and romance from the past' – David Crane in the *Spectator*

'As a travel book, it is vintage Young. One does not have to be a Conrad enthusiast to enjoy it, but those who enjoy it are likely to become Conrad enthusiasts' – Chaim Bermant in the *Sunday Telegraph*

'It contains vivid characterizations ... conveys the pullulating fecundity of Celebes, where at times you can hear the caterpillars eating. It limns the lethal beauty of coral reefs, which glow in the sunshine but disappear in cloud ... Resonant with *hommages*, the book also succeeds on another, deeper level; as "a kind of collaboration with the dead writer". Perhaps this is because Indonesia, in Young's portrayal, is heavy with magic. It is *hantu*, peopled with spirits. None are more vital than Conrad's creations' – Piers Brendon in the *Observer*

D0967900

ABOUT THE AUTHOR

Gavin Young spent most of his youth in Cornwall and South Wales. He studied modern history at Oxford University and spent two years with a shipping company in Basra, Iraq, before setting out to live in wilder places – first with the Marsh Arabs in southern Iraq, between the Tigris and Euphrates rivers, and then with the obscure people of the plains and mountains of south-western Arabia. From Tunis he joined the *Observer* as a foreign correspondent in 1960 and subsequently covered fifteen wars and revolutions throughout the world. He has also been the *Observer* correspondent in Paris and in New York. He is a Fellow of the Royal Society of Literature.

Gavin Young's first book, *Return to the Marshes* (1977), describes his adventures in Iraq with the Marsh Arabs who inhabit the ancient lands of Sumer and Babylonia; it was the basis of a BBC film in 1979. His second book, *Iraq: Land of Two Rivers*, an account of a journey through the historic landscape of Mesopotamia, was published in 1980. Gavin Young then travelled around the world by whatever waterborne transport he could find at the time. The story of that extraordinary voyage was told in his next two bestselling books, *Slow Boats to China* (1981, Penguin 1983) and *Slow Boats Home* (1985, Penguin 1986). *Worlds Apart* (1987, Penguin 1988) is a collection of pieces, most of them written for the *Observer*, that summon up more than twenty years of travel and adventure in some of the world's most remote and exciting places, while *Beyond Lion Rock* (1988, Penguin 1990) is the remarkable story of one of the world's greatest international airlines, Cathay Pacific Airways. He is currently working on a book on America, past and present.

In Search of Conrad was joint winner of the 1992 Thomas Cook Travel Book Award.

In Search of Conrad

Gavin Young

Illustrations by
Salim

Ah, Davidson, woe to the man whose heart
has not learned while young to hope,
to love – and to put its trust in life.

JOSEPH CONRAD, *Victory*

PENGUIN BOOKS

For Gillon and Cari Aitken

PENGUIN BOOKS

Published by the Penguin Group
Penguin Books Ltd, 27 Wrights Lane, London W8 5TZ, England
Penguin Books USA Inc., 375 Hudson Street, New York, New York 10014, USA
Penguin Books Australia Ltd, Ringwood, Victoria, Australia
Penguin Books Canada Ltd, 10 Alcorn Avenue, Toronto, Ontario, Canada M4V 3B2
Penguin Books (NZ) Ltd, 182–190 Wairau Road, Auckland 10, New Zealand

Penguin Books Ltd, Registered Offices: Harmondsworth, Middlesex, England

First published by Hutchinson Publishing Co Ltd 1991
Published in Penguin Books 1992
  3 5 7 9 10 8 6 4 2

Copyright © Gavin Young, 1991
All rights reserved

The moral right of the author has been asserted

Printed in England by Clays Ltd, St Ives plc

Except in the United States of America, this book is sold subject
to the condition that it shall not, by way of trade or otherwise, be lent,
re-sold, hired out, or otherwise circulated without the publisher's
prior consent in any form of binding or cover other than that in
which it is published and without a similar condition including this
condition being imposed on the subsequent purchaser

Contents

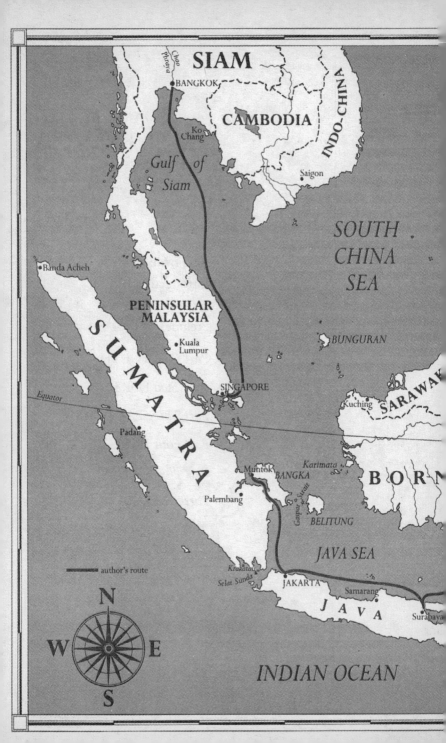

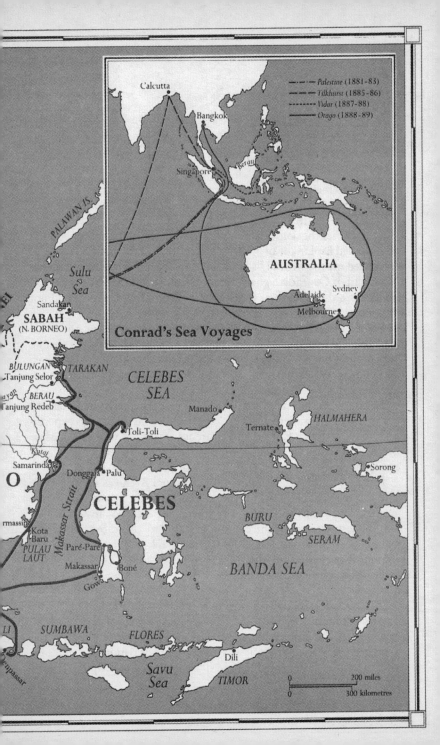

Calcutta

Bangkok

------- *Palestine* (1881-83)
------- *Tilkhurst* (1885-86)
.... *Vidar* (1887-88)
------- *Otago* (1888-89)

Singapore

Berau

AUSTRALIA

Sydney
Adelaide
Melbourne

Conrad's Sea Voyages

PALAWAN IS.

Sulu
Sea

Sandakan

SABAH
(N. BORNEO)

BULUNGAN
Tanjung Selor

TARAKAN

CELEBES
SEA

BERAU
Tanjung Redeb

Manado

HALMAHERA

Toli-Toli

Ternate

Kutai

Samarinda

Donggala Palu

Sorong

O

CELEBES

BURU

rmassin

Kota
Baru

Paré-Paré

SERAM

PULAU
LAUT

Makassar Boné

Makassar Strait

Gow

BANDA SEA

LI

SUMBAWA

FLORES

Savu
Sea

Dili

TIMOR

0   200 miles
0   300 kilometres

ACKNOWLEDGEMENTS

It is hard to thank sufficiently Norman Sherry, whose meticulous and brilliant work of literary detection, *Conrad's Eastern World*, inspired my decision to attempt this adventure. Norman Sherry saw before I did the ghosts that move among the solid office buildings and on the tree-shaded Esplanade of modern Singapore, and, without knowing it, he passed me the word. His book gave me the final shove that sent me in pursuit of Conradian characters to far more distant places where in some cases they met their bitter ends – places Sherry, alas, could not visit because of the circumstances of a lively local war.

I asked Norman to come with me on the old ketch *Fiona*, and in his reply he said how sorry he was – 'down to my heart's blood' – that he was too busy in an equally engrossing project that kept him in Texas. Now, in place of that trip, all I can do is to offer him inadequate thanks. A poor substitute.

Next to Sherry's *Eastern World* I am particularly beholden to Jocelyn Baines's superb *Joseph Conrad* and to his *Letters* so expertly edited by Frederick R. Karl and Laurence Davies, as well as Zdzislaw Najder's *Joseph Conrad: A Chronicle*. I am also grateful for the miscellaneous writings of G. J. Resink of Jakarta and The Hague.

I spent a good deal of time in the National Archives of Singapore and I have to thank Mrs Lily Tan, the enthusiastic lady in charge, for her help in tracing the past in a city where the past is not always held in the highest esteem. I am equally grateful to the directors of the National Archives in Bangkok where, thank heavens, the past is seldom forgotten, and where I also received much assistance from ladies and gentlemen of the Siam Society and the Neilson-Hays Library.

In Jakarta I was lucky enough to meet Dr Jacob Vredenbregt, who knows southern Celebes – the Bugis lands – well after five years' teaching at the University of Makassar, and my way through the region of the Makassar Strait was made a good deal more enjoyable by the cheerful Master of the PELNI steamer *Tidar*, Captain Harry

Subardi. Indeed all the officers of PELNI were extraordinarily helpful, starting with Captain Abrahams of the *Lawit* who took me through the Bangka Strait.

To Mr Richard Bull, until recently Headmaster of Rugby, my thanks for all his great hospitality when I revisited my old school. And Graeme Laird and Willem van den Wall Bake gave me much appreciated house space in Bangkok and Jakarta respectively, waiting with exemplary patience for me to complete my research.

Boundless thanks are due, as always, to my 'sea anchor' Gritta Weil, and to Sheila Colton, who has considerable personal knowledge of the area of Conrad's South-East Asia and whose Malay is so much better than mine. Salim has excelled even himself with his drawings. Roddy Bloomfield, of course, remains one of the world's most sympathetic editors.

From the Oxford Companion to English Literature:

CONRAD, Joseph (Teodor Josef Konrad Korzeniowski) (1857–1924), novelist and short story writer, was born of Polish parents in the Russian-dominated Ukraine. His father's political sympathies caused the family to be exiled to Volagda in northern Russia, where Conrad's mother died when he was seven. After their return to Poland his father, a well-known patriot, poet, and translator of Shakespeare and Victor Hugo, also died and Conrad was taken under the wing of his uncle, Thaddeus Bobrowski, who was to be a continuing influence on his life. From an early age he longed to go to sea and in 1874 he went to Marseilles, embarked on a French vessel, and began the career as a sailor which was to supply so much material for his writing. In 1886 he became a British subject and a master mariner and in 1894, after twenty years at sea, he settled in England and devoted himself to writing. He published his first novel at the age of 38, writing in English, his third language.

In 1895 Conrad married Jessie George, by whom he was to have two sons, and his novel Almayer's Folly *appeared in the same year. This was followed by* An Outcast of the Islands (1896). With The Nigger of the Narcissus (1897) and Lord Jim (1900) he showed himself a master of his craft. The sea continued to supply the setting for most of his novels and short stories. His narrative technique is characterised by a skilful use of breaks in time-sequence and he uses a narrator, Marlow, who provides a commentary on the action not unlike that of a Greek chorus. Conrad has been called an Impressionist and the movement of the stories, of the images and emotions, are portrayed through each character's private vision of reality. It was the novel Chance (1913) that brought Conrad his first popular and financial success. His other major works include Youth (1902), The Mirror of the Sea (1906), Victory (1915), The Shadow Line (1917), The Rescue (1920), and The Rover (1923). Conrad's autobiography, A Personal Record appeared in book form in 1912 and his unfinished novel Suspense was published in 1925.

He died of a heart attack on 3 August 1924, at Oswalds, Bishopsbourne, near Canterbury, and was buried at St Thomas's Roman Catholic Church there.

Introduction

My obsession with Joseph Conrad got into its stride, as I explain later on, after my Headmaster read a passage from the story *Youth* – a story that said in so many words, 'Catch life on the wing – but hurry!' A message I took in at full strength.

Conrad was not entirely new to me. My grandmother had a shelf full of the complete novels and stories at her house in Cornwall, blue volumes with tantalising titles in gold: I particularly remember *Victory* and a book with a fascinating name, *The Nigger of the Narcissus*. And the day my father died, about ten years ago, I found on his bedside table a battered copy of *The Mirror of the Sea* which from an inscription I saw he had bought at the Savoy Hotel in London in the middle of the war. Passing through London in the Blitz, and spotting it in that unlikely place, he had, I suppose, decided to carry it with him as a talisman for the rest of the war – and then, having done so, kept it by him for the rest of his life.

As a war correspondent I, too, took to carrying a Conrad novel about with me, both as a talisman and as a reminder that my hectic life was probably on the right track – that is, the one *Youth* had pointed out to me. Conrad had taught me that there was really no question of choice when a romantically inclined young man is faced with adventure and life on the one hand and a battened-down existence on the other.

My first job as a war reporter took me to the Congo and Katanga, the scene of Conrad's *Heart of Darkness*, and subsequently to pleasanter places than that doom-laden centre of Africa that had done for poor horror-stricken Kurtz. Several of those places I went to had been well known to Conrad – places like Bangkok, Borneo and Singapore, all three settings for his novels and stories. In those places I

1

began in my mind's eye to 'see' the world of the novels; it wasn't difficult to see through their modern disguise. I began to feel I was surrounded by almost palpable spectres from *Lord Jim*, *Victory* and *Falk* whenever I was in Singapore or Bangkok – I would catch the flick of Marlow's nautical jacket or a whiff of his cheroot, or get a glimpse of Captain Whalley's bushy whiskers on Singapore's sunlit Esplanade, and hear the rattle of the horse-tramway down Bangkok's New Road passing Schomberg's hotel. From a steamer's deck a white sail, veiled by a rain squall, slipped between two islands in the Java Sea, and what ship could it be but Lingard's *Flash* or the *Rajah Laut*?

The more I thought about them, the more characters like William Lingard, Jim, Schomberg the innkeeper, the miserable Almayer and the rest of them seemed to be there, lounging in wait for me under a seafront awning or in the porticoed doorway of Emmerson's tiffin room. They became as real as actual Singaporeans or Thais passing me in the street.

Until my reporting career came to an end I never had time to go chasing after them. But one can only cover wars for so long without sickening of the whole business of death, destruction and refugees, and only then did I find time to fulfil the ambition to follow full-time in Conrad's steps. That was quite a tall order because the world does not stand still. Was I too late? These days, places change very quickly.

With Conrad's books open before me, I could see how skilfully he had laid a fresh layer of history on the places he had written about. Certain rivers he knew – particularly the Berau – are still relatively unknown. One or two Conrad scholars have been to the Berau, but not, as far as I know, for some time. The admirable Norman Sherry wanted to go there. It wasn't his fault that he did most of his research in the middle of the war of confrontation between Indonesia and Malaysia and so found the islands inaccessible to him. My account of them, however inadequate, may therefore be the last. Soon the grave of 'Almayer's' sons may be devoured anew by the jungle, and the tombstones at Bulungan may very well disappear.

And the change was not all one way. Conrad, in a passage stating his extreme admiration for James Brooke, the first White Rajah of Sarawak, wrote:

> there were others – obscure adventurers who had not [Brooke's] advantages of birth, position, and intelligence; who had only his sympathy with the people of forests and sea he understood and loved so well. They can not be said to be forgotten since they have not been known at all. They were lost in the common crowd of seamen-traders of the Archipelago.

Such a one, *par excellence*, was William Lingard ('Tom Lingard' in the novels), 'a man once so well known, and now so completely forgotten amongst those charming and heartless shores'.

Men like him, said Conrad,

> for the few who know, have tinged with romance the region of shallow waters and forest-clad islands that lie far east and still mysterious between the deep waters of two oceans.

Of course Conrad himself, more than anyone, has changed the region, 'tinging it with romance' for ever. The East will never be the same since he wrote about it and fictionalised the real world of Olmeijer, Lingard, the Bugis and Syed Abdullah.

Some of the places they haunted still take some getting to. Norman Sherry's wonderful work of literary detection, *Conrad's Eastern World*, had told me that the grave of Austin Williams, the 'original' of Jim, might still be found in an abandoned graveyard. It can be found there still, but for how much longer? Of course national archives, registries, libraries remain full of records of people and events of a hundred years ago – of the world in which Conrad and his characters moved. But a grave is something personal.

Of all these elements I have tried to make an appetising *pot au feu*. I have often used bits of Conrad's own dialogue, and occasionally his own descriptions of people and places. I wanted to avoid a lot of imitation nineteenth century sailors' jargon, and after all, Conrad knew how his contemporaries spoke better than I do.

I must warn readers familiar with Conrad's works that now and again they may be startled to recognise the Master's own voice in the pages that follow. The truth is that I am attempting a kind of collaboration with the dead writer – his Past, my Present – without his permission, alas, but with the greatest reverence. Before I am accused of crass plagiarism, I should like to make that clear.

What follows is a pilgrimage – a search for scenes and ghosts known to that heavily accented foreigner from Eastern Europe, whose English shipmates nicknamed him 'Polish Joe' and who became one of the greatest novelists in the English language. I hope I can attract others to his world; to entice others to venture among the echoes and flickering shadows of the past, and among the swashbuckling ghosts, some evil, some noble, of strong men Conrad knew and made as familiar to us as if we had encountered them in real life.

Eager to meet them, I packed my old metal suitcase with the works of Joseph Conrad, and set off to the East.

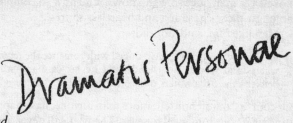

Dramatis Personae

Abdullah, Syed

Conrad's fictional representation (as Abdulla) of the real Syed Abdullah Al Joofree. Wrested commercial control of the Berau and Bulungan rivers from Lingard and Almayer.

AL JOOFREE, Syed ABDULLAH

Eldest son of Syed Mohsin bin Salleh Al Joofree, Straits Arab merchant and owner of steamers, including the *Vidar* on which Joseph Conrad served as First Officer on four voyages to the Berau in 1887–8. Syed Abdullah was his father's agent in the Berau-Bulungan area and broke William Lingard's monopoly of the Berau trade.

Almayer, Kaspar

Fictional character based closely on Charles Olmeijer. In An Outcast of the Islands and Almayer's Folly. In the latter novel he dies worn out and a failure on the Berau.

Falk, Christian

Fictional tug master – 'the only tug master in Bangkok', according to Conrad – in the short story Falk.

Jim

Fictional character loosely based on A. P. Williams.

LINGARD, Captain WILLIAM

Nicknamed 'Rajah Laut' (King of the Sea) by admiring Malay sailors. A generous, daring, successful privateer and owner-captain of a succession of Singapore-based sailing ships, successfully trading throughout the Eastern Archipelago. Discovered and commercially exploited the Berau and Bulungan rivers in east Borneo – Charles Olmeijer was his representative there. Finally lost his trading monopoly on the Berau to Syed

Abdullah Al Joofree, son of Syed Mohsin, the Singapore Arab trader and steamer-owner. His end was mysterious. Probably he returned to England and died there, but where and when is not known.

Lingard, Captain Tom
Fictional character based very closely on William Lingard.

Marlow, Captain
Joseph Conrad's alter ego in Lord Jim.

OLMEIJER, CHARLES
Born in Surabaya in 1848. Eurasian bookkeeper in Makassar, employed by William Lingard to represent him in the Berau office of Lingard & Co. for thirty years. Retired to Surabaya where he died after a cancer operation in 1900.

Schomberg, Wilhelm
Fictional innkeeper; a Conrad invention in Lord Jim *and* Victory.

WILLIAMS, A. P.
First officer (1880) of pilgrim-ship *Jeddah* at the time of her abandonment, blamed by the official inquiry as 'unfitted for his position as First Mate'. Returned to Singapore in disgrace. Died in Singapore on 17 April 1916.

'A man has got to learn everything – that's what so many of these youngsters don't understand.'

'Well I am no longer a youngster.'

'No,' he conceded.

JOSEPH CONRAD, *The Shadow-Line*

Prelude

We were discussing Joseph Conrad over tea at School House – they knew I had just returned from exploring his old haunts in South-East Asia – and the classics tutor was searching for a quotation. Between sips of the housemaster's Earl Grey he said, 'What was it exactly? – "I always thought that if a fellow could begin with a clean slate." Now which of Conrad's characters was speaking?'

'He's word-perfect,' I thought admiringly and answered, 'It comes from *Lord Jim*. Jim is sitting with Captain Marlow over drinks at the Malabar Hotel in Singapore, wondering how to start a new life.'

I could see the scene as if I was staring at an old photograph: a cigar butt arcing like a shooting star from the hotel's shadowy terrace; the two men choosing their words carefully, each for his own reasons; the black shoulder of the Harbour Office against the sky; the riding lights of sailing ships and steamers in the Anchorage.

'That's right! And Marlow – well, Conrad in fact – answers with something about one's fate being hewn in stone.'

My eye followed a jetliner far above the Rugby School playing fields as it ruled a straight white line through the pale, untropical blue of the Warwickshire sky. I quoted, ' "A clean slate, did he say? As if the initial word of each our destiny were not graven in imperishable characters upon the face of a rock." '

It sounded like showing off, but it wasn't much of a feat of memory. I have lost count of the times I have read and re-read Conrad's novels about the East, and that book in particular was vivid in my mind. As a matter of fact, it was a mere three weeks since I had said goodbye to the obscure river in Indonesian Borneo where Marlow had finally parted from Jim – Jim, silhouetted all in white on a strip of sand against the black and sombre wall of coastline behind him, the western horizon 'one great blaze of gold and crimson'.

I had just come back from that river, that coast, that sunset. How different from the scene I was contemplating now. I looked at it with interest. The Close was sharply lit by an unclouded sky and the housemaster's tall drawing room windows looked directly on to it. I had not stared at that view for forty years yet it was almost shockingly familiar. For a weekend in Shakespeare's mid-England I could hardly have chosen better weather. Sunlight flooded into the angles of the old drawing room, making its yellow walls glow like honey, and washed gently over the flat greenness beyond, over the boyish figures in white and the square white sightscreens over the darker background of tall, straight poplars and the needle-like spire of the Tolly Church. Nothing like the violent Eastern sunshine and the stronger vibrant colours I had come to know.

> I saw a bay, a wide bay, smooth as glass and polished like ice, shimmering in the dark . . . a puff of wind, faint and tepid and laden with strange odours of blossoms, of aromatic wood – the first sigh of the East on my face . . . .

I too had seen such bays; I had anchored and swum in them.

There were nine of us in the drawing room: the housemaster of School House, two of his tutors, five of his senior boys and myself. Across the Close a bowler ran with loping strides towards the wicket and the breeze brought us the faint click of a bat.

'See any changes?' The Senior Tutor was a clean-shaven, rather military-looking man, and of course as he asked I realised that what I had thought was familiar was in fact almost but not quite the same. Yes: the oak tree on the right of the garden wall had grown. And something else. Of course! – the static water tank had gone. No one

had ever had to put that dirty water to its intended use, which was to douse German incendiary bombs. Night after night in the early days of the Second World War the German bombers had throbbed above us on their way to pulverise Coventry, but although Rugby had an important railway junction I didn't recall any bombs falling – incendiary or otherwise. I remembered food rationing (meals of gristly mince), 'reconstituted' eggs, and bathwater limited to a few tepid inches. But no bombs. No 'enemy action'. No excitements at all. And then in our wartime backwater, one evening at Prayers the Headmaster had taken up his favourite anthology and read to us from Joseph Conrad.

In my day, our Headmaster took Prayers in Hall every weekday evening – one or two prayers, a hymn, a reading from his favourite anthology of uplifting poetry or prose: fifteen minutes of routine boredom. That evening began like any other. The boys sat at the long tables, all except a few senior boys who flanked the Headmaster on the dais under windows heavily masked by blackout curtains.

Prayers over, the single hymn ended, the Head of House carefully closed the lid of the upright piano and in the silence that followed the Headmaster rose with a book open in his hands. Murmuring, 'This is an extract from *Youth* by Joseph Conrad,' bowing a head haloed by strands of receding white hair, he began to read:

> I need not tell you what it is to be knocking about in an open boat. I remember nights and days of calm, when we pulled, we pulled, and the boat seemed to stand still, as if bewitched within the circle of the sea horizon. I remember the heat, the deluge of rain-squalls that kept us baling for dear life (but filled our water-cask), and I remember sixteen hours on end with a mouth dry as a cinder and a steering-oar over the stern to keep my first command head on to a breaking sea. I did not know what a good man I was till then. I remember the drawn faces, the dejected figures of my two men, and I remember my youth and the feeling that will never come back any more – the feeling that I could last for ever, outlast the sea, the earth, and all men; the deceitful feeling that lures us on to joys, to perils, to love, to vain effort – to death; the triumphant conviction of strength, the heat of life in the handful of dust, the glow in the heart that with every year grows dim, grows cold, grows small, and expires, too soon, too soon – before life itself.

I was fifteen years old and the words rushed to my head like strong drink. Who was this unknown author telling us to wake up and start living? Telling us, in fact, just what we wanted to hear: that we were young (I am not sure that that fact had really struck us before) and, as Conrad put it, 'had closed behind us the little gate of mere boyishness, and entered an enchanted garden'. Now, as I stood with my teacup in the sunlit window, the quiet voice of my late Headmaster reading those words came and went in my head like a distant but very distinct echo.

A cheerful, fair-haired boy – next term's Head of House – said to me politely, 'We hear you'll be reading some Conrad to us in Hall tomorrow. Some of us are taking Conrad for 'A' Levels, did you know?'

'I hope I won't put you off him,' I said.

I panned my mind's eye to that austere dining room-cum-auditorium like a movie camera – out of the elegant drawing room, across the carpeted hallway, through a self-closing door that led out of the Housemaster's private quarters into School House proper. I remembered a long, low passage lined by the gnarled wooden doors of boys' studies, cramped as cells of solitary confinement, and a steep corkscrew staircase that led down to great double doors, heavy and forbidding. Beyond these doors you were in Hall, an echoing, high-ceilinged, ancient, barnlike refectory. Here Dr Thomas Arnold, Rugby's early Victorian Headmaster, gowned and severely whiskered, had preached Muscular Christianity under the tall, ecclesiastical windows, looking sternly down at the long tables running the length of Hall, past the old black fireplace where the bully Flashman and his friends had roasted Tom Brown.

A Billy Bunterish boy in glasses blinked up at me. 'We're doing *Heart of Darkness* this term. What are you going to read to us?'

'Something from *Youth*,' I said.

How had I come to be here? Had I made an embarrassing mistake?

A few months earlier I had dared to write to the present housemaster of School House, explaining that I had spent some considerable time searching for traces of Conrad in the ports and on the waters of Thailand, Singapore and Indonesia – the countries Conrad had known as a ship's officer a hundred years ago. I explained how, at Prayers in Hall forty years ago, my obsession with Conrad had begun, that I hadn't been back to Rugby since, and that now at last I wanted to revisit that never-to-be-forgotten scene. To my surprise he had replied at once, 'Do come,' adding, as a *quid pro quo* – 'And by the way, because that passage from *Youth* had so much effect on *you*, would you be so kind as to read it to us?' The result was I was now apologising nervously to the little group of tea-drinkers in his drawing room.

grizzly bear, nicknamed 'Polish Joe' by his British shipmates – could this be a future master of English literature?

The organ fell silent and I heard the invisible organist moving about the loft, putting away his music. I stood up and edged out of the narrow pew, and the sound of my footsteps echoed through the nave as I made my way to the door into the Close.

The following evening fifty or sixty boys arranged on rows of metal chairs looked up at me like a large and hostile jury. I felt as if I were walking the plank as I followed the classics tutor down the twisting staircase to the new Hall, smaller than the old one, with the straight-backed chairs instead of benches and tables. He waved me to a chair and – kind man – gave me a flattering introduction. I had come to the end of the plank. There was nothing left to do but jump.

I explained about my Headmaster's reading from *Youth*, then spoke briefly of my own travels, and how Conrad's idea of life as an enchanted garden, its very shades glowing with promise, every turn of its path a seduction, had haunted me since that reading. 'Your housemaster has invited me to read the same passage. It may leave you cold, but – cross fingers . . . .' *Youth* fell open at the turned-down page, and I began to read:

'I need not tell you what it is to be knocking about in an open boat . . . .' No sound interrupted me; there was no applause; on the other hand there were no snores or giggles either. My audience was a blur of faces among which I could dimly make out the blond quiff of next year's Head of House, and now and again a flash of glasses and Billy Bunter's grin of encouragement. For the rest, as a preacher has faith in the power of his god, I had faith in Conrad. As I read I saw once again the boat motionless on the water, the rain filling the water cask, the drenched and dejected figures of the seamen, and young Conrad exulting in this initiation into the fellowship of the sea – of the East – of Life.

When I stopped reading I had no idea how it had gone. I could only hope that *someone* in my young audience had been made forever aware of the 'heat of life in the handful of dust' and how with every passing year it grows dimmer and colder, and expires – always too soon. And often long before life itself.

Part One

Youth

Let a young man voyage, speculate, see all that he can, do all that he may; his soul has as many lives as a cat; he will live in all weathers, and never be a halfpenny the worse.

It is as natural and as right for a young man to be imprudent and exaggerated, to live in swoops and circles . . . as it is for old men to turn grey, or mothers to love their offspring, or heroes to die for something worthier than their lives.

ROBERT LOUIS STEVENSON

You doubt that the Divine Spark is within you. In this, you are like the others. Will you differ from them in faith which fans the spark into a brilliant fire?. . . .

Why are you afraid? Of what? Is it solitude or death? O strange fear! The only two things that make life bearable!

JOSEPH CONRAD
Letters to Marguerite Poradowska

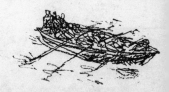

Early in March 1883, the old British barque Palestine (Captain Beard, First Officer Mahon, Second Officer Conrad Korzeniowski) entered the Sunda Strait, approaching Java Head. She had taken her time, having set sail from Newcastle-upon-Tyne as long ago as 29 November 1881 with 557 tons of West Hartley coal bound for Bangkok and a crew of thirteen hands all told. There had been mishaps on the way. At Newcastle the Palestine had been rammed by a steamer and delayed for three weeks. Beset in the chops of the English Channel by a succession of heavy gales, she lost sail and sprang a leak that almost did for her and shattered the nerves of her crew. She was delayed for thorough repairs in Falmouth for almost nine months. This was time enough for Conrad to receive (and ignore) a letter of advice from Uncle Thaddeus, his guardian, in Poland:

> Dear boy ... such a wretched ship. If you succeed in drowning yourself it won't profit you to arrive in the Valley of Jehosophat in the rank of a third or second officer! ... Both your Captain Beard and you strike me as desperate men, who go out of their way to see knocks and wounds. I shall not come down on you if you go back to London.

Second Officer Korzeniowski did not go back to London. With him aboard, the Palestine – the Judaea of Youth – creaked out to sea on her last voyage on 17 September 1882, and Conrad was destined to get his first sight of the East from an open boat.

one

According to the schedule the *Lawit*'s sailing time from Tanjung Priok, the port of Jakarta, was 1600 hours. Just two hours to go.

I had arrived in plenty of time, obeying the advice on my ticket, allowing for traffic jams. It was just as well I had. In the passengers' waiting area on the wharf – a cement box with a high ceiling supported by square pillars – scores of men, women and children were confined within a plate glass inferno. I doubt if there was a square yard of empty floor-space. Standing, sitting, squatting, some lying full-length, propped against hillocks of bags, boxes and baskets of woven leaves, they chatted and laughed, ceaselessly offering each other small, thin cigarettes that filled the thick, humid air with sweet, clove-scented smoke.

I stood like a sweating zombie: loosely to attention, immobile, my feet imprisoned by elbows and knees, a zip bag on my shoulder, my grip in one hand and my ticket turning slowly to sweaty pulp between the fingers of the other. I felt like a man who has painted himself into the corner of a Turkish bath. If I stooped a little to peer through the locked plate glass doors I could see the steep side of a big ship, but it wasn't the *Lawit*; there was another name on her lifeboats. The *Lawit*, I supposed, was some way further along the wharf.

I caught my companion's eye and gave him a smile of encouragement. He winked mutely back. There was no point in my saying anything: he would not have understood. That was the snag. Waiting to board ship, my mind wrestled with the problem. What on earth was I going to do with him?

It had seemed such a good idea. 'Do take Tomi with you,' an Indonesian friend had said. 'His English is not bad and he does so want to improve it.' So, even though I much prefer travelling alone, I had

19

agreed to take him with me, sight unseen, as an interpreter. My knowledge of the Indonesian language – *bahasa Indonesia* – is minimal and I would be lucky, I thought, to find many people in Bangka Island who spoke English. So an interpreter would come in useful, and Tomi would be worth his fare. But meeting him for the first time in the taxi to the wharf I knew within two minutes that my Indonesian friend had been talking rubbish and that Tomi's English was non-existent. With 'yes' and 'thank you', Tomi just about reached the limit of his spoken English.

The knowledge came too late. For one thing, the tickets were bought, but for another – and far more importantly – it was obvious that Tomi was pathetically excited by the prospect of his first sea journey, so that when we reached Tanjung Priok passenger terminal I hadn't the heart to tell him to take the taxi back to the city and forget the whole thing. With a flurry of flamboyant mime (I could see the driver's startled eyes in the mirror), he had conveyed that he was a student at a Jakarta school for ballet dancers. Confirmation followed in a remarkable fistful of Polaroids. At what looked like a particularly lively private party, he and his friends were shown doing spectacular high kicks in tights or, with wide smiles, posing coyly for the flashlight. 'Very nice, Tomi,' I had said, and he had murmured 'Shank you'.

So there he was, tall, slim and muscular, clutching an elegant new shoulder bag, in new white shoes, black and white sports shirt and jeans, waiting patiently to embark for Muntok.

With a roar of static, the port's loudspeaker began to bellow. For me, catching one word in twenty, it might have been announcing a bomb in the waiting room. Since Tomi could do nothing to enlighten me it was a relief to see policemen unlocking the glass doors. Barely waiting for them to open, several hundred passengers exploded, yelling, on to the wharf, heading in a jostling mob towards our ship's bows glimpsed vaguely at the far end of it. We followed more slowly, myself gloomily, Tomi with the straight-backed dignity of the prince in *Swan Lake*.

He could not keep that up for long. Our boarding was anything but dignified. A human scrum fought for footholds on the *Lawit*'s extremely steep and overcrowded gangway. In the ruck at its foot policemen strode importantly up and down, blowing whistles and shouting fiercely, '*Dua! Dua!*' ('Two-by-two! Two-by-two!'). Paying no attention, we pressed forward in fives and sixes, battered and bumped by other people's baggage, clutched at by other people's hands, toes squashed by countless stumbling feet. Near the top of the gangway, Tomi's bag staggered me with a hefty clout from behind that buckled my knees and I had a fleeting vision of my swift descent to the quayside, sweeping a dozen passengers with me in a mêlée of arms, legs, sarongs, parasols and large cardboard boxes. '*Hati-hati!*' I snapped over my shoulder – 'Careful!' – and heard Tomi's apologetic murmur. Sweating and dishevelled, a few steps later I handed our tickets to a ship's officer in an impeccable white uniform with two shining gold bars on his shoulderboards.

'Deck Number 7. Take key from information office.' he said, smiling sleepily, his English almost as impeccable as his uniform. I didn't need an interpreter at all. I collected the cabin key and followed a steward to the cabin. There, dumping my bags on one bunk, I pointed Tomi to the other. I showed him the shower, the washbasin and toilet and he murmured 'Hot-and-cold' with a smile.

I splashed cold water on my face. 'I'll be back,' I said, and went out and up on to the boat deck. People with baggage bustled about. Indonesian pop music, much amplified, rose from a deck or two below. The ship had come alive. I wanted to look her over and watch her take to the sea. She was the first Indonesian vessel I had ever been on.

The *Lawit* was relatively small – a neat 1400 tons, perhaps – but modern and German-built and belonging to the Indonesian government's shipping company, PELNI. I liked the look of her. She was clean and freshly painted; her officers and crew looked neat and businesslike. In due course she hooted three times to signal our departure, and several hundred other passengers rushed up from her bowels to see what would happen. A tug, the *Selat Sanding*, nosed close to our stern, and fat, muscular men in oily denims wrestled our stern cable on to the great hook on her deck. A second tug moved to our bows; another cable splashed down and was made fast. Silently, infinitely slowly, we were eased out parallel to the quayside, inching with seamanly caution away from a Thai ship lying astern of us, the *Bua Thip* of Bangkok, loading or offloading scrap – and looking like a lump of scrap herself from the rust on her.

The Indonesian passengers watched all this intently, standing three-deep at the *Lawit*'s rails. All ages, sexes and sizes, they were determined to get a view of the harbour, laughing and shouting, elbowing and shouldering. Soon they began pointing and coyly winking at me, the only *orang putih* (white man) aboard, evidently regarding me as an unusual bonus to their sea-going adventure.

Indonesians – anyway, Sumatrans and Javanese, as these mostly were – are a moderately sized people, and at six foot three I loomed over them like Gulliver in Lilliput. Smiling people came up one after another to gaze at this human skyscraper from Europe, to smile, to say, 'Hello, Misterrr' – their English went no further – to ask politely in Indonesian where I was going (I knew enough to answer that), how old I was, how many children I had, if I were Dutch, and if they could have a look through my old Leitz binoculars.

I answered them all, shook their hands, returned their smiles and lent them my binoculars. One very dark, very long-haired youth stared straight down at the water through them intently for a long time, then said, '*Terima kasih*' and, still holding them, began to walk away. I took back the glasses firmly but gently and offered him a Mentos mint from a crumpled packet in exchange; he accepted the mint and grinned widely. Perhaps he thought I had given the glasses to him and had been too surprised to hand them back. Later he shyly approached me and presented me with a can of Coca-Cola.

Shedding the tugs, the *Lawit* now moved forward under her own steam through the dock's thick, scummy water towards the sea. A heron flew over derricks, cranes and radio masts. Almost at once we had slipped out into the Java Sea, turned west and picked up speed – I estimated twenty knots – through the small armada of foreign cargo vessels at anchor in the roads. More heron and a wedge of dark birds with curved beaks like ibis skimmed low over a maze of bamboo fish-traps and reefs, heading for the swamps that surround Jakarta. Black storm clouds were massing over the hills behind the sprawl of the city but our bows were aimed north, towards the entrance to the Sunda Strait and beyond that – ah! – to the Bangka Strait where the *Palestine* had gone down in flames. That thought reminded me that I needed to make the acquaintance of my ship's captain.

I went below to make sure the ballet dancer knew where he could find something to eat and drink. He was lying on his bunk studying an English phrasebook. I made eating and drinking gestures – '*Makan, Tomi*' – and gave him some money. He smiled a thank you and skipped off down the passageway towards a 'Cafeteria' sign, no interpreter, it was true, but at least good-natured.

In the empty cabin reeking of Tomi's powerful *eau de toilette*, I penned a note to the captain asking for permission to see Bangka Strait as Conrad had seen it: to watch our progress up the Strait to Muntok from the *Lawit*'s bridge – I could go into the details of why later, if he wanted to know.

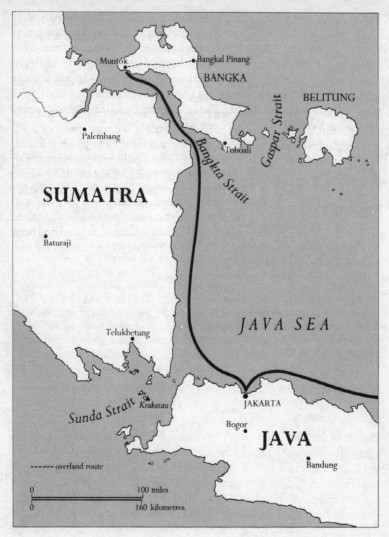

I thought the smiling chief steward would be the man to deliver my message and I went to find him. The information office was on the deck below mine, a long counter between a water-cooler and a small shop selling sweets, Coca-Cola, bottles of water and ice cream. Passengers clustered round the water cooler, crowded into the shop or lolled on the few easy chairs around it. Behind the counter I found the chief steward – an elderly man, I now saw, who told me his name was

John and that he came from Menado City in the largely Christian north of the island of Celebes. Through the grille I explained what was in the letter. 'It's a question of ghosts – '

'Ghosts?'

'It's a long story, I'm afraid. It's for a book. A famous ship burned and sank near here a hundred years ago.'

'A book? Ship sink? Oh, then I certainly give captain your letter.' He added, 'But we shall not see the Sunda Strait. We pass north of it.'

Never mind. He confirmed we would sail up the Bangka Strait and, most important as far as I was concerned, I would see the approach to Muntok. Back in my cabin I felt the light tremor, the lift of the choppy, shallow Java Sea as of a firm but gentle hand under the *Lawit*'s hull, and felt my own spirits lift accordingly. I took out my copy of *Youth*, lay down on my bunk and read:

> The first thing I did was to put my head down the square of the midship ventilator. As I lifted the lid a visible breath, something like a thin fog, a puff of faint haze, rose from the opening. The ascending air was hot, and had a heavy, sooty, paraffiny smell. I gave one sniff, and put down the lid gently. It was no use choking myself. The cargo was on fire . . . . On the lustre of the great calm waters the ship glided imperceptibly, enveloped in languid and unclean vapours, a pestiferous cloud defiling the splendour of sea and sky. Things began to look bad. We put the long-boat into the water. The second boat was ready to swing out. We had also another, a 14-foot thing, on davits aft, where it was quite safe.

Not long after that the *Palestine*'s cargo exploded.

Towards sunset Tomi burst excitedly into the cabin, indicating in high-spirited mime that he had been making all sorts of friends on deck. He carried a little bag looped round his wrist to safeguard his valuables, including the snaps of himself and his friends. He was extremely proud of them, that was obvious, and clearly he had been showing them to all and sundry on board – with what effect God alone knew. Indonesians, in my experience, are extremely broad-minded and also exceptionally polite, but I had no inkling of how they might react to pictures of young Javanese practising daring Western dance postures. Still, I felt no animosity towards Tomi or our mutual friend who had foisted on to me a fairly expensive (the *Lawit*'s cabins were not especially cheap), non-English-speaking interpreter I could well have done without. I did not want Tomi to feel badly about my mistake; it was not his fault. In fact, I wanted him to remain happy until the end of the voyage, which in any case would come soon enough since we were due to reach Muntok next day at about two o'clock in the afternoon.

A little later there was dinner of soup, rice, fish and some sort of sweet course served in a low, wide dining room by obliging stewards in high-collared red tunics, dark trousers and the round black Indonesian pillbox hats called songkoks. Later still, when darkness fell, a loudspeaker announced that a Jakarta-based pop group would perform in the mess room. In no time, scores of young men and one or two young women trooped eagerly up the companionways to sit in long rows facing a dance floor and a dais on which four musicians – keyboard, drums, two electric guitars – played 'Smoke Gets in Your Eyes'. An appropriate number, for they sat staring stolidly at the players through a fog of their own cigarette smoke, in silence, barely applauding. They sat up a bit when a girl singer in a short skirt and too much make-up began to move sinuously up and down under a couple of rosy spotlights, alternately crooning and shouting into a hand-held microphone. Her remote, don't-lay-a-finger-on-*me* sort of sex appeal drew excited whispers from the audience, yet nobody applauded her much either. Not that the audience looked bored. Perhaps it was simply that they were *kampong* – village – people unaccustomed to this sort of show, who felt that shouting and whistling at girl singers was undignified. One of them, anyway, was having the time of his life. I could see Tomi in the centre of the third row, grinning and swaying about on his seat to the rhythm of the music. Perhaps in a little while, I thought, he will leap up and astonish them all. Before he could do so I went for a stroll on deck.

At the door I met the chief steward and he introduced me to the ship's first officer, a surprisingly young man who said at once, 'Oh, the captain has seen your note. Okay to go to bridge when you like. Tomorrow? Six a.m.? We enter Bangka Strait then.' He nodded and smiled. 'You just come up.'

'Will I be able to look at the charts, do you think?'

'See the charts, see anything. No secrets on *Lawit*.' He laughed. 'You write *buku*?'

'Yes.' I told him my book would be partly about Indonesia today, partly about the past – for instance, about the sinking of an old British sailing barque, the *Palestine*, a little more than a hundred years ago and just about where we were now, near the Sumatra coast. The crew had escaped by boat to Muntok, I added.

'Just come up any time,' he said, looking interested. 'See you.'

Out of the dark to starboard, tall, thick flames wavered against the night sky. 'Oil recks,' the first officer said, meaning 'rigs'. They made a dramatic sight, like sea-going will-o'-the-wisps, the flares seeming to burst out of the water itself, flecking the rippling waves with red and orange. It struck me that the biggest of them looked very like a ship on fire – a ship full of burning coal. Within a very few hours we would be on the spot where the old barque had finally gone down. The ghost of the *Palestine* had every right to make a display.

When I went down to bed I felt as I had felt as a boy waiting for Santa Claus on the night before Christmas. Tomorrow something exciting was going to happen. But unlike the boy, I slept well.

TWO

Early next morning Tomi lay lightly snoring under his blanket; he had been considerate enough to creep into the cabin after the non-dancing disco without waking me. I tip-toed about, splashed water on my face and pulled on my clothes. Then I opened my zip bag and dug out a file – the report on the Marine Court of Enquiry into the loss of the *Palestine* 'held at the Police Court, in Singapore, on the 2nd day of April 1883, by order of His Excellency Sir Frederick Aloysius Weld, KCMG, Governor and Commander-in-Chief of the Colony of the Straits Settlements'.

Spreading it on the cabin's little table, I went through it again. The report began with details of the *Palestine*: 427 tons and built of wood at Sunderland in 1857 – so she had been twenty-six years old when she went down. She had been laid up in Shadwell Basin in the Port of London for a very long time before her final adventure – she was all rusty bolts, dust and grime – and the report referred to a number of misfortunes and long delays she had had to suffer at the outset of this voyage to 'Bang Kok'. The ship was doomed; one could feel it. In the Atlantic, Conrad had noticed, she wallowed like an old candle box. And then there it was – the beginning of the end: on 11 March

> a strong smell resembling paraffin oil was perceived; at this time the ship's position was lat. 2 36 S and long. 105 45 E Banca Strait. Next day smoke was discovered issuing from the coals on the port side of the main hatch. Water was thrown over them until the smoke abated, the boats were lowered, water placed in them. On the 13th some coals were thrown overboard, almost 4 tons, and more water poured down the hold. On the 14th, the hatches being on but not battened down, the decks blew up fore and aft as far as the poop . . . .

27

It was 6.30 a.m. and I climbed up two decks to the *Lawit*'s bridge. The young officer of the watch welcomed me with a cheerful wave of his hand.

'*Selamat pagi.*'

'*Pagi.* 'Morning.'

The *Lawit*'s wheelhouse was wide and high, with plenty of room to move about: I could walk from the port to the starboard windows without getting in any officer's way. Standing at the forward window (it sloped outward from bottom to top in modern fashion) I saw at once the light that I recognised from the chart, marked Tanjung Langgen, the southwest point of Bangka Island. Behind it stretched a jungle outline, still indistinct at this early hour, of dark ridges broken here and there by giant trees that raised their ragged heads like the crests of dark green cockatoos. On the other side of us, the Sumatran coast was quite different: low, flat and almost treeless, half lost in heavy, bruise-like storm clouds beneath which it would soon vanish altogether. There had been rain in the night. Now, suddenly, there was more of it, a roaring descent of water – a flash storm known locally as a 'Sumatra'; opaque walls of rain sweeping across the Strait before a strong wind. Soon the Bangka shore vanished, too, so that within minutes the entire scene before us – both shores and the Strait – had turned a watery green-grey colour and disappeared as though it had never been.

The officer on duty, peering intently ahead, reached for a lever and the *Lawit* gave out a warning hoot for the benefit of any craft that might be ahead. Torrents of rain beat down with the sound of pebbles against the windows and bulkheads of the *Lawit*'s bridge, reducing visibility almost to nil. When it could be seen at all, the sea was a grey-green blur of furrows ridged with white. It looked sad, wrinkled and old. We hooted again. And again. It was just as well. All of a sudden, a great black shape reared up out of the murk. Arrogant and indifferent as an iron-clad angel of death, with only a weak foremast light to warn us, a large cargo ship, the *Black Bird* of Adelaide churned past and was instantly swallowed up by the curtain of rain.

Does it seem unlikely that at this moment my mind was invaded by the sound of crashing Wagnerian chords – played, to be precise, on a Steyn and Ebhart piano by a vision of pale northern beauty called Freya? We were sailing just then very near the scene of Conrad's *Freya of the Seven Isles* – and Wagner's music was an appropriate background to the storm around us.

Violet-eyed Freya lived with her father, bumbling old Nielsen (some called him Nelson), a retired trader, an old Eastern hand. About twenty, she had a perfectly oval face, a most happy disposition, lovely round, solid arms and hair so long she could sit on it. In the big, hospitable bungalow her father had built on a shelving point of land on one of the islands not far north of Bangka, Freya loved in almost equal measure her piano, Wagner and an English privateer captain and adventurer called Jasper Allen.

There was no doubt that Allen, chestnut-haired, long-limbed, with an eager glint in his eye, was sweet on her, too. Anyone could see that. He paid regular and tempestuous court to Freya, sailing his wonderfully fast and pretty brig, the Bonito, up to her peaceful island retreat as though he was about to board an enemy vessel. To impress Freya, he would anchor the Bonito foolishly close to the dangerous point of the island, disregarding pointed comments from Conrad on the wisdom of paying heed to the uncharted rocks and shoals hereabouts.

'A perfect darling of a ship,' enthused Miss Freya, ignorant of rocks and shoals, as she gazed at the Bonito's snowy awnings, flashing brasses and gold-leaf mouldings.

Allen was impetuous to a fault, and impetuosity did indeed do for him. He ended up a ruined man, his beautiful Bonito impaled for ever on a reef off Makassar.

In precisely the sort of weather the Lawit was now experiencing, Freya had been driven by those hot Wagnerian passions.

> With the lowered rattan-screens rattling desperately in the wind and the bungalow shaking all over, Freya would sit down to the piano – the Steyn and Ebhart – and play fierce Wagner music in the flicker of blinding flashes, with thunderbolts falling all round, enough to make your hair stand on end.

And, as is typical with a 'Sumatra', within an hour the rain had swept by to the northwest, the clouds had lifted, light and visibility were restored. We had been spared thunderbolts, and now the piano chords ceased to echo in my mind.

Alas, old Nielsen (or Nelson) succumbed to senility and a broken heart in a boarding house in Bayswater, London; and, sad to say, Freya had died a little before him of love for poor, ruined Jasper – or was it merely pneumonia? – in wintry Hong Kong.

The master came onto the bridge as if he had timed his appearance by the return of clear weather. A youngish man, or at least young-looking, Captain Joseph Abrahams, originally of Timor but long resident in Jakarta, was bareheaded, wore casual green overalls and strode across the wheelhouse with his hand outstretched and an air of renewing my acquaintance. What sea-rover's spirit was it that made these Indonesian officers so uniformly courteous and friendly? He was about medium height with a cheerful, round, clean-shaven face and spoke nearly perfect English: 'I was at the Merchant Marine Academy in Jakarta. We all learned English there, I think you may find.' Then he patted my elbow, saying, 'And you want to see . . . come,' and led me to a table in the chart room behind the wheelhouse where the chart of the Bangka Strait lay spread open. I ran my finger up the coast from Tanjung Langgen to Muntok, opposite the Musi river channel to Palembang, explaining to him the reasons for my search. The predicament of the *Palestine*, Conrad, and her crew raised an immediate response from Captain Abrahams.

'The ship was on fire,' he mused. 'What position, exactly?'

I consulted my notes: '. . . umm . . . the position was latitude 2 36 S and longitude 105 45 E. The date and time – noon, 11 March 1883.'

'1883? Over a hundred years ago. Phew!' He worked a pair of dividers across the chart, finding where the bearings converged. He pointed. 'Here. In line with Tanjung Bedawi on the Bangka Island side, and Tanjung Tiram in Sumatra.' He straightened up, smiling. 'We'll be there in a few minutes.'

The Strait was narrowing here and swinging northwest; the Sumatra coast was the same low, mangrove-lined smudge and on Bangka Island a mountain was burying its head in cloud. It was a fair, clear day, but on *that* day, over a hundred years ago, the weather, Conrad remembered, had apparently been 'serene' – the sky 'a miracle of purity', and the sea had 'sparkled like a precious stone'. Not that fine weather could have helped the *Palestine*. The smoke kept pouring out of her, forcing itself through bulkheads and covers, making 'a pestiferous cloud defiling the splendour of sea and sky'.

I gave the captain a few more details – how the holds exploded and how the survivors had rowed for thirteen and a half hours, according to the Court of Inquiry's report, to reach Muntok. Puzzled, he said, 'But it's fifty miles. I don't think they could have made it.'

I consulted my notes again. Fire had been discovered on 11 March, the explosion had come on the 14th, so the ship had moved on, despite its difficulties and the calm weather. Abrahams nodded. 'No doubt.'

And then the decks blew up, tossing Second Officer Korzeniowski bodily into the air.

No doubt about it — I was in the air, and my body was describing a short parabola . . . . I picked myself up . . . . The deck was a wilderness of smashed timber, lying crosswise like trees in a wood after a hurricane . . . . I thought, the masts will be toppling over directly; and to get out of the way bolted on all-fours towards the poop-ladder. The first person I saw was Mahon [the elderly First Mate] who stared at me with a queer kind of shocked curiosity. I did not know that I had no hair, no eyebrows, no eyelashes, that my young moustache was burnt off, that my face was black, one cheek laid open, my nose cut, and my chin bleeding. I had lost my cap, one of my slippers, and my shirt was torn to rags.

'And after that she was towed?' Captain Joseph Abrahams was running his finger over the chart, estimating distances and speeds.

'Yes. By a steamer coming up from Australia to Singapore. For about five hours.' But the towing fanned the flames even higher, and old Captain Beard of the *Palestine* had had to issue the order to cut the towline.

'Cut?'

'Cut, yes. They couldn't attract the attention of the men on the steamer to get them to slip it, you see. By the time they could, the *Palestine* was really burning. Too late.'

The steamer's captain gave Beard one last chance.

'Come along: Look sharp. I have mail bags on board. I will take you and your boats to Singapore.'

'Thank you! No!' said our skipper. 'We must see the last of the ship.'

'I can't stand by any longer,' shouted the other. 'Mails — you know
. . . . I'll report you in Singapore . . . . Good-bye.'

The *Palestine* was a mass of fire; she would go down shortly. Officers
and crew had to hurry to the boats, and the exhausting haul to
Muntok began: *days* of rowing, according to *Youth*; *hours*, according
to the official Report. Back-breaking, anyhow. 'We pulled, we pulled
. . . I remember the heat, the deluge of rain squalls . . . . I did not know
how good a man I was till then.'

The chart of Muntok showed six wrecks, four of them clustered round
the entrance to a narrow channel leading to a small wharf. The *Lawit*
would anchor about a mile outside, Captain Abrahams said. Not
because of the wrecks; the exceptionally muddy water could ruin the
ship's engine-cooling system.

In the chart room I took down the volume of the *Indonesia Pilot*, the
indispensable guide to every port, bay, inlet and islet in the entire
archipelago, including the Bangka Strait — 'the best route between
Sunda Strait and Singapore', it said.

'The town of Muntok, which stands at the mouth of Sungai Muntok
is a local administrative centre. The climate is considered unhealthy.
There is a small harbour or refuge for praus [locally-built sailing
vessels]. Anchorage for large vessels with good holding ground may be
obtained from 1 to 1¾ miles offshore . . . . *Facilities*. Loading and
unloading is carried out by praus. *Supplies*. Fresh provisions, fuel and
fresh water are NOT available.'

'We off-load on to barges now, not praus,' the captain said, reading
over my shoulder.

Beacons were scattered along the Bangka shore, an occasional
huddle of houses marked the mouth of a small river, and beyond the
shore mountain and forest. '*Timah* all around here — what you call
tin,' Abrahams said. 'Tin ashore; tin under the sea. And *pasir quarsa* —
the sand they make into glass.'

By the time Conrad's boat had reached our present position, the
Palestine would have gone under, head first, in a great hiss of steam, at
the last minute shooting out, viciously, a slim 'dart of fire' at the men
pulling the boats across her stern. 'We drag at the oars with aching
arms . . . . 'And I see a bay, a wide bay, smooth as glass, a high outline
of mountains.' And here was that wide, shallow bay. I was *on* it,
moving in the *Lawit* across it, towards that high outline of mountains
and Muntok.

An order barked over the loudspeakers. Breakfast. I left the bridge and went below – to be halted outside the information office by the sight of Tomi, dressed in his tight black jeans and an even tighter T-shirt patterned with black and white zig-zags. The over-sweet aroma of his *eau de toilette* filled the area around them and I could see the chief steward's nose wrinkling as Tomi held his attention like a high-spirited and much rejuvenated Ancient Mariner. He was demonstrating something of great importance. With the sense of foreboding only strengthened by the seeping aroma of his *eau de toilette*, I recognised the portfolio of dancing-party snaps. The chief steward was being offered a detailed commentary on them. I somehow doubted whether that amiable old sea-dog was an *aficionado* of modern, Western dance, but his expression could fairly be described as inscrutable.

Tomi turned to face me, holding out a photograph of himself in full *entrechat*. 'You like?' he asked.

'One of my favourites,' I said wearily.

I tapped him gently on the shoulder and led him away to join the stream of other passengers at breakfast.

The meal – chicken-porridge and thick, sweet Java coffee – was soon over. I was eager to get back to the bridge but so as not to seem unfriendly I accompanied Tomi on a short stroll among the crowds on Deck 6. There I left him, in the open, lightly spray-spattered area below the bridge, happily chatting to a group of young people. He may have spotted a few potential balletomanes among them. When I looked back from the companionway leading to the wheelhouse he was reaching ominously into his handbag. I kept on going. I did not want to miss our approach to Muntok, Joseph Conrad's first Eastern landfall.

Across the big, shallow bay I could see a long sweep of beach ending in a prominent white lighthouse. It had been night when the survivors of the *Palestine* had reached this bay; they saw an outline of mountains, the beach gleaming in the dark and dimly made out the light at the end of the wharf and steered for it . . . .

> This is how I see the East. I see it always from a small boat . . . I have the feel of an oar in my hand . . . and I see a bay, a wide bay, smooth as glass and polished like ice, shimmering in the dark. A red light burns far off upon the gloom of the land, and the night is soft and warm. We drag at the oars with aching arms, and suddenly a puff of wind comes out of the still night – the first sigh of the East on my face. That I can never forget.

Even from a mile away, the shore looked surprisingly unpopulated. As we drew in from the middle of the strait to anchor, I could see a few red roofs half hidden among trees, two longish ramshackle buildings (where, the captain said, tin was processed for export), one or two godowns and a spindly, iron-strutted jetty. There were some barges alongside it and an anonymous white mast. And that was all.

The *Lawit*'s smartly painted nose swung towards the unbroken line of tall trees; slowed; stopped. The hook went down, and after a while I saw through my binoculars a tug setting off from the jetty. As it approached, I could see it was towing an iron barge – no, two barges side by side, one with a makeshift awning and both red with rust and almost top-heavy with passengers and baggage.

'We take on those passengers. Then we offload you,' Captain Abrahams said, smiling.

'I had better go down, then,' I said.

We paused to exchange addresses, and shook hands. From the rail I watched the barges rocking on the current behind their tug and clashing against each other repeatedly, like opposing shields in a battle, their thin iron sides banging together, sending hollow clangs like the sound of great cracked bells across the water. Their passengers, perhaps a hundred altogether, squatted among bundles and boxes, clinging to each other or to bollards on the metal decks. The tug's name, *Timah II*, in white paint on her bows, swung gently alongside. The ship's gangway came down, was made fast and the second storming of the *Lawit* began.

Like a column of ants, the embarking passengers shouldered their belongings and clambered unsteadily up the side of the ship, shouting advice or warnings to each other as they went, the tumult increased by encouraging yells from the impatient crowd already on board.

One night a hundred years ago, a disembodied cry had rung out across this patch of water: *What steamer is this, pray?* – the voice of Second Officer Conrad Korzeniowski, fatigue emphasising his thick Polish accent.

'Eh? What's this? And who are you?'
'Castaway crew of an English barque burnt at sea. We came here tonight. I am the second mate. The captain is in the long-boat, and wishes to know if you would give us passage somewhere.'

'Oh, my goodness! I say . . . . This is the *Celestial* from Singapore on her return trip. I'll arrange with your captain in the morning . . . .'

Now I was surrounded by hubbub. The shouting, milling crowd at the top of the gangway descended in a struggling mass into the barges, hugging children who howled and huge suitcases and crates that weighed a ton. I went to the cabin and found Tomi lying on his bunk. He raised his head as I came in, blinked and smiled, ready at once for a new round of encounters. In a few minutes, having dropped the cabin key in the information office on the way, we were back on deck.

I shook hands with the chief steward and elbowed my way through the jostling throng at the head of the gangway. Soon we were on a swaying barge, being towed towards Muntok's spindly jetty and those red roofs half hidden behind the clumps of vegetation on the sickle-shaped beach. There – precisely there – the three boats from the *Palestine* had lain; the sleeping seamen sprawling in the careless attitudes of death; the head of the old skipper leaning back in the stern of the long-boat filled with the burning image of the death of his last command; the face of Mahon, the first mate, upturned to the sky, long white beard spread out on his breast as though he had been shot, 'and the East looking at the tired men from the West without a sound'.

A bit different from my own arrival. Our barge swung alongside the jetty with a last mournful clang, its hawsers made fast and I looked up. The jetty was thronged with waving, chattering Bangka people, excited men and women and many children, brown-skinned, soft-eyed people, inquisitive to see who was landing here today – the *Lawit* only called once a week, I believe. The many paler faces I took to be Bangka Chinese. When Conrad at last reached Muntok, he saw

the whole length of the jetty was full of people. I saw brown, bronze, yellow faces, the black eyes, the glitter, the colour of an Eastern crowd . . . . The fronds of palms stood still against the sky. Not a branch stirred along the shore, and the brown roofs of hidden houses peeped through the green foliage . . . . I see it now – the wide sweep of the bay, the sands, the wealth of green infinite and varied, the sea blue like the sea of a dream, the crowd of attentive faces, the blaze of vivid colour – the water reflecting it all, the curve of the shore, the jetty . . . .

I could see for myself that hardly anything had changed. The attentive faces, brown, bronze, yellow, the black eyes, the curve of the shore, the palms and the roofs of hidden houses, the jetty – all these things were the same. What was new? Baseball caps, jeans, Tomi's white trainers, the minibuses beyond the crowd. For Conrad all the East had been contained in that vision, which had lasted no more than a moment: *'a moment of romance – of youth!'*

I slung my bag over my shoulder and stretched up a hand. Someone grasped it and heaved me up on to Muntok's crowded jetty.

Three

On the *Lawit*, and again on the barge, I had talked briefly with a dark, Indian-looking man wearing a grey 'wideawake' that gave him the look of a river-boat gambler. 'This is Mr Helmi, the PELNI Company's agent on Bangka Island,' Captain Abrahams had said. And Mr Helmi had responded warmly. 'When you come to Bangkal Pinang, the capital of this island, please come to my house and my office. Next to the Hotel Wisma Jaya. I will look after you.'

At the jetty Mr Helmi took me by the hand and led me to the driver of a battered minibus. 'This is Benny. He will bring you to Bangkal Pinang. See you there.'

Benny was bright, sensible and spoke English. I said to him, 'A quick tour of Muntok please. Then to Bangkal Pinang.'

'No problem.'

There is not much of Muntok to see. Probably there never was: many years after the thrill of his first Eastern landfall Conrad had called the place 'a damned hole without any beach and without any glamour'. Muntok does have a beach, which is a narrow one but also very long: it skirts the whole rim of the bay. Conrad and the rest of the *Palestine*'s crew had had to spend nearly a week here before the British steamer *Sissie* arrived to take them to Singapore, and that must have seemed an interminable time if you have just been shipwrecked.

Benny warned that another rainstorm could block the long, bad road to Bangkal Pinang, so we were no more than an hour in Muntok.

Below the jetty there was a tin works of some sort, but I was more interested in the little town that Conrad had seen. It had a battered, picturesque quality. Canals ran inland through rows of wooden houses, many of them on stilts with battered roofs of red tiles or rusty corrugated iron. A good many small motor launches floated on the creeks' greenish water, and sometimes a larger wooden barge. A red-tiled mosque occupied one side of an untidy main square which was unpaved and presumably became a morass of mud in the rainy season. It was surprising to find that down narrow streets once-gracious Chinese residences still survived, though sadly crumbling now, with rotting gables and chipped stone temple dogs at their doorways, and one or two old brick villas of former Dutch merchants and officials.

Unused now by big ships (which anchor like the *Lawit* out in the Strait), the old port of Muntok was no more than a tiny pocket of water tucked away north of the jetty, with the narrow strip of yellow beach Conrad had ignored running uninterrupted to the lighthouse at the top of the bay.

Two stone breakwaters had been built years ago to protect a prau harbour, and now at low tide a few big-bottomed, wooden vessels lolled there on their sides in the mud like stranded whales, and one big white sailing ship propped up on piles was under repair. Long, ancient brick warehouses matched in style the old Dutch buildings in the town. There was little sign of life. Three elderly men sitting idly talking under a tree paid no attention to us.

'Four hours' driving, bad for the back,' Benny announced as we set

38

off for Bangkal Pinang. Tomi, stretched out in the back seat, may have slept, but the drive was an ordeal. The narrow road was pitted with potholes as big as small shell craters, across the worst of which local people had laid miniature bridges of branches and palm fronds. As Benny had warned, it was a spine-punishing four-hour drive.

Bangka Island was generally flat with patches of wild vegetation alternating with rows of pepper plants clinging to long poles, and villages standing among bananas, bamboos and palms.

Bangkal Pinang was a good deal bigger than Muntok; a garden town, with a certain charm. The 'new' hotel – I am not sure how new it was – was a bungalow patronised by Indonesian commercial travellers and the occasional official and his wife, and the youngish staff gambolled out to meet us like puppies. 'Tomorrow,' I told Benny before he drove off to see his girlfriend, 'we go to see Mr Helmi.'

For breakfast there was *bubur ayam* (chicken-porridge) and *nasi goreng* (fried rice), set out in metal dishes and stone-cold. The methylated spirit had run out, a waitress said, and she had no money to buy more. 'Now you have.' I gave her some money and set off irritably, to Mr Helmi's office next door.

Mr Helmi had not yet arrived. Perhaps, his clerks warned, he was still asleep – after all, it was only eight o'clock. Urgent childish shouts of 'Papa!' arose as I approached the front door of his house through a garden, and almost at once he appeared, his hat on his head, looking more darkly Indian than ever.

'No, no! I am not sleeping,' he protested, smiling. 'Did they say I was asleep? No, no. Have some tea.' He led the way into a small study that connected his house with the main PELNI office. It was sparsely furnished with a desk, a telephone, a telex machine, a couple of easy chairs, a filing cabinet and on the walls numerous photographs of Mr Helmi and his PELNI colleagues, some of them hanging askew. The room strove for an air of relaxed efficiency, and Mr Helmi, wide awake and sipping tea sat behind his desk, smiled serenely.

'I am from Acheh,' he said by way of introduction. 'An unusual place on the extreme northwestern tip of Sumatra. The Achinese are Muslims of rather an extreme kind. They defeated the Dutch armies, and for many years the Dutch kept strong garrisons in the region.' Mr Helmi did not look like a fanatic.

'Acheh,' Mr Helmi said again. 'A-c-h-e-h, you see. A for Arabian. CH for Chinese. E for European. H for Hindustan or Hindu. Islam came from Arabians. The Chinese came for trade. Hindustan – India –

came because was nearby. Of course, the Europeans came later. Quite a mix-up, you might say.'

He suddenly turned to Tomi. 'And you are from?'

'Jakarta,' replied Tomi. with a shy wriggle of his shoulders. Mr Helmi looked at him for a moment with interest but without a word.

Mr Helmi insisted that as a friend of Captain Abraham he would like to help me in any way possible. It was hot in his little office so he rose, reached up to pull the switch on the air conditioning fixture in the wall and sat down again, wiping his dark brow with a coloured handkerchief. The air conditioning, I noticed, was not plugged in. We continued to swelter.

Muntok, said Mr Helmi, the sweat glistening on his dark skin, was smaller than Bangkal Pinang but it had always been the port of Bangka, exporting the island's tin and pepper. Bangkal Pinang was where the merchants actually lived. In the old days the Dutch had liked it here and business had followed them: pepper business and tin. The island had a Javanese Governor, although in the old days, of course, the Governor had been a Dutchman: 'A charming, peppery, hearty, retired rear admiral.' A friend of old Neilsen.

Mr Helmi broke off our conversation to try to telex his main office in Jakarta. After a long wait he gave up. 'Here, communication no good,' he said. He tried a telephone call to Padang in Sumatra next, but he was obliged to give that up, too.

'Oh, this is nothing,' he shrugged.

Before his posting to Bangka Island, he explained, he had suffered for three seemingly endless years as PELNI's representative in Sorong, a port of Irian Jaya in New Guinea; after that awful experience, what were a few delays here with the telephone. 'It was,' he told me, assuming an almost boastful expression, '*impossible*! The people of Irian Jaya had no *learning*. The Dutch taught them to be *drunk* most of the time.'

They refused to work. In despair Mr Helmi had thought of trying to look like them, of growing his hair long and drawing interesting patterns all over his face with his wife's lipstick. Perhaps that would win them over. Perhaps then the people of Irian Jaya might say, 'Oh-ho, Mr Helmi, now you are one of us – a brother! We will *work* for you now!'

No, he had not cared for Sorong. His Chinese wife had hated it.

Now he offered to help me get a flight back to Jakarta, and he peered in his office mirror, straightening his grey wideawake before going into town. The hat meant status like his tie, his white shirt and his shining shoes, and at the Garuda airline office he needed every bit of status he could summon up. Rough, Chinese-looking businessmen rudely shouldered their way to a counter, ignoring those who were already there. They demanded reservations and tickets from the hard-pressed staff with the threatening air of bank-robbers demanding the contents of the till. Mr Helmi, in his hat, maintained his dignity. He courteously addressed himself to a clerk in his proper turn; self-contained, saturnine, dark-skinned Mississippi gambler cashing in his chips. An hour and a half later we emerged.

'Mr Helmi,' I said, 'You know in Arabic they say *"Ajela min esh Shaitan, es subur min er Rahman."* Haste is from the Devil, patience is from God.'

'Ah, *rahman*, yes,' he cried in delight. '*Rahma* means "love". God loves everyone.'

Allah was very important to him, Mr Helmi assured me. When I told him that Europeans had a saying, 'God helps those who help themselves,' he immediately agreed. 'Oh, yes. I don't want only to sit and not working, waiting for God to help me. Oh, no.'

After a pause he smiled. 'You go to many places by sea. I am not surprised. I read history. Britain once ruled the waves. I learned that. British are very at home at sea.'

'We used to be.'

Back in his house, Mr Helmi served rich Javanese coffee and rice with a sauce of creamy coconut milk and durian – a plump, delicious fruit that smells like a drain but is adored by all Indonesians.

Mr Helmi put a bottle of warm beer on the table for me, explaining, 'I gave up drinking whisky and beer, doctor warned me of high blood pressure.' He smiled and emphasised his point: 'Doctor, I say, not Allah.'

I found Mr Helmi's candour engaging. When it was time to part he said: 'I would like to write to you. I would like a . . . .'

'A correspondence?'

'Yah, yah. A correspondence. I write to you in London . . . you write to me here.'

He wrote out his address, opened a drawer and took out a photograph of himself. 'You see my face,' he laughed, 'you think of Muntok!' Then he grasped my hand with both of his, and gave me the Indonesian *salaam*, palms pressed together vertically, under his nose.

Instead of heading straight for the airport we drove out to a beach not far away. The sand was white here where the South China Sea joins the Java Sea, and the water shallow. Lifeless little waves plucked anaemically at the shore.

I bought Benny and Tomi soft drinks and we stood in brilliant sunshine beside fishing boats drawn up on the sand. There was a fair stretch of water facing us; barely any solid land between us and Indonesian Borneo. To the southwest, just out of sight, was the other large island of the Bangka group, Belitung, and separated from us by the Gaspar Strait, another route from Sunda to Singapore but less safe than the Bangka Strait because of its reefs and rocks. They had a fascinating name. The Hippogriffe reefs, the *Pilot* said, were marked by rip tides and congregations of sea-birds; the Belvedere Rock was black and surrounded by coral; the Warren Hastings reef was a menacing cluster of six coral patches. Canning Rock; Rifleman reef; and Wild Pigeon reef – all, I supposed, took their names from ships that wrecked on them or from survey ships that charted them. Nemesis Shoal at the south entrance to Bangka Strait sounded as if it had already taken its toll. In *An Outcast of the Islands*, Captain Tom Lingard had planted his brilliant little brig *Flash* for ever on a ledge of rock in the Gaspar Strait. He never recovered from that bit of carelessness.

At Jakarta airport I thanked Tomi for his company. He took my hand, grinning, and pumped it up and down, saying '*Baik*!' and '*Bagus*! Good' – and then launched into a long, rapid and passionate speech, a lot of gratitude for a short journey, until I pressed a parting present of rupiahs into his hand. I said, 'On your way, big boy.' I said it gently, and with a smile. And at last he turned and went off with a cheerful wave and his springy dancer's stride.

During the flight back to Java I peered down at the entrance to the Bangka Strait; in the sunlight it was very clear, very blue. A large freighter was crawling up the calm sea, slowly unfurling its wake like a silver thread. Wistfully I searched the water for the *Palestine*; for a plume of smoke with a heart of glowing coal, for an old wooden barque, dismasted, her decks blown into matchwood, sinking into the sea like a funeral pyre. And for three dots – three open boats – creeping painfully away from it, northwest towards Muntok. Of course there was nothing like that. The wide, sunlit Strait, smiling innocently back at me, seemed to deny that such a disaster could ever have happened.

A man should stand up to his bad luck, to his mistakes, to his conscience, and all that sort of thing. Why – what else would you have to fight against?

JOSEPH CONRAD, *The Shadow-Line*

Part Two

Port

The Sissie *(not the* Celestial, *as he said in* Youth*) took Conrad on to Singapore where he was paid off with $171.12 on 22 March 1883. Then he returned to England on a passenger steamer. He sailed out to Singapore – a very brief visit – in 1885 on board the* Tilkhurst. *His third and by far the longest period in and around Singapore ran from 6 July 1887, when he arrived, injured, from Samarang in Java aboard the* Celestial, *until 3 March 1888. On that day he left for Australia as master of the 367-ton sailing barque* Otago, *his first and last command of a sea-going vessel.*

Set squarely on the main west-east shipping route, Singapore is a great Eastern port and was populated then (as now) by an extraordinarily colourful mixture of races. It represented a turning-point for Conrad. From the merchants and ship's officers who frequented the Sailors' Home, the Harbour Office, Emmerson's Tiffin Rooms and other places he heard, for example, the scandalous story of the young English Merchant Navy officer, who was then still working there, who was to become Conrad's fictional 'Lord Jim'. He heard, too, much excited talk of the famous trading captain and adventurer Captain William Lingard, who (as Tom Lingard) appears as a major character in Almayer's Folly, *An* Outcast of the Islands, *and* The Rescue. *And in Singapore he took a fateful step in signing on as first mate of the* Vidar, *a small steamer that plied between Singapore, the ports of the Java Sea and the remote Berau River in Borneo. The* Vidar *belonged to a Straits Arab shipowner, Syed Mohsin bin Salleh Al Joofree, whose son Syed Abdullah finally broke the trading supremacy of William Lingard and his agent, Charles Olmeijer, in eastern Borneo. Resigning that position, Conrad went to Bangkok to take charge of the* Otago *after the sudden death of her captain.*

Four

What a contrast to humble, unglamorous Muntok! The skyscrapers on Singapore's newly created seafront shoot up in almost invariable sunshine, like dragons' teeth. They have a self-satisfied look, proclaiming both the rewards of hard work and a new hard-headed Singaporean – Confucian attitude to the wicked layabout modern world. At the same time one cannot deny that those icing-sugar towers, those shiny dominoes announcing 'Money' make a spectacular background to the scores of cargo ships and tankers of all sizes and nationalities that spread themselves across the Anchorage in neat rows like a fleet waiting for some cocked-hatted admiral to review it.

The view from the water is memorable; but from the office towers on the reclaimed land in the area of Shenton Way and Collyer Quay round to the massive, unimaginative, neo-Babylonian shapes of the ultra-smart hotels near the confluence of venerable Beach Road and upstart Raffles Avenue there's nothing – no domed mosque, no pagoda, no palm tree – to tell you that you are in the East. You must strain your eyes from the ship's rail, through binoculars preferably, to make out odd bits of the city Conrad knew – the formal colonial front of the City Hall behind the leafy avenues of Esplanade Park, the stately wedding-cake façade of Parliament House, or the regal mass of Victoria Memorial Hall. The elegant white spire of St Andrew's Cathedral is today crudely dwarfed by a huge hotel and a shopping complex called Raffles Plaza.

So coming back to look for Conrad's world I wondered: 'Have I come ghost-hunting too late?'

Singapore had most dramatically achieved the future that its founding genius, Stamford Raffles, had predicted for it. It was already the emporium and multiracial pride of the East by the time Joseph

Conrad arrived there, first in the *Sissie*, then two years later aboard the *Tilkhurst* from Hull and, finally, after three years more, on the British steamer *Celestial*, coming up from Samarang. Since full independence in 1965 Singapore's government had spent much time and energy demolishing the Past. Architectural relics had been tumbled down as if they harboured some deadly plague, but now the government was feverishly trying to preserve what was still standing.

Arriving at Changi airport from Jakarta, I drove into the city down the East Coast Highway between lawns that looked as if they had been trimmed with nail scissors. Well, was I too late? How much of what Henry James called the 'visitable past' remained behind the cosmetics? Partial reassurance came with the sight of Fort Canning Park, the gentle slope of land behind the modern seafront, reinforced later on by the clumps of trees that still broke through the concrete uniformity like gay green buttonholes, and the old-world elegance of the tiny shops and tea houses in the rabbit-warren districts known since Raffles' time as Kampong Glam and Kampong Bugis. The harbour was still there, of course, and the river.

In the past I had stayed at Raffles Hotel or at the Cockpit, successor to the old Hotel de l'Europe that once faced the sea across the Esplanade. Raffles gloriously survives but now it was in the throes of a facelift, half-gutted and alive with workmen; so I went to the Cockpit, once a cosy little place with panelled stairs, a timbered bar and chalets in a garden, but all that had gone and now it was a high-rise slab. Pale ghosts of a sort lurked there, recent ghosts from my earliest days as a Foreign Correspondent in Singapore when I rested at the Cockpit between one Asian war and another.

I thought of the shades of Conrad's days, and the seamen, harbour masters, pilots, merchants, ship brokers and ship chandlers who had made Singapore bustle a hundred years ago – nothing pale about them. Or about the shades of the robed and white-capped Straits Arabs, rich and powerful men who owned steamers and traded with Palembang, Makassar, Surabaya and a dozen other places in the region; and of the dangerous, dark-skinned sea-rovers, saronged and armed with fine krisses – the *orang laut*, traders or scavengers, Bugis or otherwise that Conrad knew and had written about. Like him, I had a large cast to handle – if I could find them.

Above all, in Singapore I had one aim in particular: to find what I could of the man Conrad called Lord Jim. What relics would there be of Jim – the young English Merchant Marine officer, the country parson's son from Cornwall, universally disgraced in 1880 for having, with his captain and fellow officers, done the unthinkable – deserted a ship full of passengers in the middle of a storm, an act of cowardice that caused an explosion of outrage and contempt not only in Singapore but far beyond? Conrad gave the young seaman no surname, so Jim he remained until the death Conrad contrived for him – shot through the chest on a river in darkest Borneo.

The Jim who really lived had a surname like any other Englishman and more than one Christian name, too. George Augustine Podmore Williams was, I believe, sometimes called simply Austin by his parents. Despite his disgrace he did not change a single one of his names. Unlike fictional Jim, he did not attempt to hide himself from men's taunts in darkest Borneo or anywhere else. He stuck it out in the East and had guts enough to return to Singapore and start a new life there, where every European would be bound to point and stare.

'Lily Tan,' said my friend Dennis Bloodworth, sipping his evening vodka on the rocks. 'She's the one to help your research.'

'Miss Tan?' I asked.

'Mrs Tan. In charge of the National Archives. Most helpful. I'll give her a call if you like.'

We were sitting, as so many times before, in the little patio of the maisonette on the city's outskirts which is Dennis's home in Singapore. New high-rise flats cast long shadows, and across green lawns we could hear laughing children and the plonk-plonk of tennis balls. The heavy heat of the day was beginning to subside. The *amah* had lit the anti-mosquito coils; soon the insects would begin to whine. Small birds flew in and out of the dwarf tropical garden of orchids, bamboo and a dozen different shrubs in big Chinese jars and pots that Judy Bloodworth invariably and miraculously creates around her wherever she settles. Judy is Chinese and otherwise known as Ching Ping, which Dennis says means Apprehensive Ice; mysteriously, since I have never seen Judy particularly apprehensive and she has a personality as warm as toast.

It was nice to be back in Singapore, a little like coming home. We sat in that familiar garden and watched a Jumbo jet like a silver whale overhead, reflecting the setting sun, sinking towards the east and Changi airport.

Whenever I am in Singapore I visit the Bloodworths. I have known them since the Sixties and a brief encounter which, it turned out, has lasted for many years. He wanted time off to write a batch of books on the area, so I took over his 'beat' and covered a variety of wars in and around South-East Asia for the newspaper we both worked for. I could see those books now, ranged like souvenirs on a shelf between the television set and a tiny bar, as I followed Dennis through the sliding glass screen separating the patio from the living room, a cosy room full of Chinese scrolls, carpets, paintings and ceramics.

Dennis filled our glasses and we walked back to the patio where the light was slowly fading. 'How exactly are you going to set about it?'

My plan of action seemed almost absurdly simple. 'First, do a good bit of strolling about,' I said. 'The Battery Road area, around the river mouth where the old salts used to gather. There should be some well-preserved ghosts there, don't you think?'

There was going to be a lot of research into old records, too, newspapers of the 1880s and 1890s, books and so on. That was the base of it. 'And,' I added, 'I want to find some trace of the man Conrad turned into Lord Jim. He was married in the Anglican Cathedral. His tomb is in some old graveyard here. I would like to see it.'

'The man who was Lord Jim,' Dennis said, 'sounds like the title of a novel. To find his grave – that would be something. Well,' he went on, 'one way or another you're going to need Lily Tan.'

True as usual to his word, he telephoned her next morning and I arranged at once to go down to the Hill Street offices of the National Archives of Singapore. In an office at the top of a flight of stone stairs I found a handsome, well-dressed Chinese woman who came round her desk to meet me in a brisk and friendly sort of way that was immediately encouraging. The postcards and cheerfully coloured drawings pinned around her office walls looked like the work of imaginative children; her own, probably. Over a cup of coffee I explained again what I was trying to do. Lily Tan was not a reader of Joseph Conrad, but she was interested in Singapore's past. She was obviously the right woman in the right job.

After a while she introduced me to her staff and they in turn introduced me, with the proud air of people displaying a particularly fine collection of antiques, to rows of filing cabinets full of historical records going back to 1819. They could hardly go back any further: that was the year Stamford Raffles raised the Union Jack over what was then no more than a little Malay village above a beach. Among the archives there were fine old watercolour sketches of that little village, a series of beautifully engraved maps showing the village growing into a city, and old black and white and sepia photographs of dead notables

50

—Europeans in pompous top hats, solar topees and fierce mutton-chop whiskers, Arabs in turbans, Chinese in slippers and Malay merchants wearing songkoks, the black, round Malay hats.

Perhaps, Lily Tan suggested, I would want to start with the newspaper 'morgue', the collection of old Singapore newspapers microfilmed and housed in the National Library. When I agreed, she phoned the chief librarian and a moment later she smiled, 'He's waiting for you.'

In the large building overlooking Stamford Road from the slope of Fort Canning Park, up two more flights of stairs, I found the chief librarian, ready and welcoming. He led me straight to the index of old newspapers. '*Straits Times*, *Singapore Free Press* . . . I know what you want. And here they are.' I took out four rolls of microfilm – 1880 to 1888 – and threaded them through the spools of the viewer. On the illuminated screen the past began to revolve before me in page after page of newsprint. In a moment, like Alice passing through the looking-glass, I was transported to another world.

Day after day I walked from the Cockpit Hotel, passing first the old Presbyterian church and then the National Museum; day after day I climbed the Library steps, switched on the microfilm viewer and, oblivious of the Chinese, Malay and Indian students at the tables around me, plunged into a world of ships and spars and solar topees; of punkahs, patent medicines and men with whiskers in white suits and panama hats who suddenly seemed very real indeed. Rendered temporarily schizophrenic, as if by some exhilarating drug, my mind began to spend a large part of its time in the bustle and clamour of a great nineteenth-century Eastern port, a world in which Dennis and

Judy Bloodworth and Lily Tan were no more real than Captain Henry Ellis or William Lingard – or Lord Jim for that matter – were in this one. We shared a secret, the Ghosts of the Microfilms and I, and the secret was the Past.

Five

Captain Henry Ellis, the Master Attendant (a 'superior sort of Harbour Master' and a very great and tyrannical person), sat like a bad-tempered Irish Buddha at his desk. Through the high windows of Singapore's Harbour Office he could look out over the Anchorage and contemplate the ships spread across it. They seemed to him like toys that he could scatter with a sweep of his hand. He was even then as a matter of duty calculating the number of ships that had arrived in Singapore Harbour over the previous twelve months, and from what he saw every day from his window he was certain they would add up to a surprising number.

Change was in the air. Steam was 'in', and each year the harbour became busier. The swift, new mail steamers from Europe bustled down the Strait of Malacca with surprising speed, but these days they had to edge their way into the Singapore Anchorage with an unprecedented degree of caution. The Anchorage was a very wide piece of water, but the possibility of collision was growing year by year. At this moment upwards of fifty-six vessels were anchored there: men-of-war, sailing ships and steamers – more and more steamers had been arriving ever since the Suez Canal was opened in 1869.

In fact, Captain Ellis's Annual Report to the Marine Department would 'respectfully state' that no fewer than 2236 vessels had sailed into it during the past year. What a shame to be obliged 'to have the honour' to report eighty-eight desertions by European seamen, four Courts of Inquiry convened to consider the total loss of three British schooners, and the stranding of one British steamer – the *Celestial*.

'Damn it,' the Master Attendant said to himself, running a large, rough hand through hair like white candyfloss. He was due to retire in three or four years – and would be glad to be gone. Every day sea-

53

going people badgered him about controlling the new-fangled steam vessels. They were everywhere, the smaller ones plying about in almost every creek like a swarm of wasps. Even without those wasps, an arriving mailship's passenger launch had to dodge innumerable Malay sampans, Chinese *tongkangs* (sailing barges) and official pilot boats before coming safely alongside the slippery stone steps of Johnston's Pier, near Captain Ellis's personal steam launch and the government's paddle gunboat *Pluto*.

Ah! That reminded Captain Ellis of something. Puffing out his fat, white cheeks and grabbing up his pen, he added a postscript to his report: '*Government Vessels*. The *Pluto*'s boiler cannot last more than another year from this date.' That would learn 'em. He was about to add his initials when an extraordinary hubbub broke out beneath his window.

'Piggi punch house! Piggi punch house!' To his Irish ears the hullabaloo had an irritating Home Counties bray. He had no need to ask the reason for it. There was no cause for alarm; he knew that no angry mob was attacking the General Post Office next door. In fact he knew exactly what the hubbub was about. As usual, a hallooing throng of disembarking British officers were thrusting lists of their baggage at the poor besieged agent of the Hotel de l'Europe before bundling their wives, their portmanteaux and themselves, laughing and shouting, into a waiting cluster of ramshackle gharries driven by droop-eyed natives and drawn by snorting ponies. 'Piggi' was the nearest most British sahibs could get to pronouncing the Malay word *pergi* meaning 'go'; and if, to the pidgin expression 'punch house' (meaning 'bar' or 'hotel'), they added the Malay word *besar* (big), their gharry wallahs knew they were expected to aim for the palatial Hotel de l'Europe on the Esplanade rather than for one of the many seedy grog shops down the road.

Captain Ellis was perfectly aware of the mailboat's arrival – he was awesomely well informed of the smallest ripple on the surface of the harbour. Three of the Marine Office's lofty windows gave on to it, and simply by swivelling his well-shaven face with its top-knot of silver hair through forty degrees he could see for himself whatever big ship was just arriving – a mailboat from Liverpool, a cargo steamer from London, or possibly a sailing ship gliding in after three months at sea to fold her white wings and have a bit of a rest.

If he wanted to know their names, the Master Attendant had only to bellow for his shipping master, a mincing Eurasian with rich olive skin and a skinny neck, who would bring him the schedules in which ships' arrivals and departures were daily registered. Obedient to the voice of his god, the shipping master would skip out from the rows of industrious quill drivers, hop nimbly through a pair of tall, important doors, and lay the schedules on his master's desk with an obsequious flourish. From these schedules the editors of the *Straits Times, Overland Journal* or the *Singapore Free Press*, just round the corner in Raffles Place and Battery Road respectively, composed their harbour columns. Today one column read in part:

SHIPPING IN HARBOUR.

Rajah Laut	Dut.barque.	Capt. Lingard
		Destn: East Coast of Borneo
Vidar	Br.str. 606 tons.	Capt. Vincent from Samarang
		(consignee: Syed Mohsin al Joofree)
Jeddah	Br.str. 996 tons.	Capt. Clark. Agent Bun Hin & Co.
		Destns: Saigon, Amoy, Penang.

Opening the *Overland Journal* that lay on his office table, Captain Ellis had already clamped his pince-nez – his nose-nipper he called it – firmly into place and run his eye over the following (delayed) news item:

The *Jeddah* appears to have met with more than one accident on her recent voyage. The *China Mail* of Hong Kong says:– She left yesterday for Swatow, having in tow a steam-launch purchased for the owners, and put back this p.m. The launch had broken adrift and Captain Clark thought it best to bring her back.

Well, the Master Attendant thought, the *Jeddah* was safe and sound among today's list of 'Shipping in Harbour' – he could see her through his window. It was a dangerous region, he mused, what with the reefs and shoals, typhoons and pirates. The *Celestial*, too, had had troubles; she had got herself stranded. But, after all, she was still alive. Some ships were like cats; they had nine lives. Think of that other British ship – what was her name? – the *Palestine*. Reported lost and done for in early 1879, sixty days out from Mauritius laden with timber, apparently lost – gone – *finito*, yet she had turned up again. Nevertheless, when it came to ships and the sea he would never say, even to himself, 'All's well that ends well.'

Early years of service in the Indian Marine, then the command of a gunboat keeping down piracy in the Strait of Malacca, after which

55

years as Harbour Master at Penang had led to his present position as Master Attendant and Marine Magistrate in Singapore. Henry Ellis had a Donegal Irish temper that many people said could set the Singapore river on fire, but his experience had taught him immense caution. He prided himself that he knew all there was to know about the sea's perfidy and man's weakness. He might think of himself occasionally as some sort of pagan divinity, but even he realised that he could not rule the waves. How could he have foreseen, for instance, that the *Palestine*, having miraculously turned up intact after her reported loss, would, after a few more voyages, burn to a cinder in the Bangka Strait? 'Her captain had a funny name – Beard, was it? – Elijah Beard! And that young second officer – something damnably long and ending in "ski". Russian? Polish? God knows.'

And how could he foresee that the *Jeddah*, the same steamer that Captain Ellis could see lying so safe and so sound on the blue waters of the Anchorage, was soon to be at the heart of the shipping scandal of a lifetime. The Master Attendant's office would be involved in it; and the Governor, Sir Frederick Weld; even the British government. Although Conrad's novel would be published eight years before he died, the name 'Lord Jim' would never mean anything to Captain Ellis. As far as he would ever be aware, the *Jeddah*'s chief mate was a man called Augustine (or Austin) Podmore Williams, a resident of Singapore. 'Oh, him!' the deputy-Neptune would growl scornfully. 'I know him all right. Do I not!'

It was half-past twelve. The Library's reading room was filling up noisily. Chinese, Malay and Indian schoolboys and girls, released from class for the noon break, whispered and giggled over their school books. I carried the reels of the microfilmed Past to the assistant librarian's counter, saying, 'I'll be back for these at two o'clock.' There was an open-air noodle stall near the Library entrance. The day was very humid but luckily a cooling breeze curled up Stamford Road from the sea, and the chicken-noodle soup was filling and cheap.

By two o'clock I felt I could switch my mind into Time Past almost as if I was changing gear in a car. Strolling about the streets of Singapore I seemed, like Tennyson, 'to move among a world of ghosts'. A number of old buildings *had* survived demolition, and from what I had seen of old street maps I could recreate in my imagination others that had vanished. Sometimes I even confused news items of today with those of a hundred years ago; certain things had not changed that much. Press announcements of a 'Special Curry Tiffin' at Raffles Hotel could have referred to a luncheon menu there two days ago. It was with genuine regret that I read of a 'Chinaman' killed by a durian tree falling on him during the storm yesterday – though, of course, I could not recall the storm. I felt mild outrage that another 'Chinaman', found dead in the Rochore river, had, according to the police, been pushed in 'wilfully' – I looked forward to an early arrest. And coming across a report that a James Patterson had been charged with behaving in a disorderly manner in a police lock-up and with breaking a urinal tub at the same place (fined $5 or eight days' rigorous imprisonment), my immediate thought was: 'Oh, has Scotland been playing Singapore at football?'

On rainy days I used Mr A. L. Kow's reliable Toyota taxi to get about the city. I had no reason to risk my life at the hands of Mr Hung Ah Kee who, according to an old *Straits Times*, had been charged (and fined) for drawing his ricksha in a 'careless manner and colliding with Mr E. M. Merewether's conveyance'. I told Mr Kow about this. He laughed and said, 'Oh, maybe he flying,' meaning he was drunk or drugged. But many ricksha coolies (or pullies) were opium addicts in the old days. They would drop the shafts without a word, abandoning their European passengers to sweat in the sun, while they popped into some hovel for a 'fix'. A dangerous practice, like drinking and driving. One day a Celestial (as Chinese were referred to then) ricksha wallah lost control on a downward hill and ricksha, coolie and passenger charged – crash-wallop! – through the door of a house. Drugged or not, the coolie had only arrived from China the day before and so he was judged to be blameless, though a Mr Shelford remarked in the

Legislative Council that the police should never have given him a licence 'to pull' in the first place.

Because of the opium habit – far-gone addicts ate it 'from the leaf', which was often fatal – ricksha wallahs had an average life of only thirty-five to forty years. Gharry drivers, too, died early but for a different reason: they would play at Ben Hur outside the Hotel de l'Europe, racing their vehicles up and down Esplanade Road. Once in a while two gharries would collide with a terrific smash that was very entertaining to the £100-round-the-world tourists in the hotel.

When Singapore residents were not writing outraged letters to the papers against this 'disgraceful practice' they were writing to protest about traffic congestion and the police. Hack gharries and bullock carts hogged the middle of every street, forcing horse-drawn carriages to come to a jolting full stop; and little Battery Road, leading from the majestic headquarters of Captain Henry Ellis to Raffles Place and the main European business houses, was often impassable. Why, newspaper letter columns asked, didn't the police do something? 'Police force – the most inefficient in existence. Bengalees . . . wild fellows from Amboina . . . Malays. Why, they couldn't even capture a tiger.'

Tigers, it was true, had become disconcertingly numerous on Singapore Island. They swam over from Johore, and hardly a day went by without a plantation coolie being carried bodily away by some striped monster. No one was safe. Word even went round that a tiger had been found hiding under a billiard table in Raffles Hotel. The police dug pits to trap them, and when eventually a cub fell into one in Bukit Timah a party of armed constables hurried to the spot. While they stood round the pit, the tigress suddenly sprang out on them, and one constable was shot and died the same day. The Deputy Commissioner himself had a bullet through his coat. Naturally yet another disgruntled letter followed to the *Times*: 'It is no part of the police's duty to kill tigers which they know nothing about . . . .'

Upstream from the short but handsomely pillared and balustraded Cavenagh Bridge over the mouth of the Singapore river, the creek distends womb-like, flanked on its south side by Boat Quay. In Conrad's time three-quarters of the entire shipping business of the island was based on or near Boat Quay. Strolling by the river's edge you would have had to dodge the huge cases of British machinery and manufactured goods continually being landed there, the bales of gambier, bundles of rattan, cargoes of Bangka tin (from Muntok), bags of Celebes sago and tapioca and of Borneo pepper, and boxes of spices from Ambon and Ternate.

Boats, three or four hundred of them, jammed the river gunwale to gunwale: Chinese 'shoe-boats', Malay sampans or fast-boats, and the Kling *tongkangs*, carrying the cargoes to and from the ships out in the Anchorage. The godowns of well-established British companies like Guthrie, the Borneo Company and Sime Darby resembled their owners – stolid, unadorned and self-satisfied – near the river's mouth. At night the Chinese warehouses, higher up, blazed with lanterns that reflected red, orange and yellow light on the water like dollops of liquid fire.

At night, too, a loom of light arced like a halo over the Town Hall; and lights from the rows of cast-iron lamps with globes of white porcelain ('like ostrich eggs', Conrad thought) flickered through the rain trees on the Esplanade.

On the other side of the Esplanade the long façade of the Hotel de l'Europe was a mass of lights like the flank of a great ocean liner. From the dining room well-groomed globe-trotters brayed at each other over their iced pudding, guffawing over stories of the Cairo donkeys, of being cheated in the Egyptian bazaars ('No, really – do you think I've been done?'), while on the terrace matches flared at the tips of cheroots, revealing white shirt-fronts, and a dead cigar butt arced like a shooting star from where Captain Marlow sat utterly engrossed, while Jim in matter-of-fact tones gave him the terrible details of the *Jeddah* affair.

Once when Jim gave way, bursting out under the pressure of his guilt, 'It is – hell,' a couple of tourists looked up, startled, from their pudding, and Marlow suggested to Jim that they move on to the front gallery. There candles burned in glass globes on little octagonal tables and they could see in the warm darkness of the roadstead the lights of ships winking like stars.

Nothing stirs but the shadows of the clouds. Two men stop halfway across Cavenagh Bridge: the younger one is tall, heavy-set, strong-jawed; the older one, also tall, is terribly lean and faded, almost skeletal. The big man stands gazing down at the mat roofs of the mass of sampans jammed in the river mouth. He is a man of about thirty-five, with close-cut chestnut hair, a clipped beard and heavy moustache, a straight nose and grey eyes.

'The new Rajah Tulla smokes opium,' the lean one murmurs in his ear. 'He is sometimes dangerous to speak to. There is a lot of

discontent in Wajo among the big people .... Drop it, Captain Lingard!' Few people in Singapore would dare to tell Captain Lingard, the 'Rajah Laut', the King of the Sea, as the Malay sea-rovers called him, to drop anything.

'Never dropped anything in my life. How the devil do you know anything about it?'

The faded skeleton points at the confusion of sampans in the river beneath them. 'They know me,' says Captain Jörgenson, once the dashing owner-master of the barque *Wild Rose*, who lives now in the native quarter with a Malay woman with a wrinkled brown face and a mouthful of blackened stumps, he calls his 'old girl'.

'I was like you once,' he murmurs to Lingard. 'And look at me now. I came out a boy of eighteen. I can speak English, I can speak Dutch, I can speak every cursed lingo of these islands. I remember things that would make your hair stand on end. I never broke my word to white or native. And look at me ....'

He clutches at the rail of the bridge. 'Are you very deep in this thing?'

'To the very last cent.'

Below them, a dim glow appears among the sampans: a boatman lighting his lantern. 'This thing' that Jörgenson refers to is a daredevil scheme of Lingard's to buy gunpowder, arms and warriors — the mounting of a sort of small military campaign, in fact, to restore his friend Prince Pata Hassim to the Bugis kingdom from which civil war and Dutch intrigues have expelled him. A debt has to be repaid: not long ago, Hassim saved Lingard from death.

Only the omniscient old scarecrow, Captain Jörgenson, knows the danger in all this. And maybe one other.

A drawling New England voice, echoing from the pages of *The Rescue*, floats through the cabin skylight of a ship out in the Anchorage. 'Yes, siree! Mexican war rifles – good as new – six in a case – my people in Baltimore. . . . Now, look ahere, these Colt pistols I am selling – See – you load – and see?' [Rapid clicks] 'Simple, isn't it? And if any trouble – ' [click! click! click!] 'Through and through – like a sieve – warranted to cure the worst kind of cussedness in any nigger . . . . Yes, siree! . . . . I could do a deal with that Lingard. Where d'ye catch him? Everywhere – eh? Waal – that's nowhere. But I shall find him . . . yes, siree!'

Leaning towards his companion on Cavenagh Bridge, old Jörgenson whispers, 'You say you don't want to interfere with the Dutch. But suppose the Dutch want things just so?' And urgently: 'Drop it!'

Lingard's reply is barely audible. 'Look here. When you save people from death you take a share in their life. That's how I look at it.'

In silence the two dim silhouettes, one thickset and walking confidently, the other gaunt and wilting, move away and vanish among the deep shadows of the Harbour Office.

Six

The Cockpit Hotel, comfortable, not too expensive, was a short walk from the National Library, but after a while I moved to one nearer the centre of Conrad's Singapore – the area with a view of the Anchorage around Raffles Place, the Esplanade and the river. The River View Hotel was perched on the southern bank well above Cavenagh Bridge facing some handsome old warehouses. It was managed by a friend of mine, Roberto Pregarz, who for years had been the general manager at Raffles. From this new base I could spend more time patrolling streets that not all that long ago had been alleys packed with sweating bodies, thick with dust, or running with mud.

Despite modern skyscraper office blocks along the waterfront the area was a natural hang-out for phantoms. For example, when I put my mind to it I could see Captain Lingard, florid and burly, alighting from a ramshackle gharry, crossing the cricket pitch from the Harbour Office and disappearing down the street of Chinese shops behind Coleman Street. An older Lingard than the one old Jörgenson had told to 'drop it'.

One major result of that adventure which Conrad recounted in *The Rescue* – the one Lingard had refused to drop – was that Jörgenson, the old used-up former captain of the *Wild Rose* who thought his days of adventure had ended long ago, went out of this world in what was literally a blaze of glory. On the Shore of Refuge down Carimata way, he found himself surrounded by Lingard's enemies on the deck of the *Emma*, an old mastless hulk which Lingard had packed with all the arms and gunpowder he had bought. Lingard was far away and twenty spears could in an instant have been driven into Jörgenson's heart. But the old ghost had shuffled inch-by-inch under hostile eyes towards the open powder magazine, and reaching it, this disregarded wreck of a man in the most casual way in the world had put his lighted cigar in his mouth – and jumped down the hatchway.

By the time the rain of shattered timbers and mangled corpses had finished falling into the lagoon, many lives, Jörgenson's included, had come to an end.

Lingard had gone back to more or less peaceful trading after that.

Lily Tan's assistants led me to the few mementoes of Captain William Lingard's earthly existence. He was not unlike the almost unbelievably heroic privateer, James Brooke, who became the first White Rajah of Sarawak. Conrad says Lingard was a Devon man – so was Brooke – but his background is not important. He was a sailor – a sailing man; a man very much of his time out East. He revelled in his mastery of the sea, and in his deep sympathy with the people of the waters and islands he understood so well. There was danger galore and he took it as it came.

He must have seemed a romantic and sometimes daunting figure to those who glimpsed him on Battery Road or crossing the Esplanade. Reports in the *Singapore Free Press* or the *Straits Times* kept readers informed about what Captain Lingard was up to next.

One day he was reported to have rescued a party of shipwrecked Javanese sailors in the Strait of Makassar. Another day he had fought off heavily armed Illanun pirates near the east coast of Borneo with the *West Indian*'s brass cannon. He could hardly avoid frequent clashes with pirates and slavers from the Sulu Sea. There was far too much piracy about; it was ubiquitous. They were a menace to every honest trader. Lingard even put pen to paper on the subject: 'It is high time,' he wrote in a blunt letter to the Makassar *Handelsblad* after one particularly outrageous act of villainy, 'you Dutch maintained the honour of your flag more effectually.'

Of course, his life was not all pirates and long voyages to the ends of the Archipelago. He could hardly have been such a well-known local figure if he had always been away in Papua or Sulu. He had a gentler side. He was often a star performer at Singapore's Aquatic Sports and this, too, the press reported. 'The race for Six-oared Gigs was won by a P&O boat from Captain Lingard's *No Name* crewed by Malays, and flying the flag of "Brow and Bulongan" — a splendid race notwithstanding Lingard's boat broke an oar in coming in second.' Everyone remarked how generous Lingard was, giving what seemed like Lord Mayor's banquets to the whole of Singapore.

'Brow and Bulongan' — spelt 'Berau' and 'Bulungan' on the modern charts on my table as I write — were the mysterious rivers from which much of Lingard's wealth derived. 'He has discovered a river,' people whispered in hushed tones behind his back. In fact he had discovered two, both of them remote and little known, high up on the broken coastline of northeast Borneo. There local rajahs seemed always to be locked in a savage war with rival rulers or alternatively battling or collaborating with the sea-rovers who sailed down in their great warpraus to loot, to kill and to carry off villagers and fishermen as slaves. Even so, Lingard had immediately recognised the rich trading possibilities in that waterlogged region and energetically set about exploring them, charting the estuaries, establishing a tiny office far up the Berau.

The press briefly noted his mysterious comings and goings:

West Indian, Master: Lingard. Departed for: Macassar.

Arrived from: Brow; Eng. Schooner *Coeran*, Master: Lingard. Destination: Sourabaya June 21, 1868.

From Berau, June 3, 1868. *Rajah Laut*, Master: Captain Lingard.

From: Bollongan . . . .

Lingard made fortunes, lost them, made them again. Year after year trading captains were killed by pirates or wasted away and died of drink or fever, but Lingard survived. Finally, after decades in the East, he simply faded out of men's sight, vanishing back to the fogs and cold air of Europe to die without leaving a trace. He left his ghost in Singapore but no grave. There is only one personal relic of him to be found.

A few years ago, at the Presbyterian church in Orchard Road, the minister showed me a document that one of his predecessors had stored there. It is a Certificate of Marriage and it proclaims to whom it may concern that William Lingard, being of full age, a bachelor and by profession master mariner, had been married by the minister, Mr John Mathison on 26 November 1864 to Miss Johanna Carolina Olmeyor, spinster, the residence of both parties being given as 'On board the *Coeran*'. Lingard's father is named as William Lingard, innkeeper, and Johanna Olmeyor's father as Mathys Olmeyor, clerk.

Certified True Copy

Registrar of Marriages

SUMMONS 13/4/15.

Certificate of Marriage.

No.	When Married.	Name and Surname.	Whether of full age or a minor.	Condition.	Rank or Profession.	Residence at the time of Marriage.	Father's name and Surname.	Rank or Profession of Father.
30	26th Nov 1842.	William Lingard	Of full age	Bachelor	Grocers Draaman	Erskinville Port Corran	William Lingard McKefer	
		Johanna Caroline Van Gyen	Of full age	Spinster	—	Oie Corner Port Corran	Christopher George Clark	Clerk

Married in the Presbyterian Church, by me. Jno. Wm Grahame MARRIAGE REGISTRAR.

This Marriage was solemnized between us { William Lingard, Johanna Caroline Van Gyen } in the presence of us { William ..., William C. Benson }

65

The signatures of the newly-weds are interesting. Lingard's writing, as one might expect, is big and brave, the capital 'L' particularly bold, the final 'D' high and rounded, like the eye at the end of a ship's cable. As for the bride, her signature contradicts the surname printed on the certificate; she spells it correctly – 'Olmeijer'. Thirty years later Conrad would immortalise it as 'Almayer'.

In Conrad's time a rambling two-storey building with a colonnaded façade and high-shuttered windows stood on the point of Cavenagh Bridge where Flint Street meets Battery Road. It contained the premises of James Motion & Co., Jeweller, Watchmaker and Optician, of McAlister & Co., Ship Chandlers, Sailmakers, Ship Brokers and General Merchants; and, most importantly, of Emmerson's Tiffin, Billiard, and Reading Rooms ('Established 1866'). Not one brick or beam of the building remains today, but to me that was not important. I made a beeline to its former site at the Battery Road end of the bridge, more or less where the Bank of China is now.

Strangers, merchants and seamen were drawn to it by the enticing notice, taking up ample space, that regularly appeared in one newspaper or another. So was I – I had seen them in the Library:

An Ordinary Daily at one O'clock,
or
TIFFIN à LA CARTE.

English, Colonial and American Newspapers
and Periodicals
Wines, Beer, Spirits & of first quality
Arctic Soda Fountain, American Drinks
CIGARS.
Three First Class Billiard Tables,
(by Burroughs & Watts, London.)

Emmerson's was not in the least grand – but far more reputable than the tumbledown grog shop and billiard room at the slummy end of Denham Street owned by Carlo Mariani, commonly known as Paunchy Charlie and in Conrad's view an 'unspeakable Maltese vagabond', Emmerson's was nonetheless overawed by the ponderous colonial buildings facing it, the nearest of which was the Harbour Office, lair of the 'deputy-Neptune' Captain Ellis. Around its arched and curtained entrance the Malay coxswain and crew of the Master Attendant's steam launch lounged in the heat among punkah pullers, policemen and sweepers; inside the big, high offices and above the

clerks at their heavy, polished desks, enormous punkahs stirred hot air thick enough to stand a spoon in.

From *The End of the Tether* a vision comes to me:

A burly old salt, like a sea-going Santa Claus, is often to be seen descending the steps of one of the most important post offices in the East. He sports a great spreading white beard, an old panama hat with black band round it, a spotless white shirt and a baggy suit of thin grey flannel. He clutches a thick stick as if it were a weapon. The bluish slip of paper tucked into his waistcoat pocket is the receipt of a registered letter containing £200 that he has just posted to his daughter, a struggling landlady in Melbourne. Captain Whalley – 'Daredevil Harry' Whalley of the *Condor*, a clipper once famous throughout the Malay Archipelago – removes his hat to mop his brow and stumps heavily off down the long straight pavement of Collyer Quay, where banks and offices overlook the forest of masts in the Anchorage, and then turns into the sweating crowds of Almeida and Market Streets.

Half-naked coolies stumble under impossible loads among potholes and dust; saronged, bare-footed Malays dart among rickshas and bullock carts; and old Indian gentlemen, clutching parasols, skip to avoid death under the wheels of the hooting cable tramcar pushing relentlessly through the human torrent. Bedlam and the Inferno combined. With relief you turn into the watery spaces of Boat Quay as you might turn into Paradise.

At the Hotel de l'Europe the sight of Captain Whalley among his few possessions – two sea chests and a roll of charts – sadly counting his dollars, might have made you weep. How many days could he stay here? Not too long to judge by the mere handful of coins on the bed.

After fifty years at sea he had been obliged to sell the *Condor*, his first love after his daughter, to raise that £200 she needed so badly. It was all he had. A sailor's life was a hazardous affair in those days – even in the East, where things were made easy for white men, even if, as Conrad said, you went on 'acting white'. Not every ship's officer – not by a long chalk – made fortunes as Captain Lingard did.

Probably no one in Emmerson's would have noticed Captain Whalley emerging from the post office. Near tiffin time, Charlie Emmerson's customers are collapsed in their chairs clutching iced drinks, mopping their faces. Some are already stirring sherry into their mulligatawny soup, or sipping iced hock over curry and *sambals*. It is very hot despite the punkahs.

Who are Emmerson's customers? – traders, owners of pearling schooners in for stores, agents for Dutch crockery houses, masters and officers of ships just in from the Bay of Bengal or the South China Sea, captain-owners of pioneer-trading vessels, like Lingard, arrived from Surabaya or Samarang, Palembang or Dilli. After the silent spaces of the sea they like Emmerson's smoke-filled, jolly atmosphere, the gossip of lost ships and piracy, the voices shouting boisterously for service.

'Hey, Colonel. Two more sherry and bitters, if you please.'

'Colonel' – that was Emmerson's nickname. A veterinary surgeon by training, he had taken to barkeeping and was as happy as a rajah keeping bar on his own premises. A bit of a wag, a popular 'low' comedian, a pillar of the amateur dramatic society, he had enough jokes, he boasted, to please everyone from a drunken skipper to a

teetotal parson. He was generous. With Charlie you could sign chits and pay monthly if you were short of cash. 'I only worry when the building burns down,' he used to say, laughing. And now and again it did.

At lunch time the tiffin rooms seemed to have become a bundle of voices – a breeding ground of rumours and stories, most of them violent.

'D'ye read about that Gordon, the American captain who tried to kill himself last night in the Hotel de la Paix?' a bald captain with a Tyneside accent might be saying: 'Daft as a brush. Took a bottle of painkiller. Then a bottle of quinine. No effect. Then put an old revolver to his head, pulled the trigger. Nothing happened. Then took a razor and cut his throat. Still no good. The quack came and sewed him up – and he'll live. Can you beat that?'

Lingard is often there, grizzled and alert, a brandy and soda at his elbow, a small charred meerschaum pipe in his hand. To some people, who resent the respect in which he is held, he is a scamp, a rogue-adventurer, a friend to Malays irresponsibly provoking the Dutch colonial authorities of the Eastern Archipelago. Never mind. Calm, assured, a match for most dangers, he can afford to ignore them.

Lingard is getting to his feet. He pats his companion's shoulder, ending a business conversation.

'I don't forget,' he says reassuringly. 'I am not that kind of man.'

He walks out into the sun. An elderly, aristocratic-looking Arab in a pure white headcloth is passing and Lingard, with a broad smile, goes up to him, his hand out. Syed Mohsin Al Joofree is the owner of four steamers, one of which, the *Vidar*, is in the harbour for engine repairs. The Arab, wisely, has put his money into steam, while Lingard clings obstinately to old-fashioned sail. These two men, descendant of the Prophet and British son of an innkeeper, are engaged in a win-all, lose-all struggle for control of the profitable Berau and Bulungan trade, but they respect one another.

Syed Mohsin gravely takes Lingard's hand and asks politely, 'What do you want, Captain Lingard?'

Lingard's smile broadens. 'First, your long life,' he replies. 'And then – your help.'

They stroll off down Battery Road towards Syed Mohsin's office in Raffles Place, heads together, talking business and casting abrupt shadows under the vertical sun.

Like everyone else connected with the ports Conrad was often in Emmerson's Tiffin Rooms. Poorer than poor old Captain Harry Whalley who even after fifty years at sea still had to count his dollars, Conrad, as a young officer, could never afford to stay at the Europe or at Raffles, where in any case he would feel uncomfortably like a potential passenger. He dined there now and again but slept on board the ships he belonged to; on board Syed Mohsin Al Joofree's *Vidar* when he was her first officer, and later in the cuddy of his 'first command', the barque *Otago*. If he stayed ashore he slept at the Sailors' Home.

The Sailors' Home looked good for $1 a day – a large bungalow with a wide verandah and a suburban-looking little garden of bushes and trees. A wizened, jockey-like creature ran it, a dreary retired sergeant of artillery named Phillips. He called himself 'Chief Steward' and in his spare time found his true calling as evangelist (mainly devoted to Malay missions, God help them), temperance worker and inspector of brothels. Inside the Home the beds – rough wooden benches covered with hard mattresses – harboured an impressive variety of diseases and although the Home's mosquitoes were of a most ferocious type according to sailors who had been mauled by them, there were no mosquito nets. Rooms were bleak and curtainless, unimproved by the religious texts nailed to their otherwise bare walls.

Phillips himself had appropriated comparatively luxurious quarters; though they smelled almost intolerably of decaying coral and oriental dust, they contained a horsehair sofa and armchairs with antimacassars. He despised his lodgers – 'a very rough lot,' he was heard to moan – and in the end someone signing himself 'Jack Tar' took him up on this in a letter to the *Straits Times*: 'Who wouldn't soon *become* rough, by looks if not by nature, if he is to sleep on next to no bed with all his clothes on?'

What did Phillips care for letters? He hated these sailors lolling about the house, some of whom did not even cough up what they owed. For example, a fellow called Hamilton had not paid a cent for months – although he complained loudly and continually that the food was unfit for a gentleman. He was no doubt right about that: soup and curry at Emmerson's was better any day than a dry lamb chop and a piece of desiccated pineapple dumped under your nose by unsmiling Chinese waiters at the Sailors' Home. And as you chewed the steward spied drearily on you from the verandah; you could hear him sighing as he cast up despairing eyes to the punkah: 'This job will be the death of me.' It was a dismal place all right.

'It is always the unforeseen that happens,' Conrad liked to think. 'After all, *la vida es sueño* – Life is a dream.' And now the unforeseen comes to pay him a visit. It comes in the form of a voice – a voice echoing deep and loud through Emmerson's, a doggedly self-assertive voice among the click of billiard balls, Charlie's jokes and the sweet smell of Manila cigars. Hearing it, Conrad – everybody – looks up. Its owner makes his way through the tables across the room, ignoring the stir his entrance has caused; he has become used to that. Customers nudge their neighbours, lay down glasses or their cards, to stare at a

man in his early thirties, a ship's officer – oh, yes, 'one of us', Conrad thinks – with a bit too much of a swagger. Dressed in smart white duck buttoned to the neck, he is tall, powerful and carries his head unusually high, and his clear, confident blue eyes unmistakably convey that anyone who wants trouble will get it – double-quick.

The men at the table he has shouldered his way to make room for him, boisterously.

'Mornin', Austin.'

'What's the news from McAlister's today, Daddy?'

'Sherry and bitters or a pink gin – what's it to be, old fellow?'

The man addressed affectionately as 'Daddy', laughs, says something to his seated friends, waves a hand to an acquaintance at a nearby table, sits down. When things have settled, he lets his eyes wander round the crowded room in a quite unfocused way, as though he is seeking something very far from here. There is a strange pause. Suddenly fearful that that heavy, distracted gaze may settle on them, those staring at him duck their heads and get back to their game or their gossip.

'Hey, Austin.' One of his friends lays a hand a little timidly on his white sleeve. 'Come back to us, old fellow, will you?'

'Jove! Sorry, old chap.' Frowning, Williams shakes his head as if throwing off an evil dream. And, slowly, the charming smile returns.

'One sunny morning in the commonplace surrounds of an Eastern roadstead, I saw his form – appealing – significant – under a cloud . . . .' From Austin Williams, once the most reviled figure in Singapore – in the whole wide world of seamen – the idea of *Lord Jim* came to Conrad.   When the *Sissie*, Conrad on board, sailed in from Muntok, Austin Williams's disgrace was already two and a half years old and he was doing his best to 'go respectable' with McAlister & Co., the ship chandlers. Soon his name would be in the *Singapore Directory*: 'McAlister & Co., Partner: C. C. N. Glass . . . Assistant: A. Williams.' A few doors up Battery Road was the office of Alsagoff & Co., owners of the *Jeddah*, the ship of his disgrace, and right next door was Emmerson's. He had only a few paces to walk for his lunch. Everyone lunched there; Conrad, too. It was a small world, this world of dreams and the sea.

Seven

I was sitting in my hotel room wondering what on this earth remained
to be seen of Lord Jim when someone telephoned from the Registry of
Births and Deaths.

'I am told you have made an application to have a take-away copy of
an entry here, Mr Young,' she said, briskly businesslike. 'Concerning
the death of a Mr – let me see – Mr A. P. Williams. Will you tell me the
reasons you want it? You see, it's the first time anyone has asked for
such a thing. We will have to know the reasons.'

Having explained my interest in Williams at length two days before
to another lady official at the Registry, I said, 'The gentleman in
question has been dead since 1916. The entry will confirm that.'

'Well, it's never come up before. I must check with the Registrar
General. I'll call you back, Mr Young.'

Next day the same lady telephoned again, sharper now. 'Your
request is most unusual, Mr Young, as I said yesterday. Would you put
your reasons for wanting to see the entry for Mr Williams in writing?
Then I can take it to my superior, the Registrar General. State *exactly*
what you want it for and how you propose to use it.'

I wondered what would happen if I asked permission for something
really unusual. Like photographing the Registrar General in a
bubble-bath.

'You haven't seen your boss yet?'

'I need your reasons in writing, then I'll see him. Please state exactly
what you want it for, and – '

'– how I propose to use it. I don't propose to do anything with it.' I
kept my voice calm. 'I just want to see a copy of Mr A. P. Williams's
death certificate. I am very interested in all that concerns him. It's a
matter of historical research. As I have explained.'

The voice on the line was impatient now. 'Well, Mr Williams – '

'Young.'

' – Mr Young. I have to tell you that all deaths are wholly confidential. Except maybe to the next of kin they cannot be divulged. Are you related to Mr Williams?'

For a moment I wondered whether to claim poor old A.P. as my black sheep cousin but instead I said, 'As I explained, I am researching a book. This gentleman died in 1916. That's seventy-four years ago. Could divulging such information possibly threaten the security of Singapore?'

I heard a giggle, then the voice snapped, 'We must obey our orders.'

'Oh, indeed.' To hell with it, I thought.

'Will you write, then, Mr Young?'

'I'll send you a Christmas card,' I said, and rang off.

At the office extension to St Andrew's Cathedral, a brisk young Chinese priest received me in his air-conditioned office. The Reverend Dr Tay had a smooth face and expensive spectacles. His well-tailored beige shirt was short-sleeved, revealing rounded arms; he had a pager attached to the belt round his beige trousers. Listening politely, he heard what I had to say about A. P. Williams and why I wanted a copy of his marriage registration – and of his death registration for that matter. Taking up a ballpoint pen, he wrote on a pad: 'A. P. Williams and his bride 22 January 1883.' The date of death, I told him, was 17 April 1916; he wrote that down, too.

'Mr Williams was a novelist, you say? If we give you a copy of these, will you write an explanation of your request and send it to us?' Well, perhaps it all seemed a bit bizarre: a fictional character based on a real one, and a novelist called Joseph Conrad who seemed to have known Singapore people rather well. Not many people in Singapore knew of Conrad; but I did not blame anyone for that.

'By all means, vicar,' I replied, and he smiled.

'Very well, then.'

A plump girl assistant brought me two large registry books, one of marriages and one of deaths. When I opened them they appeared to be in fair shape, but there was considerable blemishing from blotches of thick ink that had seeped through the heavy, old-fashioned paper. Still, the registrations were easy to read.

Marriage solemnised at St Andrew's Cathedral, Singapore.
When married: 22 Jan. 1883. George Augustine Podmore Williams.

74

Age: 30. Condition: Bachelor. Rank or Profession: Master Mariner. Elizabeth Jane Robinson. Age: 16. Condition: Spinster.

Williams's father's name was given as Thomas Lockyer, and Austin had signed his own name boldly, with an elaborate flourish.

In the second book, under 'Burials at Singapore', I found:

When died: 1916 April 17th. Christian Names: Augustine Podmore. Surname: Williams. Age: 64 years. Quality, Trade or Profession, etc., etc., etc.,: Master Mariner. When buried: 1916 April 17th. Cause of death: Bulbar Paralysis.

As I was making a note of these entries and elaborately named diseases, the plump girl came running.

'You want photocopies, you said?'

'Yes.'

'The vicar says photocopying a Death is all right, but a Marriage is a legal document, so permission to copy it is necessary from the Registrar of Marriages. In writing, of course. It will take time.'

'You know, this marriage took place in 1883, not in 1983.'

Yes, she did know, she informed me with a sweet smile.

Sweating, I ploughed back to the River View Hotel, cursing bureaucrats. It was nonsensical that the record of a remote death could be photocopied in one part of Singapore but not in another and that the record of a distant marriage between persons long dead was a document that had to be guarded until the end of time, or until the records rotted away.

There was a related question. Was every Singaporean functionary a misanthrope? During my first foray into the Registry of Births and Deaths I had been confronted by a bad-mannered clerk whose expression said very plainly that *he* wasn't going to give away any hundred-year-old deaths to unauthorised persons, and he had dismissed me by continuing to write a letter as if he were alone in the room.

Perhaps it was *me*. I looked in the hotel mirror and examined what I saw. What I saw was a man who looked as if he might try to strangle the next Singaporean official who told him to state his reasons in writing. That wouldn't do. I went down to the bar. Drinking a silent toast to Mrs Lily Tan, I began to feel much better.

Next day I walked slowly down a paved path under the beautiful trees that surround the Cathedral, killing time. Mynah birds whistled and fluttered noisily in the branches. Near the gate an old Malay was sitting on a bench, shirtless in the heat, his wrinkled brown skin glistening. Buses roared in procession down North Bridge Road from Kampong Glam, past the corner where the Capitol cinema stood on the former site of the Sailors' Home, its posters advertising a horror film with decomposing faces and a bloodstained claw. I found a bench near a bus-stop, sat down and considered the cruel case of Lord Jim, as it really happened to Austin Williams, from its beginning on 19 July 1880.

You would not have paid particular attention to the announcement in that morning's *Singapore Free Press* under 'Shipping Departures':

Brit. steamer *Jeddah*, Clark, for Jeddah, via Penang.

The *Jeddah* came and went, a familiar sight in Singapore's harbour. Registered there and flying the Red Ensign, she belonged to the Singapore Steamship Company, owned by Syed Mohamed Alsagoff. Her captain, Joseph Clark, was well known, too. Over the years he had carried hundreds of Muslims making the Mecca pilgrimage to the Red Sea port of Jeddah. Why should this voyage be any different?

The story is succinctly set out in the report of the Court of Inquiry, consisting of one session judge and one nautical surveyor, held at Aden on 20 August 1880. Briefly the *Jeddah*, having set sail from Singapore on 18 July, filled up at Penang with 953 passengers – Muslim pilgrims – and set off again heading towards the Red Sea. On 3 August she found herself in something very like a hurricane, with high seas breaking over her. The weather worsened as the voyage progressed, and her boilers started from their fastenings and became totally useless; the ship began to leak quite badly and soon the engine room became an untenable wreck. Volunteers among the passengers helped the ship's firemen to bale water out of it, but the water still gained.

At this point Captain Clark lost his nerve, suddenly convinced that the ship was doomed, that it was going to founder. He was also guiltily aware of two all-important factors – there were insufficient boats to take off everyone aboard – indeed only a quarter of the souls on board could have been accommodated in them; and he had his wife with him. He later claimed that as the desperation of the ship's situation began to dawn on the passengers they became hostile and clustered round his cabin, threatening to murder Mrs Clark. Whether this was really so is doubtful, but in any case when night fell Captain Clark – without considering the possibility of organising and arming his officers to suppress any uprising among the passengers – ordered a boat to be hung out astern and manned; placed his wife and the chief engineer in it; and then clambered into it himself.

His panic was encouraged to a great extent by Austin Williams, chief mate. He earnestly assured him that the *Jeddah* was bound to sink and that it was his duty to save his wife, himself and his officers, and with such hysterical advice, physically thrust him over the side and into the boat. I cannot imagine he met with much resistance.

Pandemonium on deck increased as the passengers grasped the fact that those whom they relied on to keep the ship afloat were abandoning them to die. The report said:

> The pilgrims commenced to throw pots and pans, and anything that they could lay hands on, into the boat, and pulled the first officer, who was lowering the boat, off the rails; and seeing they could not prevent the lowering of the boat, they attempted to swamp it.

The Court of Inquiry was quite clear that no violence had been threatened until the moment when it became quite obvious that the captain was ignominiously running away. His actions induced panic, when order and leadership might well have saved the day. Austin Williams pulled off the rails, found himself in the water, and was probably quite happy to be there. Helped into the captain's boat, he drew a pistol and coolly loosed off a couple of shots which drove the furious pilgrims back from the rail. The boat was then cut adrift.

The second officer was not quick enough. He appears to have attempted to leave the ship by going to the boat to which he was appointed which was manned and ready for lowering. 'On the pilgrims ordering the people to come out of the boats, and on their refusal, some of the pilgrims cut the falls, and it fell into the sea bow first from the fore fall being cut first, and all in it appear to have perished.' The second engineer was luckier. He had been sleeping but managed to clamber into a boat from which he and all the others in it were thrown back on board by angry pilgrims. Yet he was not harmed.

With the master, the chief officer and the chief engineer gone, the passengers on the *Jeddah* resumed their baling and pumping. Next morning the skies cleared and the sea was smooth. They sighted land at Cape Guardafui and, having set sail, made for it, flying signals of distress. That afternoon, the Alfred Holt Line steamship *Antenor* sighted the *Jeddah* and came alongside. After a good look at her disabled condition, the *Antenor*'s captain sent his chief officer aboard for a closer inspection. Convinced that she could be saved, he reported back to his captain that the only crew men still aboard were three sailors, one topman, one *serang*, eleven firemen, one clerk and one fireman working his passage plus the second engineer and supercargo.

There were also 992 passengers: 778 men, 147 women and 67 children, not counting infants in arms. Everything on board was still in confusion and everyone was panic-stricken. Since the ship was now being driven before an east wind towards the coast of Africa, on which a heavy surf was breaking, they had every reason to be.

With patience, skill and ingenuity, the captain of the *Antenor* took the *Jeddah* in tow and three days later the two ships arrived at Aden. The sight of them must have been a shock to some of those already there: Austin Williams, Captain Clark and the rest had been picked up by another British ship, the *Scindia*, and had spent the previous twelve hours assuring the British authorities in Aden that the *Jeddah* had gone down with all aboard her, that there was no point in looking for her, and that the second officer and second engineer had been murdered by the pilgrims.

Singapore heard of the disastrous affair when a cable arrived from Aden addressed to the Singapore Steamship Company: 'To Alsagoff, Singapore. Aden, 10th August 8.20 p.m. *Jeddah* foundered. Self, wife, Syed Omar, 18 others saved. Clark.' [Syed Omar was Alsagoff's nephew.] A second cable came next day: '*Antenor* towed down here *Jeddah* full of water. All life saved, now in charge of government . . . .'

That set Singapore buzzing all right – those cables were immediately published in the *Daily Times*. In *Lord Jim* 'the whole waterside talked of nothing else – every confounded loafer in the town came in for a harvest of drinks over this affair . . . .' You heard it in the Harbour Office – imagine Captain Ellis's reaction. You heard it 'at every ship-broker's, at your agents, from whites, from natives, from half-castes, from the very boatmen squatting half-naked on the stone steps as you went up'.

As for Captain Joseph Lucas Clark, the Singapore man, the Court was 'reluctantly compelled to state' that it considered he had shown a painful want of nerve as well as the most ordinary judgment, and had allowed his feelings to master 'the sense of duty it is the pride of every British shipmaster to vaunt.' It considered that he had been guilty of gross misconduct in being the indirect cause of the deaths of the second mate and ten natives, seven crew and three passengers, and in abandoning his disabled ship and leaving nearly a thousand souls aboard to their fate. The Court also felt compelled to mark its sense of his poor conduct by suspending his certificate of competence as master for a period of three years. Only three years; people considered Clark to be a lucky man. He would be able to take command of other ships when his suspension was up.

Augustine (or Austin) Podmore Williams, twenty-eight years old, was dealt with next:

> The Court consider it necessary to place on record their disapprobation of the conduct of the first officer of the *Jeddah*, Mr Williams, who may be said to have more than aided and abetted the master in the abandonment of his vessel .... But for Mr Williams's officious behaviour and unseamanlike conduct, the master would probably have done his duty by remaining on the ship.

Harsh, deeply damaging words: 'officious ... unseamanlike'. Williams was fortunate to get away with a mere reprimand, when in many people's opinion – including that of His Excellency the Governor of the Straits Settlements and, I would lay odds, of the deputy-Neptune and 90 per cent of all those sherry and bitters drinkers and Manila cigar smokers at Emmerson's – both Captain Clark and Chief Officer Williams should have been banned from any position of responsibility on any ship whatever for the rest of their lives.

Some, like young, vain, disdainful Captain Montague Brierly of the Blue Star Line – Big Brierly, master of the *Ossa* at only thirty-two – would have taken much tougher measures with Williams (so he said) than that: 'Let him creep twenty feet underground and stay there! By heavens! *I* would.' Brierly had another idea, too: 'I tell you what,' he proposed to Conrad, 'I will put up 200 rupees if you put up another hundred and undertake to make the beggar clear out early tomorrow morning. Frankly, I don't care a snap for all the pilgrims that ever came out of Asia, but a decent man would not have behaved like this to a full cargo of old rags in bales . . . .'

So a 'decent' man should have cut and run, according to Brierly. How strange that when shortly afterwards something similar (no one knew just what) happened to him, big, brassbound, pompous Brierly told his chief officer, Mr Jones, to lock his dog in the chart room and put four belaying pins into his pockets to help him down, and deliberately jumped off the stern of the *Ossa* into the sea. 'Committed his reality and his shame together to the keeping of the sea', as Conrad put it – off Borneo, not far from the Hector Bank. Another unsolved mystery of the sea.

Austin Williams, branded a coward in full sight and hearing of the world, did not kill himself. He might have returned to face his parson father in England – it would have been a brave action in its way. But he was adamant: 'No. My dad has seen it all in the home papers by this time. He would never understand.' You can see what he meant in an old photograph: Austin's father, strong, bushy-bearded, had the forbidding look of a Victorian clergyman who had 'found' the God of Wrath, which indeed he had.

Yes, he did know about it; had indeed read all about the *Jeddah* scandal in the British press. The first reports in the *Globe* announced 'Dreadful Disaster at Sea. Loss of nearly 1000 Lives', and then, when this was found to be untrue, that the captain, the chief engineer, the chief officers, the assistant engineer – all British – had abandoned the ship and her thousand passengers.

'It is to be feared' – the *Daily Chronicle* went so far as to say – 'that pilgrim ships are officered by unprincipled and cowardly men who disgrace the traditions of seamanship. We sincerely trust that no Englishman was among the boatload of cowards who left the *Jeddah* and her thousand passengers to shift for themselves.'

But they *were* all Englishmen and not least the chief mate, Austin Williams, who was born in Porthleven, Cornwall, on 22 May 1852.

The *Globe* pointed out that because the ship did not sink, there clearly was not the extremity of peril the officers claimed – and that therefore the charge against those absconding officers 'became one of over-timidity as well as simple *lâches*'. And the *Daily News* professed 'feelings of indignation and horror at what seems the cowardly desertion of their post and trust by the master and seamen of the ship'. And of course there were more comments in that vein.

Austin returned to Singapore – Johnston's Pier, Battery Road, and Emmerson's. (What sinking-ship jokes would the genial colonel have been concocting there? What gags about absconding rats?) And he returned there the day after – the day *after* – a determined attempt to bring criminal charges against him and Captain Clark had failed in the Singapore Legislative Council, solely for want of witnesses. He served on Syed Mohsin's *Vidar* for a few months more – then left the sea for good.

So Williams was a brave man – of a certain kind. After what had happened you would have to be brave to take a job with McAlister and Co., the ship chandlers next door to Emmerson's and opposite the front door of the Master Attendant of Singapore, the *Jeddah*'s home port.

Austin Williams became a water-clerk. A job, Conrad said, which meant 'racing under sail, steam, or oars against other water-clerks for any ship about to anchor, greeting her captain cheerily, forcing upon him a card – the business card of the ship chandler – and on his first visit on shore piloting him firmly but without ostentation to the firm's

shop', It was a job for which no examination was necessary. It did not need intellect; it was a job requiring ability, agility and stamina. And it required Presence. Williams – tall and powerful, carrying his head forward with a 'fixed from-under stare' which made Conrad, watching him over his tiffin, think of a charging bull – undoubtedly had Presence.

Almost every noon he emerged into that busy convergence of narrow streets in front of the Harbour Office, either landing from McAlister's launch on to the stone steps of Johnston's Pier, or stepping from McAlister's vast, cavern-like shop, full of things that are eaten and drunk on board a ship, and everything to make her seaworthy and beautiful, from a set of chain-hooks for her cable to a book of gold-leaf for the carvings of her stern. In McAlister's cool parlour there were easy chairs, bottles, cigars, writing material, the latest newspaper and, if you really wanted one, a copy of harbour regulations (courtesy of Captain Henry Ellis). If you were hungry – then tiffin was at Emmerson's: a matter of out one door and in through the next.

It was there that Williams fell under the thoughtful but sympathetic scrutiny of a dark-complexioned, rather small man with black hair and a clipped black beard, very broad in the shoulder and long in the arm: Second Officer Korzeniowski, reborn, you might say, since the death of the *Palestine* and the rigours of the open boat. And later at the Hotel de l'Europe Conrad got to know the private anguish in the man with the fixed stare of a charging bull.

> At times I stole a sidelong glance. Jim [or Austin], while he pretended to be writing letters, was rooted to the spot, but convulsive shudders ran down his back; his shoulders would heave suddenly. He was fighting, he was fighting – mostly for his breath, as it seemed . . . . Suddenly, as I was taking up a fresh sheet of notepaper, I heard a low sound. Those who have kept vigil by a sickbed have heard such faint sounds wrung from a wracked body, from a weary soul . . . . He went to the door in a hurry, paused with his head down, and came back. 'I always thought that if a fellow could begin with a clean slate . . . .' A clean slate, did he say? As if the initial word of each our destiny were not graven in imperishable characters upon the face of a rock!

In the National Library, among the pages of the *Singapore Free Press* between an advertisement for motor cars – 'The Argo Standard low cost with utility and beauty' – and a report of a speech from Winston Churchill on the Opposition Front Bench, I had found this announcement:

> There passed away yesterday morning, at his residence Shamrock, Barker Road, Mr Austin Podmore Williams, who for 27 years was employed at Messrs McAlister & Co., as their chief outside superintendent in the Dubash and Shipchandlery Department. He severed his connection with this firm some three to four years ago and set up on his own account in a ship-chandlery business in the Arcade, but this not proving as flourishing as expected, Mr Williams joined the firm of Dawood & Co., and it was while he was employed in his duties there, that on the 15th of March, he slipped and fell, which resulted in a fractured hip bone. The deceased never really rallied from this accident and died at 3.45 yesterday morning of paralysis of the brain. The late Mr Williams was chief officer of the Singapore Steamship Co's *Jeddah*, a pilgrim ship which met with an accident in the Red Sea and was abandoned with about 1,000 coolies aboard. He held a chief officer's certificate and was for some time the Singapore representative of the Imperial Merchant Service Guild. Many wreaths were sent to the funeral having reference to his nautical career, besides many others from private friends. The deceased leaves a wife and nine children to mourn his loss.

Everyone had liked Williams's Eurasian wife, Jane. Partly half-caste Singapore-Indian, she had been sixteen when she married him, very well-educated, hair drawn back in a neat bun, a tiny waist. It is unlikely that her family – or she herself – had been unaware of her husband's unfortunate past. She must have known very well why people looked at him, why they averted their gaze, avoided asking him when he was going 'Home'. At his death, seven of the sixteen children she bore him had 'gone before'. People who knew her and Austin said that in that household, despite his formidable presence, it was she who had the upper hand, that he listened to her and was a good husband. When he died she was left to think, as she read the obituary and the cards on the many loving floral tributes to 'Austin' or to 'Daddy', that although much had never been forgotten, a great deal had been forgiven.

There was one more thing I wanted to find in the archives: a review of *Lord Jim*, published in 1900. In a column called 'London Day and Night' someone had written: 'Novel reading is a waste of time, but for those with time to waste *Lord Jim* is a story with a plot laid in Malaya, but "Tuan Jim" is an impossible person who flings over his dusky beauty for an unattractive specimen of "Poor White Trash".'

This travesty of a review has nothing to do with the tenor of Conrad's novel and the reviewer completely missed out the first part of *Lord Jim*, which contains the story of the *Jeddah*. So it seems doubtful that the review would have tempted Williams to dip into it. And anyone who did have 'time to waste on novels' – lured on in this case, no doubt, by the 'dusky beauty' reference – would never have risked pointing out to him the account of the *Jeddah* incident. That would have earned whoever it was a black eye, at the very least. So perhaps Williams – leading the quiet domesticated life of a ship chandler, busy buying houses, making money in a land boom, losing it in rubber and coping with all those children – was spared the knowledge that such a book had ever resurrected the shame of his youth.

Walking down Stamford Road from the Library, I thought of the strange case of A. P. Williams, and particularly his end. As I passed the Supreme Court – where the Malabar Hotel had stood in *Lord Jim* – I wondered if Williams had had more of Jim hidden inside him than anyone knew. More of the romantic Jim, I mean. If Williams had read *Lord Jim* Part Two he might actually have fancied himself in the role of

Jim Triumphant, dying tragically but heroically up a river in remotest Borneo.

'He came! He came!' was running from lip to lip, making a murmur to which he moved. 'He hath taken it upon his own head', a voice said aloud. He heard this and turned to the crowd. 'Yes. Upon my own head.' A few people recoiled. Jim waited awhile before Doramin, and then said gently, 'I am come in sorrow'. He waited again. 'I am come ready and unarmed,' he repeated.

The unwieldy old man made an effort to rise, clutching the flintlock pistols on his knees. clung heavily with his left arm round the neck of a bowed youth, and lifting deliberately his right, shot his son's friend through the chest.

The crowd, which had fallen apart behind Jim as soon as Doramin had raised his hand, rushed tumultuously forward after the shot. They say the white man sent right and left at all those faces a proud and unflinching glance. Then with his hand over his lips he fell forward, dead.

Had he thought of it, had he had sufficient romantic imagination, Austin Williams might have deemed that a worthy death for the disgraced son of a high-minded Anglican churchman from Cornwall. I certainly would not spurn such an end. But what is written is written, as the ancient Arabs used to say. And the imperishable characters engraved by destiny on that rock said not 'Borneo' but 'Bulbar Paralysis' and 'Bidadari Cemetery'.

Eight

The first time I went to the old disused Bidadari Cemetery in the northeast part of Singapore, Mr Kow took me in his Toyota, just to see if it was still there.

Not only was it there, it was enormous. Like a dilapidated park it spread out behind what looked like red-brick gatehouses on the main road and disappeared over the brow of a hill beyond rows of shattered crosses and mutilated angels half-hidden in grass. Half of it seemed never to have been implanted with tombs or anything else – which was strange because in Singapore if anything is left untended for more than five seconds something usually springs up, a bus stop or a shopping centre. But here there were fine trees and red paths, some of them wide enough to drive a car on, though round the cemetery's limits the urban sprawl was encroaching fast.

The gatehouses had once housed the registries of the graves in the cemetery but gardeners used them now to stow their belongings in and

to sleep in when they came off duty. When I asked one of them, an Indian, who was responsible for looking after the place now, he replied, 'I think the Ministry of Environment, Cemetery Affairs, sir. Sometimes a man comes and looks around.' He thought the ministry had grave registries, but he was not sure.

In default of them, I walked for an hour or two through the cemetery, with grass up to my knees, and only part of my mind on A. P. Williams; the other part was on snakes. When the gardener waved to me and called, 'Here! Here!' I thought he had stumbled on Austin, but he had only found a cluster of anonymous tombs from 1916. Some had anchors on them, others had not and all were buried in deep grass or creepers. To make things worse, the chronological arrangement of the graves appeared distinctly haphazard: those of 1916, 1917, 1911 were followed suddenly by one from 1946 and an assassinated Governor of Sarawak from 1949.

It would take us a week of looking, and suppose Williams had been moved? I thanked the gardener and asked Mr Kow to drive me to the ministry. 'We might find a registry there,' I said. But before returning to the city we stopped at an imposing shop-front with 'The Singapore Casket Company' over it. Mr Kow said he had a friend here who was well acquainted with the cemetery. Perhaps the distinguished Indian with grey hair and a gold chain round his neck who came to the front desk to meet me thought I had come to place a lucrative order. 'Established 1926,' he said, running a professional eye over me, when I asked about the Singapore Casket Company. 'The biggest in the state. Very distinguished.' When I apologised and explained that I wanted to know about the Bidadari Cemetery rather than order a coffin he remained as well-disposed as ever.

'They've exhumed some bodies,' he warned me. 'Perhaps even the one you are looking for.'

'Exhumed? And where did they move them to?'

'Oh, they burned them, I think. After exhumation, no reburial.' Seeing my look of disappointment, he changed the subject. 'There's a lot of vandalism. There's a lot of things broken into and all that.'

'Aren't vandals frightened of ghosts? Those tombs must be full of them.'

'Well, I've been there, even at night, and I've never seen a ghost. People do see them, of course. Even in our mortuary here. No, my advice to you is, go to see the ministry. They'll tell you if the grave you're looking for has gone or not.'

*

Stephen de Souza of the Ministry of the Environment was a big improvement on the officials of the Registry of Births and Deaths. When I said I knew one or two de Souzas in Singapore, he laughed. 'Oh, Mr Young, you only have to throw a stone in Singapore and you are sure to hit a de Souza.' He consulted his files and returned with advice. 'You should go to the National Archives – do you know them? Ask for Mrs Lily Tan. Come back to me with the grave number.'

In next to no time, so it seemed, Mrs Tan was showing me a microfilmed registry of graves, and there I found the following entry:

2559. Augustine Podmore Williams. 64. Male. 32 Barker Road. English. Master Mariner. Bulbar Paralysis (duration 1 month).

Mr de Souza came with me to the Bidadari Cemetery. I wrote the grave number on a card and handed it to the gardener I had met before, and once more we began the slow, difficult, up-and-down perambulation of the graves, the lumpy earth, the tall grass. Tombs gaped under roots and small bushes; it would have been easy to turn an ankle on a lump of marble or an angel's sword lying buried in the undergrowth.

'Those so-called gatehouses were chapels once. The bells were stolen,' de Souza said as we poked and prodded in the undergrowth. Malays wearing headbands and wielding besoms patrolled the paths, sweeping leaves. The cemetery had a number of the beautiful trees Malays call *tembusu*, with tiny post-impressionist leaves, a good many rain trees and some trees I did not know, whose leaves were dark and shiny. Small white butterflies danced about one of the grandest tombs: a stone canopy sheltering someone named Cornelius Lozanne who had died in 1912.

After a while a Singaporean Indian joined us. Having heard from one of the gardeners that de Souza was from the ministry he wanted to take the opportunity to make a complaint. He was middle-aged, short, fat and wearing a sort of waterproof deerstalker. He had been cleaning up his mother's grave, he said. I saw it later. A huge slab of black stone which looked as if it had cost a small fortune, it was covered with an extraordinary profusion of ceramic roses and a small army of marble angels standing guard.

'Look at the branches round my mother's grave. They are always falling down,' he cried, pointing to the trees. 'Are you from the ministry?' he demanded of Mr de Souza. 'Do you know how things are always getting vandalised? They break my angels right and left.' He dropped his voice, perhaps out of respect to his mother. 'Sometimes they even rape people here. Take drugs, do y'know?' He shook his head. 'Do you know, sometimes I've found fellows sitting on top of the graves, drunk. I say to them, "There's a body under there. Be careful." And you know what they reply? "What are you worrying about? He's dead!"'

All this half-serious complaining left de Souza smiling and unperturbed, and the Indian politely introduced himself.

'My name is Laurence Handy,' he went on. 'A well-known name; my father was a famous doctor here. There's even a Handy Road near the Cathay cinema. I would like to invite you. You must come for *makan*, you know.'

He broke off to address de Souza again with mock severity. 'Have you told this gentleman about snakes? Well,' he turned to me, 'the other day I got the fright of my life. A cobra as big as my wrist went by my dear mother's grave. A black one. I said to the gardeners, "Suppose I stamp on that by mistake?" The thing is, the snakes come out to sleep in the grass, for a morning bask. I'm not against that. Only what will happen, I mean to say, if they bite someone?'

De Souza agreed: 'We've seen cobras in the Muslim cemetery, too. I had to stop going there.'

Handy insisted, 'They're in the Chinese cemeteries just as much.' He smiled. 'They don't differentiate between religions, cobras don't!' He turned back to me. 'Look here, sir, only the tail part of that cobra was long as my arm. Just imagine – when you are putting flowers out for the dead, you're in a pensive mood. And suddenly these cobras rise up at you – and maybe spit at you. Five minutes – and you're dead.'

'At least you die in the right place,' I said, and we all laughed, standing there among the snakes and the broken tombs.

Handy, coming down to business, turned to me again. 'Now, sir, who are you looking for, if I may ask?'

De Souza answered for me. 'Lord Jim,' he said, 'Lord Jim is who we are looking for. The famous Lord Jim.'

'The writer, Lord Jim?' asked Handy.

'Well,' I said, 'he was a character in Joseph Conrad's novel of that name.'

'Yes, yes,' Handy said, enthusiastically, 'I read Joseph Conrad at school. And his Lord Jim is buried here?'

'The man who was the original Lord Jim – the *real* Lord Jim – is buried here. At least I hope so.'

Mr de Souza had not read *Lord Jim*, but he remembered now that he had seen the feature film of the novel made some years ago. Oh, yes, he said, he had seen it and asked excitedly: 'Who was the actor now?'

Austin
Podmore
Williams

'Peter O'Toole,' I answered.

Ecstatic, he grasped me by the hand: 'Peter O'Toole! Now, we know what we're looking for – the grave of Peter O'Toole! We'll try all the harder to find the tomb, Mr Young!'

With renewed vigour we set about clearing grass and shrubs. And suddenly it was all over. There it was, calf-deep in grass and needing to be swept: the grave of Lord Jim.

I stood there looking down on that grave for a long time. I knelt down in the grass and touched the inscription, slowly and carefully as if I were reading braille.

Augustine Podmore Williams
Born 22nd May 1852
Died 17th April 1916
'Thy Will be Done'

The cemetery vanished, and the voices of Mr de Souza and Mr Handy with it. I seemed to hear instead the clamour of an awful wind, the crash of high seas breaking over a ship that dementedly pitches and rolls, her engine room awash. I saw a young man standing on a deck, clinging to a rail, white with fear, in a nightmare he had never believed fate would require him to endure. He was staring at scores of passengers huddled under awnings looking in the dim light like corpses, like the silent company of the already dead. Well, he was thinking, they *are* dead! Nothing can save them.

'Lower the boats. Quietly!'

The pilgrims were waking up.

'Hurry! Come and help, man . . . Our only chance . . . What am I going to do? Why, clear out!'

The starboard boat was in the water, and the captain was in it and his wife, the chief engineer and some of the crew. . . .

Another scene. Punkahs stirred the heavy air of a courtroom, swaying slowly over the rows of spectators seated on narrow benches, dark native faces in turbans and voluminous draperies, Europeans, red-faced and very hot in tight drill suits, clutching pith helmets on their knees. The young man now stood very upright in the witness box, feeling the stab of attentive eyes and an agonising, burning shame. There was a voice. 'The Court consider it necessary to record . . . .' Terrible words hung in the air: 'Cowardice . . . inhumanity . . . want of resource.' Then, oh God, came: 'But for Mr Williams's officious and unseamanlike conduct, the Master would probably have done his duty by remaining on the ship . . . .'

'Thy Will be Done,' said the inscription at my feet.

He lay in the long grass of a condemned cemetery while my hand rested on his ruined tomb like a consoling hand on his dead shoulder.

The headstone of the tomb was gone and, though I implored everybody to look for it and they did so, it was not in the surrounding bushes.

'Are you wanting to see any other place here, sir?' the gardener asked at last.

On a whim I said, 'Well, what is next door?'

The gardener got to work with a machete and I heard de Souza say, 'There's another Williams here.'

Thinking, 'So what? It's a common enough name,' I nonetheless scrambled to my feet and walked over.

This grave, though earlier by nearly five years, was in rather better shape than the tomb of A. P. Williams. It bore a headstone in the shape of a Maltese Cross and an engraving:

Alfred Lockyer Williams
Born 13th February 1884
Died 28th June 1911
'Only a Step Removed'

Lockyer: that was the middle name of A. P. Williams's father — Thomas Lockyer, the Cornish parson. Could there be two 'Lockyer' Williamses, separated by half the globe and yet unrelated?

I tipped the gardener and shook Laurence Handy warmly by the hand, urging him to watch out for cobras and promising that I would give him a ring. I thanked Stephen de Souza, too; he had brought me here. Then, in Mr Kow's Toyota, I sped back to the River View Hotel and hurried to my room to consult Norman Sherry's book.

In 1909, the twenty-fifth year of his marriage, A. P. Williams, I found, had done at least two things worthy of note: he had celebrated his silver wedding at the Hotel de l'Europe and he had made a Will. The Will, dated 10 March, left to 'my son Alfred Lockyer Williams my watch, large diamond ring and the family crest seal and seal with coat of arms'. But Alfred Lockyer Williams, the eldest of Austin's sixteen children, never profited from his father's Will. As I now knew, he died little more than two years later.

Next morning I wasted no time. I was in Lily Tan's office so soon after she had opened the door that she looked quite startled. I blurted out what I could about Alfred Lockyer Williams and once more sped back to the register of graves.

Alfred Lockyer Williams had died in the Tan Tock Seng Hospital of an abscess of the liver, aged twenty-seven. No profession was given; perhaps he had lost through illness whatever job he had. Such an abscess, according to the medical dictionary, is often a manifestation of dysentery, and is accompanied by 'rigors' and by a 'great-enlargement' of the liver.

There was no way of knowing if poor Alfred Lockyer had died under surgery or before it. In any case, his father had chosen an appropriate inscription for his grave. In time and place, the son would indeed be 'only a step removed' from his father.

To Bankok! Magic name,
blessed name!

JOSEPH CONRAD, *Youth*

Part Three

Pagodas

In 1887, in Singapore, Conrad had been taken on as first mate on Syed Mohsin's steamer the Vidar, and in the wake of Lingard on the remote and exotic Berau river in Borneo had found the material for his first two novels, Almayer's Folly and An Outcast of the Islands, for the second half of Lord Jim and other stories. Shouldn't I have followed him chronologically – first to Borneo, then Bangkok? Perhaps. There were two reasons why I did not.

First, there are not many obliging cargo shipowners these days, but the Pegasus Progress was ready to sail to Bangkok and her captain would take me; second, I wanted to see from the deck of a ship the approach to Bangkok through the Gulf of Thailand and up the river. So it seemed better to take chances as they came, to leave Singapore on the Pegasus Progress and return in due course to follow the ghosts of Lingard, the Straits Arabs and Lord Jim at leisure. Java, Celebes and the Makassar Strait could wait while I pursued the phantoms of Leggatt, the man-killing mate of The Secret Sharer, and the enigmatic Falk, the man-eating tug master of Bangkok who, according to Conrad, only pulled your ship over the Bar into the Chao Phraya river when he felt like it.

I knew Bangkok quite well, but I had been haunted by a desire to cross that Bar for years. Conrad's first command, the Otago, had been waiting for him in Bangkok when he had sailed there in the steamer Melita, leaving Singapore at seven in the evening of 3 March 1888. Just about a hundred years later I went aboard the Pegasus Progress about to take exactly the same route.

nine

'Welcome aboard, Mr Young.'

'You are doing me a great favour, Captain.'

'Pleasure.'

Captain Viggo Johansen of the *Pegasus Progress*, Copenhagen, was not a word-spinner. But that did not matter. The main thing was he knew the way to Bangkok as well as he knew the Skaggerak; he had been going up and down the Gulf of Thailand for months. The *Pegasus Progress*, like her officers, was Danish, operated by Knud Larsen of Copenhagen, and at the moment she was on a Singapore-to-Bangkok shuttle for P&O. Built in 1983, she was a useful size – a neat 4500 tons with, as usual these days, all the living accommodation in the stern, quite unlike anything Conrad had ever seen.

We dropped the pilot into his launch – a dapper, white-shirted figure who gave us a jolly wave before he slipped down the rope ladder – and then 'Full ahead'. Picking up speed, we headed for the roads and Singapore dwindled. The container wharf, the big Hitachi cranes straddling the quays, the Finance Building appropriately designed to suggest a pile of coins, fell behind. For a moment a pale shaft of sunlight illuminated the needle spire of St Andrew's Cathedral, picking it out of the thickets of high-rise buildings.

Passing a rust-coloured container ship, the *Malaysia*, with tugs fore and aft, the captain took the 'wheel' – a lever in this case – and began to thread a way purposefully through the armada; at a quick count sixty to seventy ships, tankers and cargo vessels. As we met the sea I felt the steady heave of deep water under our bows: the joyful rise and fall of a ship coming alive. Towards the eastern end of Singapore Island a rain squall swept down on us; when we emerged from it, the *Pegasus Progress* had begun her swing to the north up the coast of Johore.

At the wheel, Captain Johansen looked across at me. 'So here you are on your way to Bangkok,' he said.

'Thanks to you.'

He smiled thinly and shrugged his shoulders.

Nonetheless, I watched regretfully as our bows swung away from the dark islands of Indonesia, lying so close to the south and east, slowly fading, turning from deep blue to a ghostly grey. Coned like volcanoes or humped like miniature camels, they rapidly disappeared as distance and the evening haze increased. All of them pirate lairs once, and perhaps even now . . . .

'Pirates.' Captain Johansen's eyes had been following mine and he might have been replying to some remark I had made. 'We've never seen any so far. These days you have to be a little careful, you know.'

I shall be back, I told the islands.

'We have only four deck hands,' Johansen went on. 'Filipinos.'

I had come across Filipino sailors before – a jolly lot in my experience, well worth having aboard for their smile-value. Their officers I was not quite so sure about. Completely unqualified Filipino officers had been known to buy sea-going certificates for a couple of hundred dollars in Manila and in crowded waters like the Suez Canal or the Strait of Malacca, there had been horrendous accidents.

'Slow,' said the captain. 'They are very slow.'

The whole ship was 'slow' in a sense. The Danish officers were a friendly, quiet lot, and life on the *Pegasus Progress* was tranquil. To my astonishment, they were teetotal. Captain Johansen was not by temperament a drinker and at sea naturally he set the tone, so on these short voyages to and from Bangkok the others were content to abstain and save their money. Luckily, it was not a rule applying indiscriminately to all aboard. The steward, Carl, urged me to take a six-pack of beer soon after I came aboard and when I paid for it put it in the fridge for me, but I think I only drank a couple of beers during the whole voyage – with the Danes drinking nothing but Rose's Lime Juice, I did not feel like it.

So I got to know the officers over instant coffee. Apart from the captain, there was Svend, the chief officer (who seldom opened his mouth except at night on the bridge); Bendt, the first officer, who seldom stopped talking anywhere; an enormous and genial chief engineer named Eric, who spoke little English and had his Thai wife on board with him (and she spoke less); and a second engineer, Ivar Hansen, who rarely appeared but having done so lived up to his comedian's face – which looked as little like a teetotaller's as W. C. Fields's.

On the bridge next day I watched the coast of Pahang sliding by on our port side, an oil flare wavering as if thrusting up out of the swell. Bendt was on watch, and talking.

'This captain keeps a nice ship,' he said. 'I mean, well, socially things are not great. The captain keeps his distance and so on – he's old-fashioned, we respect him. But the ship's clean and works efficiently. She's well run, I think.'

Just what one would expect from a Danish company, I replied.

In Bendt that touched a nerve. 'Ah-ha!' he went on. 'The trouble is there'll be no Danish merchant sailors soon. It's wages! They're just not good enough compared to shore jobs. Why go to sea if you can earn twice as much by staying ashore? Since the captain went to sea in 1949, there's been a revolution. *Ja*. A social revolution. And not even the captain would go to sea if he had his time over again. Danish sailors are too expensive. You could employ twelve Thais for my salary. So the companies are cutting us down.'

I had heard old predictions before: of huge computerised tankers needing no more than a couple of officers to sail them. High pay, not much work and a great deal of booze ashore – that is what European seamen want, the story went.

Things were only relatively different a hundred years ago. Conrad had been summoned from the Singapore Sailors' Home to see the Master Attendant in his office and had arrived late because Phillips, the Home's dismal steward, had delayed the message. Ellis had saluted Conrad's belated arrival with a nerve-shattering, 'Where have you been all this time?' Here was a good job on offer and, as all too often, it seemed that Conrad was in no hurry to snap it up. No wonder the deputy-Neptune was irritated. It was a common occurrence; officers, not seamen, were the trouble then. 'They are all afraid to catch hold,' Ellis fumed, meaning the European officers out East.

'Are they, sir? I wonder why?'

'Afraid of the sails. Afraid of a white crew. Too much trouble. Too much work. Too long out here. Easy life and deck chairs more their mark . . . . I began to think you were funking it too.' Then seeming to recollect himself, he explained that the master of a British ship having died in Bangkok, the consul-general there had cabled him for a competent man to be sent out to take command. 'You have a good name out here,' he growled and Conrad said, 'I am very glad to hear it from you, sir . . . .'

Bendt said, 'Ever think of China? China is buying up hundreds of ships. If you go up the rivers of China, for five hours up them you see

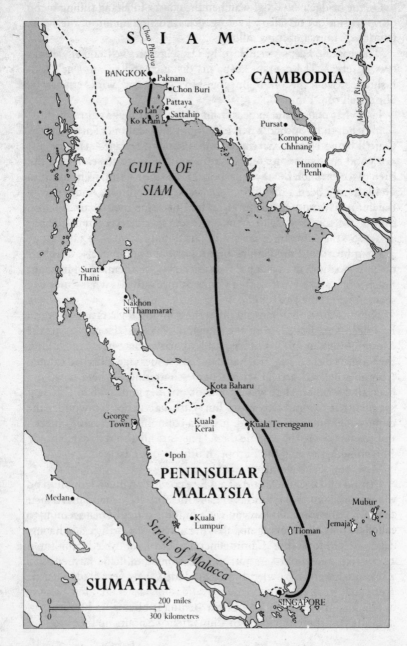

SIAM

Chao Phraya

CAMBODIA

Mekong River

BANGKOK • Paknam
• Chon Buri
Pattaya
Ko Lan •
Ko Kram • Sattahip

Pursat •

Kompong
Chhnang •

Phnom
Penh •

GULF OF
SIAM

Surat
Thani •

Nakhon
Si Thammarat •

Kota Baharu •

George
Town •

Kuala
Kerai •

Kuala Terengganu •

• Ipoh

PENINSULAR
MALAYSIA

Medan •

Mubur

Jemaja •

• Kuala
Lumpur

Tioman

SINGAPORE •

SUMATRA

Strait of Malacca

0   200 miles
0   300 kilometres

the ships stacked. Two thousand ships, maybe more. Waiting for the men to be trained for them. Twenty thousand men come out every year from the Chinese training colleges.'

'The floating yellow peril,' I smiled. I had no idea if what he said was true or false.

The night skies of the Gulf were full of stars. We moved smoothly over calm waters, the Southern Cross hanging over our stern. Just before dawn Venus swam out as bright as a diamond from wisps of cloud; and at evening a reddish Jupiter replaced her as we crossed from the Malaysian side of the Gulf towards the coasts of Cambodia and Thailand.

The Gulf of Siam is deceptive. Extreme patience and extreme care, Conrad said, are needed to see one through this region of broken land, of faint airs and dead water. 'It is full of complications and difficulties – yet simple enough in a way. One is a seaman, or one is not. And I had no doubt of being one.' An old captain in the Sailors' Home in Singapore had agreed with him: 'The gulf . . . Aye! A funny piece of water, that. Whatever you do, keep to the east of it. The west side is dangerous at this time of the year. Don't let anything tempt you over.'

It was 'this time of year' now, and evidently Captain Johansen had found nothing to tempt him to stay with the currents and reefs of the Malaysian shore. We were heading straight across to the island-embedded coast below Sattahip. There was no sign of it and no sign of Malaysia either when the chief officer said, 'We may – we don't know yet – we may have to anchor for a while before the Bangkok river. Outside the Bar.'

'Outside?'

'*Ja*. In the roads.'

That would suit me, I thought. A good look at our course on the chart had told me that we would pass due north between the islands, well away from Pattaya. That would take us to that extraordinary channel, the wide and absurdly shallow slit through the strip of mud called the Bar which every ship that ever reached Bangkok had had to negotiate. Before that Cambodia and Thailand would hold our attention to starboard – not an easy coast: 'Much indented and numerous rivers discharge through it', the *China Sea Pilot* warned. 'There are many off-lying islands and dangerous shallow coastal banks. . . .' Mangroves, too, and fishing stakes spread across a coastal bank extending nine miles offshore.

Supper that night was kippers, cold meat, mayonnaise, pâté, salad, spring onions, Danish Blue cheese – with water, of course, Rose's Lime Juice or tea. Coffee, as usual, hung in a thermos from a nail in the bulkhead. Talk among these quiet Danes was limited and I went early to my cabin – I had a bunk in the ship's diminutive hospital. Soon we would reach the islands where Conrad had played a furiously dangerous game with his new, unknown ship, an unknown crew, and a resentful and suspicious chief mate; where the mate of a British vessel who, having killed a man, had appeared out of night and the sea to ask for sanctuary: Leggatt, who reminded Conrad so much of himself. Leggatt, the 'secret sharer'.

I washed my face, took up my binoculars and went up to the wheelhouse. There were lights all over the place by now – from fishing boats mainly, hundreds of them, it seemed – pinpricks of light that pierced the darkness like electric torches and then mysteriously vanished. Just here Conrad, his ship becalmed, had remarked to his two officers at supper: 'Are you aware that there is a ship anchored inside the islands? I saw her mastheads above the ridge as the sun went down.'

It was common practice for a heavily laden ship to wait outside the Bar at low tide and offload some of her cargo on to barges. Even the *Pegasus Progress* might have to wait outside the Bar. But Conrad's young and cocky second mate made it his business to find out the ship's name: 'She's the Liverpool ship *Sephora* with a cargo of coal. Hundred and twenty-three days from Cardiff. The tugboat skipper told me.'

More or less where we were now, Conrad, all alone on deck that night, had found a rope ladder left carelessly over the side of the ship. Looking up at him from the water a naked corpse spoke to him.

'My name's Leggatt,' it said.

Conrad had little time to think. Almost automatically, he helped the dripping figure on board and down to the warmth and secrecy of his cabin. In one of Conrad's own grey-striped sleeping suits the mysterious newcomer might have been his own twin. Indeed, Conrad might have been looking at his own reflection in a mirror. What was his double doing clambering aboard a strange ship in the middle of the night? 'I've killed a man,' the stranger explained, adding, a little red-faced, 'a pretty thing to have to own up to for a Conway boy.'

His story was as follows.

After days of storm the *Sephora* had only one foresail left to keep her running. The ship needed every hand to pull his weight in weather that threatened to sink her. It had gone on and on, seemingly without end; and in this dire situation the insolence and neglect of duty of a disobedient seaman had begun to drive Leggatt to distraction. 'He was one of those creatures,' Leggatt told Conrad as he sat huddled in his rescuer's pyjamas, 'that have no business to live at all. He wouldn't do his duty and wouldn't let anybody else do theirs . . . . You know the sort.'

A final word of insolent disobedience proved too much. At the height of a devastating storm there was no time for gentlemanly reproof. The first officer grappled with him, a huge sea fell on them both, and when they were parted the seaman was dead.

'Mr Leggatt, you have killed a man,' the *Sephora*'s captain said without further ado. 'You can act no longer as chief mate of this ship.' Leggatt's action had saved the ship; yet now his captain treated him as if he had the halter round his neck already. He had to escape. For weeks he waited for an opportunity. At last, seeing a ship becalmed, he had broken out and swum for its light. He was lucky to find Conrad. In Conrad's judgment Leggatt was an exemplary sailor who had saved his ship from a rogue seaman threatening her and everyone aboard. Conrad was willing to do what he could to save him, and he took a terrifying risk to do so, allowing his ship to drift perilously close to the black mass of Koh-ring Island – close enough to enable the fugitive to have a good chance of reaching the shore. The risk paid off. The *Otago* found a breeze to keep her from grounding; Leggatt, a good swimmer, escaped to the shore. Watching him disappear in a swirl of phosphorescent water, Conrad hoped the proud swimmer would find a better destiny.

The real events that lay behind Conrad's story featuring Leggatt, *The Secret Sharer*, concerned one of the most famous sailing ships that has ever been launched – the *Cutty Sark*. What a beauty the ship was. Once on the Asia run she did 2163 miles in six days, or an average of 15 knots per hour; on occasions she managed 363 knots in twenty-four hours. She was something of a marvel – more of a marvel at times than some members of her crew. She proved a point a wise old salt makes in another Conrad story, 'Ships are all right. It is the men in them!'

In the spring of 1880 the American Navy Department put out urgent orders for the best Welsh steam coal for warships in the Pacific. At that time the *Cutty Sark*'s master was one of the most popular men

at sea, but even Captain Wallace had the devil's own difficulty in scrounging a crew at the coal port of Penarth, thanks to the black reputation of his mate – a hard and short-tempered man called Sydney Smith. The crew that Captain Wallace finally sailed with consisted of five Englishmen, three Danes, three black men (of unknown provenance), two Greeks and an Italian. One of the three blacks, John Francis, quickly fell foul of Smith, who considered him intolerably insolent and ham-fisted.

Francis was badly injured in the hand on the voyage and what with the pain and the venomous ranting of the mate, he lost control of himself. He threatened to go after Smith with a capstan bar. In the South Atlantic, relations between the mate and Francis went from bad to worse, and to avoid the men taking sides and working themselves into a mutiny, the captain quickly handed out arms to his officers and apprentices and ordered Smith and Francis to sort their problem out man-to-man with bare fists, while he himself, pistol in hand, swore he would shoot the first crewman to intervene. Unfortunately after a quarter of an hour of furious fisticuffs there was no result.

Perhaps Wallace should have put Francis – and maybe Smith, too – in irons then and there, because as the *Cutty Sark* headed for the Sunda Strait the worst happened. In the middle of a gale, Francis twice ignored an order, and Smith went for him, wrested away an iron capstan bar he was brandishing and cracked his head open with it. Francis died three days later. The mate retired to his cabin, as if to prison, for the rest of the voyage; and the crew, who preferred even Francis to the mate, vowed they would see him hanged for murder.

You cannot keep a good ship down – and despite all dramas the *Cutty Sark* passed the volcano of Krakatoa and reached Java Head only seventy-two days out from Penarth. There, off the little port of Anjer, Smith argued kind Captain Wallace into letting him escape and fled in a boat to an American ship, the *Colorado*, lying nearby and bound for Saigon. At just that time Captain Wallace received orders from his owners to proceed to Yokohama and had to get under way with only his officers and apprentices to help him – the crew had discovered the hated mate's escape and went on strike, and the proud *Cutty Sark* limped into the Java Sea manned by six boys and four men. Then came the second tragedy.

This is how Basil Lubbock puts it in his *Log of the Cutty Sark*:

> Captain Wallace had no sooner helped his mate to escape than he realised in what a predicament he had placed himself. He saw an official investigation looming ahead in Yokohama, in which there was little doubt but that he would be held responsible for the mate's escape, and the very least that he could expect was the suspension of his certificate. He had an old mother and a young wife dependent upon him, and the future for them as for himself looked black . . . . Ever since the escape of the mate he had been unable to sleep. Night and day he stood gazing out to sea or walked with bowed head up and down the poop in a misery that was plain to see.

The fourth day after leaving Anjer, in the dark at four o'clock in the morning, Captain Wallace turned to the ship's carpenter on the poop and asked, 'Is the second officer coming up, d'you think?'

'Just now, sir,' he was told.

Wallace called the helmsman's attention to the ship's course, walked calmly aft – and stepped over the side of the ship. The sea was like a millpond and a boat was quickly lowered, but however much the crew blamed themselves for having refused duty, their much-loved Captain Wallace was never found, any more than Big Brierly of the *Ossa* (who had said Jim should creep twenty feet underground) was ever found.

A small world. By chance the *Cutty Sark*, captainless now, was redirected to Singapore. She arrived there three days after another ship's mate, Austin Williams, had returned there in disgrace from the

Court of Inquiry in Aden on the *Jeddah* affair. So the *Jeddah* and the *Cutty Sark* gave Emmerson's regulars a double ration of drama. Captain Henry Ellis, the deputy-Neptune, must have been beside himself.

As for Sydney Smith, the despotic mate, was he less lucky than Leggatt or more so? You could toss a coin on that, I suppose. John Anderson, alias Sydney Smith, thirty-one, described as a seaman, was charged with the wilful murder of John Francis before Mr Justice Stephen at the Central Criminal Court in London.

CHARGE OF MURDER ON THE HIGH SEAS

The prisoner was chief mate of an English vessel, called the *Cutty Sark*, which sailed in May 1880, on a foreign voyage. The deceased, who was a black man, joined the Vessel at Cardiff as an able seaman, but . . . it was discovered that he was unable to perform the duty, and this led to a great deal of unpleasantness on board, and the deceased was not at all on good terms with the crew . . . .

The prisoner was on several occasions very angry with the deceased and used violence to him, but there does not appear to be any doubt that the deceased was very insolent to the prisoner, and had been heard to threaten that he would use a capstan bar to protect himself . . . .

The jury consequently found the prisoner guilty of manslaughter.

Numerous people spoke of Smith's good character, and when his counsel had urged in mitigation that, after all, he was responsible for the safety of the ship and the crew, and that this had been gravely endangered by the conduct of the deceased, the judge sentenced him 'with great pain' to penal servitude for seven years. Smith spent his sentence in Dover prison, working on the breakwater, of which he later used to say he knew every stone. He went back to sea after that, bravely starting again from the bottom and working his way up to captain: a 'regular hard old case', people said. He died of cancer aged seventy-two in 1922, forty-two years after that rendezvous off Krakatoa and Java Head.

The water was full of lights. Our night-time wake was straight as a torpedo's and silvered in the reflection of the moon. Fishing boats flashed torchlights at us to show that their nets were strung here, begging us to avoid them. Making small deviations in course we tried, though it was not easy. Tiny lights like makeshift 'buoys' held up the nets, so small that they were barely visible until we were up on top of them, minute oil lamps lodged somehow on palm fronds, like fairy lights bobbing on the face of the gulf.

Like a blanket, the warm windless air of Thailand crept about us. To starboard, in my binoculars, the island of Ko Khram grew to resemble a black cliff – and I thought of the dark overhanging mass of Koh-ring that had once so menaced Conrad's ship.

Carl brought up a telex message from the Borneo Company, our agents in Bangkok. 'No anchoring. Go straight up into the river.' And when I peered again through my binoculars, I saw far ahead the single light of the pilot winking at me – inviting, welcoming – at the entrance to the Bar.

Ten

'I am reducing speed now; we meet the pilot at the Bar at 2300,' the chief officer was saying.

The moon had disappeared behind cloud, and the stars seemed to have transferred themselves to the water. Countless fishing boats surrounded us with dancing flashes of light. Blocks of light like multi-storeyed houses hovered ahead, reflected in the water; these were big ships waiting in the anchorage outside the river, their derricks and masts folded and still like the long legs and motionless wings of sleeping crickets. Soon the pilot boat was under our bows, and the pilot, a small neat man in white shirt and slacks, clambered up to the bridge and gruffly showed us the way to the narrow entrance to the Bar.

From the shaded chart I could see that the Bar is not simply the very narrow strip of mud that I had supposed it to be. It is a long solid shelf stretching up and down the whole coastline, closing in on the mouth of the Chao Phraya river like the heavy claws of a giant sky blue lobster. The channel through it is amazingly narrow – so very narrow that as soon as we entered it the ship's bows, forcing their way through, created a wave of water that roared past amidships with a jumble of noise so unexpected that I looked over the side to see what on earth was happening. It was not so much a roar as the purposeful drive of a strong incoming tide against a steep breakwater, and it drowned out every other sound. The channel is so shallow here that the bulk of the ship, relentlessly pushing through it and thrusting the water aside, exposed the muddy edges of a trench. A close avenue of red and green buoys led us towards the dim, dark line of the shore, the roar of the water combining with the unwavering throb of our engine thudding like a metallic heart.

And then – the climax to this drama – I saw a tall spire and, shimmering ghost-like in the blackness, the outline of a great temple.

Customs men in blue uniforms came aboard at Paknam, a little town a short way up the river. They sat expectantly at a table in the *Pegasus Progress*'s 'smoking room', greeting the cans of Foster's lager and the cartons of cigarettes with expressions of grateful surprise. When the thanks turned to hints and pleading, Carl handed out a second armful of cigarette cartons he kept in reserve. He knew the form.

We moved on up the river, through infinite flatness, twisting and turning for twenty miles or more, watching the high, distant lights of Bangkok appearing, now here, now there, according to the windings of the water. At last, at Terminal 20, just after Bang Chak on the east bank, we tied up opposite a wilderness of palm trees and a few one-storey wooden huts on stilts.

'When we had more time we used to meet girls in those huts,' the first officer said, winking. But it was difficult to imagine girls seducing anyone into these ramshackle, waterbound hovels.

It had been dark when we arrived but the day came up fast, bright and cool with high clouds. Big grey birds, like heron, flapped slowly down the still dim bank, and a furious little tug fumed upriver like an impatient urchin, forcing a puttering skiff with an outboard motor to escape from its wake among the nipa palms along the bank. I could see a tanker just astern of us; upstream the derricks of a big cargo vessel poked up from behind a line of warehouses, and a cluster of industrial chimneys smoked lazily beyond a bend in the river.

I went down to say goodbye to Captain Johansen. 'Well,' he said, 'I was in Bangkok in the 1950s as a young seaman. The Maersk Line, you know it? We did a long time in port in those days of bulk cargoes – fourteen or fifteen days. You were young. You had time to find yourself a girlfriend. You went to the Mosquito Bar. There were nothing but empty roads, and fields and water everywhere then.'

I had known the Mosquito Bar; a famous – or infamous – seamen's hang-out near the docks, well known among other things for its transvestites, as many waterside bars in the East are. But the Mosquito had disappeared at about the time the container ships appeared on the scene – into port one morning, out again the same evening, with no time for loitering in bars.

I put out my hand. 'Thanks, Captain, for the lift,' I said. 'I expect you've seen the Danish memorials in the Anglican cemetery here?

Worth a visit, you know. You Danes — the East Asiatic Company — pretty well "discovered" Siam.'

A hundred years ago Thailand's kings had employed Danish officers to sail their ships, train and drill their army, and officer their police. 'It is a special pleasure to arrive in Bangkok on a Danish ship, Captain,' I smiled at Johansen. He seemed quite surprised at that.

As the steamer *Melita* bore Conrad across the Bar and up the river towards Paknam, he could feel the piece of paper in his pocket that had changed his life. The memorandum from Captain Henry Ellis was short and to the point: 'This is to inform you,' the deputy-Neptune of Singapore had written in his most heavy and official style, 'that you are required to proceed in the S.S. *Melita* to Bangkok and you will report your arrival to the British Consul and produce this memorandum which will show that I have engaged you to be Master of the *Otago*.'

To the British Consul in Bangkok Ellis had written:

I have the honour to acknowledge the receipt of your telegram 'can you engage Master to take *Otago* from Bangkok to Melbourne salary £14 a month . . . .' The person I have engaged is Mr Conrad Korzeniowski, who holds a certificate of competency as Master from the Board of Trade. He bears a good character from the several vessels he has sailed out of this port . . . .

Signed, of course, with a heavily assertive, broad nib: 'Henry Ellis, Master Attendant'. Even Korzeniowski was spelled correctly.

For Conrad it had happened like a miracle in a fairy tale. Captain Ellis (a fierce sort of fairy, it was true) seemed to have produced Mr Korzeniowski's first command out of a hat. It was a great relief to arrive in Bangkok; it would be a greater one to be shot of the *Melita*'s atrocious captain, who had made it very plain that he did not welcome passengers. The *Melita*'s arrival in the Chao Phraya is registered in the *Bangkok Times* as follows: 'Jan. 24th, *Melita* Gr. steamer 389 tons Capt. H. S. Moretz from Singapore.' Conrad might have been mildly amused by another news item:

The following very funny 'shipping report' has been shown us. 'Arrived. *Melita* s.s. Germ from Chinese spore passed Paknam at 5.45.' A germ from Chinese spore must be a curious thing whether it has arrived at the *Melita* or other embryo state. It probably passed Paknam to go and germinate in the Klong Telah [a particularly smelly canal].

Conrad stared at Bangkok, a city he had always yearned to see, and

> . . . there it was, the oriental capital which had as yet suffered no white conqueror; an expanse of brown houses of bamboo, of mats, of leaves, of a vegetable-matter style of architecture, sprung out of the brown soil on the banks of the muddy river. It was amazing to think that in those miles of human habitations there was not probably half a dozen pounds of nails.

Some of the wooden houses, usually on stilts, seemed to cling miraculously to the low shores; others floated in long anchored rows. Here and there, as they do today, great piles of masonry towered above the brown-tiled roofs – the King's Palace, the Temple of Dawn, Wat Po where the Reclining Buddha reposes, the Temple of the Emerald Buddha: gorgeous, gilded structures, glowing serenely under the vertical sunlight, enough to bring an awestruck European heart into his mouth. Nothing very drastic has happened to change that essential scene.

Today on the wriggling muddy Chao Phraya river, the strings of heavy barges, wooden-sided, with arched roofs and awnings like ponderous Noah's Arks, pulled by tugs, strain against the tide. The canoe-like 'dragon-boats' roar in and out of the tangled islands of water-hyacinth, cutting daringly close under the noses of the barges; passenger ferries, balustraded and terraced, criss-cross from bank to bank as though threading them together; and sand barges push up and down, gaily flying the red, white and blue striped flag of Thailand, so heavily laden they are mostly under water. Nothing is ever still on this great water highway.

Otago

And there she was; Conrad's new command.

'There! There's your ship, Captain.' The voice was that of the master of the *Melita*. Conrad, leaning over the rail, hardly dared to lift his eyes. Yes, there she was: the *Otago*. At first glance his fears vanished. She was perfection; one of those craft that by virtue of their design and finish will never look old. Amongst the other ships moored alongside her, she looked like an Arab steed in a string of carthorses.

'I hope you are satisfied with her, Captain,' came the sneering voice of the *Melita*'s captain, but he didn't even turn his head. Why bother? He knew he was looking at one of those creatures whose mere existence is enough to make one feel that it is good to be in the world in which she has her being.

Half an hour later, putting his foot on her deck for the first time, he knew that nothing could equal the fullness of that moment. He walked slowly aft savouring it, ascended the poop, saw under the awning the gleaming brasses of the yacht-like fittings, the polished rails, the glass of the skylights. Below, in the cabin, a mahogany table under the skylight shone in the twilight like a dark pool of water; there was a marble-topped sideboard surmounted by a wide looking-glass in an ormolu frame; and the saloon was panelled in two kinds of wood in excellent, simple taste.

There was one drawback, at this point invisible. This was the *Otago*'s ageing first mate, a 'meagre man with a haggard expression', suffering from the belief he should have been given command after the previous master's death, although he was not legally qualified to do any such thing. But his surliness could not spoil the moment of

110

triumph for a young officer, not yet thirty, viewing his first command.

'Polish Joe' had made good.

I checked into the Royal Orchid Hotel on the river. It is a newish hotel but it has a magnificent view of the Chao Phraya and the old Portuguese Embassy's garden of tropical trees. Further downstream the old Oriental Hotel building crouched behind a new wing that might have been part of an expensive hospital, and next door to it the East Asiatic Company still occupied its turn-of-the-century building, wharf, piers and warehouses.

A hundred years ago Bangkok had meant this district, reaching up the eastern banks of the river past the sunlit pinnacle of the Royal Palace and the flashing wings of the Wat Po temple, past the soaring finger of the Temple of Dawn a little way up on the other bank. The old foreign legations, hotels, offices, and the Customs House had all been clustered here. Beyond, where now the sprawl of late twentieth century Bangkok spread hideous traffic jams and imposed a layer of polluted air so thick you could almost cut it with a blunt paddle, there had been in those days nothing but mile after square mile of rice paddies, lotus gardens and the famous Siamese *klongs* – canals – that ran in straight, narrow lines across a landscape as flat as a chessboard, only interrupted here and there by a bamboo-encircled hamlet or a golden temple.

The *Pegasus Progress*'s agent had my passport stamped and delivered to the hotel by midday. Once settled in, I picked up the telephone.

My friend Sumeit answered at once. 'Nuee is coming out of jail,' he said, 'in five days' time.'

'Amnestied?'

'Yes. The King's amnesty came.'

I had been afraid the ship would arrive too late for this great day.

I had met Sumeit in the Sixties soon after arriving in Thailand for the first time. He was in the hotel business; obviously poor; obviously hard-working. He was married then to Nuee's mother but for obscure reasons he left her soon after the son was born. There had been two other wives since then, and two other sons who had given Sumeit no trouble at all.

By now Sumeit had risen to be deputy manager of one of the best hotel restaurants in Bangkok, but he still lived very simply in the house he had bought years ago when I had first met him. It stood on a watery

111

patch on stilts, its porch tilting a little dangerously, I thought. Puppies gambolled about, eating the shoes of guests who had gone barefoot into the house. A white bird with a needle-sharp beak talked Thai briskly back at him from its wicker cage on the porch. Sumeit loved birds, dogs and snakes. Once he had proudly shown me a white cobra in a box; thank heavens, it had mysteriously disappeared. All he could think about now was the release of his eldest son.

This was Nuee, twenty-two now. He had been in prison since he was fifteen, serving a fourteen-year jail sentence for having been a member of a gang of young drug dealers. The leader of the gang, in his twenties, had been put away for much longer – for twenty or even thirty years, I believe. By now Nuee had spent virtually his entire adolescent life behind bars.

'Bring him here as soon as you can, Sumeit. And then I suggest you take him to the seaside for a holiday. To get to know each other again, you see that?'

'I see,' Sumeit said.

I had visited Nuee in the jail at Klong Prem with Sumeit a couple of years before. We had bought presents inside the prison gate: cakes, bread and biscuits, soap, dried fish, toothpaste and a toothbrush, coffee, cigarettes and washing powder – things like that. Everything had to be examined by the guards; because, Sumeit explained, the year before quantities of heroin had been discovered in packets of cigarettes. So our instant coffee was poured slowly into a transparent plastic bag, and everything else was probed and sifted, too. A warder said he would keep it until our names were called and then pass it in to be delivered to Nuee. We waited on hard benches until a loudspeaker spat our names at us and shepherded us through a deep archway, across a dusty yard to a high grille. We peered over a wide, empty gap. And there behind a second grille, but within shouting distance, we saw Nuee's pale, anxious face peering back.

What did we talk to him about? Banal things, of course. He was not forgotten, we assured him; there was hope of a royal amnesty within a year or two. What else? Our simply being there brought a wan smile to Nuee's pinched face and light into his dead eyes, and made our visit worthwhile.

Nuee had been cut with a knife in a fight. Never mind, Nuee shrugged, prison was full of hoodlums; he had been beaten up quite often. A good deal of *ganja* – pot – was smuggled in, sometimes with the help of the guards; he kept away from that and also from the *farangs* he sometimes glimpsed. Foreigners had AIDS, he had been told.

112

'Not you though, Nuee,' I said. 'I hope.'

And he said, 'Oh, no,' and laughed.

Sumeit translated. 'Nuee says the prisoners are often hungry. They like the rainy season because it brings out the toads. He says the common toad is very good to eat.'

'Well, the French like them.'

Nuee was going to need a lot of looking after. During his seven years in jail Bangkok had been transformed, bloated by immigrant populations from the countryside, by the destruction and construction of real estate developers, and by an annual invasion of hordes of globetrotters. There would be the problem of finding new friends and a steady job. Had Nuee really managed to reject drugs for good and all? We would have to wait and see. When we waved goodbye the little pale pixie face faded wistfully from sight through a metal door that shut with a clang.

'When he gets out we'll take him on the river. That's the first thing,' I had told Sumeit. We had agreed long ago that the river was the lifeline in a city as large, ugly and polluted as Bangkok had become. The 'real' Bangkok was still alongside the Chao Phraya.

Drugs and AIDS are Thailand's problems now, but in Conrad's days the problems had been fever and drink. Cholera epidemics: they came and went, with devastating effect. The *Siam Repository* reported in 1873: 'There is a rumour afloat that some 20,000 have fallen victim to the cholera.' That was nothing compared with the 30,000 deaths in 1849.

The trouble was that there were not enough sewers, deep underground drains or cesspools, so that the Siamese, who lived near the river banks not only had to put up with an indescribable stench and the sight of the corpses of plague victims floating up and down the river with the tides, but had to drink contaminated water that must have resembled a nauseously meaty kind of minestrone. Instead of building sewers they floated food, images and lighted candles on the river to appease what the newspaper called the 'imaginary power which has hurled upon them such a terrific calamity'. The cholera thrived.

Foreigners seem to have been spared the worst, which is odd when the medicines most freely used sound hardly more effective than Siamese images and lighted candles: Dr J. Collis Browne's Chlorodyne (for 'Dysentery, Cholera, Fever, Ague, Coughs, Colds, etc . . .'), Penny Davis' Pain Killer, Dr Jayne's Spirit of Camphor and Dr Beach's

Neutralizing Mixture — 'we've advertised everywhere'. Calomel and laudanum had had their day by then, but the old standby, quinine, survived. Conrad gave his crew large dollops of quinine at regular intervals as advised by the British Legation's doctor, William Willis, who often visited Conrad on board, finding him good company.

But cholera and fever had already hit the *Otago*'s crew, including her ageing first mate. The ship's steward and cook had died of choleraic symptoms a few days before Conrad arrived in the *Melita*: only two crewmen were unaffected. Now he forbade any work in the sun; only light work was to be done, under awnings.

'You seem to have a most respectable lot of seamen,' remarked Willis. It was true. The *Otago*'s crew were a sober lot; no Mosquito Bars for them. Which was unusual, seeing that they were all white men: a German first mate, an English second officer and six sailors — two English, two Norwegian, one Scot and one German. But even so, the ship's health trembled on the verge of a break-up. The fever, even though it was late January, a cool time of year by Bangkok standards, worked with 'the swiftness of an invisible monster ambushed in the air, in the water, in the mud of the river bank'.

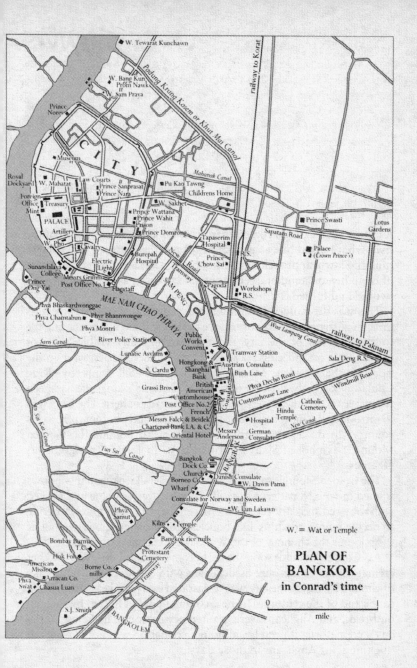

W. Tewarat Kunchawn

W. Bang Kun
Prom Nawk
W. Sam Praya

Prince Nores

CITY

Museum

Royal
Dockyard

W. Mahatat

Law Courts
Prince Sanprasat
Prince Nara

Foreign
Office
Mint

Treasury

PALACE

Artillery

Prince Wattana
Prince Wahit
Prison
Prince Domrong

W. Pho

Cavalry

Sunandalaya
College

Electric
Light

Burepah
Hospital

Prince
Ong Yai

Messrs Grimm

Post Office No. 1

Flagstaff

Phya Bhaskardwonggae

MAE NAM CHAO PHRAYA

Phya Chamtabun

Phyr Bhannwongse

Phya Montri

Sarn Canal

River Police Station

Lunatic Asylum

S. Cardu

Grassi Bros.

Hongkong &
Shanghai
Bank

British

American
Customhouse

Post Office No. 2

French

Messrs Falck & Beidek

Chartered Bank I.A. & C.

Oriental Hotel

Tun Sai Canal

Sai Kat Canal

Bangkok
Dock Co.

Church

Borneo Co.

Wharf

Consulate for Norway and Sweden

W. Lun Lakawn

Phya
Samut

Kilns

Temple

Bombay Burma
T.C.

Bangkok rice mills

Hok Foh

Protestant
Cemetery

American
Mission

Arracan Co.

Phya
Swat

Chasua Luan

Borne Co.
mills

S.J. Smith

BANGKOLEM

Podung Krung Kosem or Khut Mai Canal

railway to Korat

Mahatak Canal

Pu Kao Tawng

Childrens Home

W. Sakhet

Prince Swasti

Lotus
Gardens

Sapatam Road

Palace
(Crown Prince's)

Tapaserim
Hospital

New Road

Prince
Chow Sai

R.S.

Pagoda

Workshops
R.S.

Wat Lampang Canal

railway to Paknam

Public
Works

Convent

Tramway Station

Austrian Consulate

Bush Lane

Phya Decho Road

Windmill Road

Sala Deng R.S.

Customhouse Lane

Catholic
Cemetery

Hospital

Hindu
Temple

New Canal

German
Consulate

Messrs
Anderson

Danish Consulate

W. Dawn Pama

W. = Wat or Temple

PLAN OF
BANGKOK
in Conrad's time

0

mile

A century ago Conrad could see from as far away as the mouth of the river what looked like a celestial beacon in the centre of the Siamese capital. Slowly approaching the city by ship he saw it first on one side of him, then on another, seeming to dodge about as the Chao Phraya twisted and turned.

This was the Golden Mount temple, and today as one stands at its foot, its glistening *chedis* nose above the trees round it, dominating the southern sweep of the city and the intermittently visible loops of muddy river meandering seaward. Three hundred stairs wind up the side of the Golden Mount, the artificial hill built by King Chulalongkorn, the greatest of modern Thailand's kings; he had been twenty years on the throne by the time Conrad got here. The King was to introduce the motorcar, sewage, electricity and photography to his country; to do all that without forgetting to honour the Golden Mount, a symbol of Siam's spiritual past: therein lies a sign of his greatness.

The Golden Mount's magic is imprisoned in tall rectangular windows framed in tangled patterns of gold offset by deep sea blue and flecked with ruby-red and dark yet glimmering emerald. Golden spires, tapering to needle points, reach up like boneless golden fingers, but over all of them looms the chimney of the Wat Sakhet crematorium.

As Conrad would soon have become aware, the Wat Sakhet crematorium has macabre associations with the successive outbreaks of cholera by which the city was devastated every ten years from 1873 to the end of the century. His new command was affected by such an outbreak, and Anglicans were granted permission to make use of the city's crematoria, if need be, although cremation was not considered 'the thing' for Anglicans in those days.

Wat Sakhet is one of the largest temples in Bangkok and on the worst days of an epidemic as many as eighty corpses were lugged through its *Pratu Phi*, Ghost Gate, to the charnel plot to await a propitious season for cremation. At the fever's height bodies, tied to long splints, were hurriedly shuffled into absurdly shallow graves or simply left to decompose in the sun or rain – if they were not consumed first by vultures and hordes of famished dogs and pigs. The Siamese royal family came into their own at such times of cholera. Ignoring rank, they distributed medicines to all and sundry. Prominent temples under royal patronage provided officials with money to buy and then burn the corpses of the very poor. It was a ghoulish business; a corpse laid face down on the burning fuel tended to become loathsomely distorted in the heat, and superstitious shanty-dwellers often thought their dead relatives had come back to horrid life.

At the far end of New Road a swampy and unhealthy piece of land lay along the river bank. About the size of a football field it still runs like a frayed and soggy carpet to the river's edge. This is the Anglican cemetery which was presented by King Chulalongkorn's father to the Christian community as a burial place.

Knowing from Norman Sherry's book that the *Otago*'s steward, having died of cholera aboard, had been buried there I wanted to discover if the British Consulate kept a record of his death.

The consul was obliging.

'What was the date exactly? And the name?'

'Sixteen January, 1888,' I said. 'John Carlson.'

We searched and found written in a thin-nibbed and ornate hand:

16 January John Carlson 29 Sweedish Bark *Otago* Cholera.

Why the clerk had given Swedish two 'e's, heaven knows. The grave number was given as 424 in block E4, a note adding that it had been demolished in 1950. 'Cook and Steward' Carlson, it said, had died in the Bangkok Hospital; and his name was listed just after a middle-aged German called Captain Vock who, it said, had died of 'Decay'. Many sailors – American, Prussian, Russian and Danish – died of sunstroke or grog. Perhaps that is what 'decay' meant.

I made an appointment with the vicar of the Anglican church at the iron gates of the New Road cemetery. The Rev. Monty Morris turned out to be as helpful as the consul. An ebullient, youngish Australian in an open-necked shirt and brown slacks, enthusiastic in a sunny outback sort of way, he stood at the gates wearing a wide smile and a wide-brimmed bush hat.

'This cemetery was the biggest rubbish dump in Bangkok when I came back,' he cried, giving a good-natured thumbs up sign to a Thai gardener raking a gravel path.

The cemetery was often under an inch or two of water at high tide. Gravestones lay about higgledy-piggledy among oleanders and jacarandas; here and there a life-size marble angel ankle-deep in soggy grass brandished a scroll in honour of some long forgotten Bangkok *farang*. A pyramidical monument, dated 1870, drew immediate attention to a group of sailors: 'Rasmussen, Died at Bangkok. E. Schnoor, Died at Sea. T. Kroger, Drowned at Bangkok.' The list bore out the frequent references in the *Bangkok Times* to deaths of drunken captains who, rowing back to their ships, tipped over into the Chao Phraya and disappeared seawards, entangled alcoholically in carpets of water hyacinths.

A different case altogether was the tomb marked:

Sacred to the Memory of Admiral Sir John Bush KCWE . . . . He served His Late Majesty Maha Mongkut and his Present Majesty Chulalong-korn for a period of 40 years. Erected by the King of Siam.

I suppose you might say that Bush in Bangkok was what deputy-Neptune Captain Henry Ellis was in Singapore, for Bush ruled his port – of which he was acknowledged 'Father' – with even more of a tyrannical hand, if possible, than Ellis. He was much honoured by King Chulalongkorn, who promoted him to the rank of *Phra Visuth Sakoridith*, Siamese for Harbour Master and Master Attendant, which gave him the right to be addressed as 'Sir John Bush, Knight of the White Elephant'. Forty years before that the King had given him a house where the Royal Orchid Hotel now stands in, appropriately, Captain Bush Lane.

Bush was a successful man and towards the end of his life a very lucky one. One of the King's most trusted servants when it came to maritime affairs, he managed in his dotage to do the unthinkable. He had wrecked the King of Siam's brand-new yacht, the *Vestari*. Fearful of losing his job, he had concealed fading eyesight and insisted on sailing the royal yacht down a notoriously tricky stretch of the Malayan coast.

Witnesses swore they had seen the *Vestari* sailing far too close inshore shortly before running full tilt on to a well-charted rock at high water. She had fallen over to starboard, her afterdeck submerged, and her bows cocked up in the air with the rock straight through them. In this undignified and desperate situation, Admiral Bush had remained to try and get the *Vestari* off. He must have felt in the direst anxiety because, as the local newspapers did not fail to point out, the British district officer had placed a beacon on the rock shortly before this grounding. What is more, it had been a calm night and Bush had had a pilot on board. All his efforts to save the *Vestari* having failed – including the pouring of oil to smooth the troubled sea – the King's gold and silver plate was taken off and the handsome vessel, a British-built iron steam yacht of 92 tons, 124 feet long, and described by the press as 'a model of beauty, ardour and strength', became a total loss.

Fearing the King's wrath, the Knight Commander of the White Elephant fled to Singapore and took refuge with a daughter married to a senior British colonial servant there. No one doubted that the old sea-dog's failing eyesight had been the cause of the disaster, and the story probably inspired Conrad's tale of Captain Whalley's blindness in the *The End of the Tether*. Captains are responsible for the fate of their ships, pilot or no pilot, but it was the unfortunate pilot who took the blame for Bush, and three years later Bush returned to Bangkok to his job, his titles, his house and eventually an honourable burial in the Anglican cemetery not far from the *Otago*'s John Carlson.

'It gets terribly wet here, as you can see,' the Rev. Morris was saying in the iron gateway of the cemetery. 'We lay the coffins in a concrete box and then top it up with cement. Pointless digging holes. We end up waist-deep in water. What we really want is a dyke along the river bank.' He wrenched a waterlogged foot from the squelchy earth.

'As a matter of fact,' he went on, 'I do two burials a year these days to every hundred cremations. Cremations are *in*. I did one the other day – a young New Zealander who'd taken an overdose of drugs. The Buddhist crematoria offer their services. Luckily. Because in here,' he surveyed the angels and urns and marble obelisks, 'there's really hardly elbow room for those who will be coming in.'

Poor Carlson. His remains had been mouldering in the floodwaters of the Chao Phraya long before his modest resting place had been rooted up to make room for one of those 'coming in'. A gentle man, he would not have complained. 'Steward has been most kind,' Conrad's predecessor, Captain Snadden dying of fever at sea, had written just before his own body was shot overboard off the coast of French Indo-China, '. . . most kind.'

*

119

Before Nuee's amnesty Sumeit's father died. A disease of some kind affecting his bowels, not cholera which these days barely exists, unexpectedly swooped down and carried him off. He was not very old. I remembered him from some years back, when he had come down to Bangkok from his farm in central Thailand for a cataract operation, a man in late middle age with bandaged eyes. He had heard my voice, but had never seen me.

Now Sumeit asked me to accompany him to a small temple for his father's cremation. At three o'clock on a burning afternoon I slipped in among the two hundred or so relatives and friends seated on rows of metal chairs on two sides of a cement courtyard. From an undecorated wooden coffin on a dais in front of the crematorium the dead man's embalmed face looked calmly up to heaven, his eyes unbandaged now but sightless forever. Yellowish skin stretched like paper across his cheekbones; his bony fingers, the colour of an old billiard ball, were folded round a bunch of lotus buds and looked hard and shiny, like plastic. It was very hot and getting hotter. Sweat poured down my face and down my body under my shirt. Sumeit, in black trousers, a long-sleeved shirt and a long, thin, black tie, tried to keep our spirits up by whispering comforting misinformation. 'The burning is at 4 p.m.' Or, 'Burning is only delayed a little. Five p.m. at latest.' I bet it will be nearer 6, I thought.

Five monks with shaven heads in saffron robes, friends of Sumeit's brother from upcountry, had the seat of honour, a long, shiny sofa upholstered in what looked like red leatherette. They gazed at me, the only *farang*, with benign curiosity. Women in black dresses got up and went and knelt before them from time to time, holding up to them presents of new saffron robes folded in cellophane; an elderly man in spectacles and a suit squatted on painful joints before them to address a few respectful words. We waited. Sweat poured. A servant boy brought out tall-stemmed metal spittoons and went round placing them at strategic points. Pigeons tumbled about like dirty scraps of paper above the gracefully swooping gold and white chapel roof, over the golden snake-necked gable ends of the temple from which little bells tinkled prettily in the breeze. An ugly brick chimney rose starkly above us like a symbol of doom.

At a quarter to six we were herded up the stairs of the chapel, solemnly circled the coffin and laid paper flowers from the basket reverently in it. A large photograph of the dead man stood on an easel decked in flowers next to the coffin; the wax-like corpse, smelling vaguely of some sweetish oil, bore no resemblance to it. Temple

officials pulled a metal sheet away from the still-cold mouth of the furnace, lifted the coffin and pushed it into the depths. Almost as soon as the metal door was in place again, flames appeared through a square peephole. I wondered how soon the heat would take to reach the waxy face, the lotuses clutched in the plastic hands. We did not wait for that. Very soon there was a general and rapid dispersal. Everyone was striding to their cars without a backward glance. Someone led the monks to a minibus. Sumeit and I drove off in his red beetle car; I looked back and saw the first thin tentacle of smoke issuing from the temple's chimney.

In a book Sumeit had given me some time before, called *Aspects of Buddha* I found: *'The significance of the ceremonies* [of cremation] *is that as the component parts of the deceased are released from their bondage by the element of fire, they ascend purified into the upper and purer elements above, to be enabled there to enter into another and higher state of being.'* In a few days the urn containing the ashes of Sumeit's father would have been taken by relatives to the mouth of the Bangkok river beyond Paknam, and floated out to sea on the ebbing

121

tide. Sumeit has often talked to me about his father since that day, always with affection, never once with sadness or regret.

A particularly appealing passage in Sumeit's book ran: '*The moon appears everywhere, over a crowded city, a sleepy village, a mountain, a river. It is seen in the depths of a pond, in a jug of water, in a drop of dew, hanging on a leaf. If a man walks hundreds of miles the moon goes with him. Buddha – the Perfectly Enlightened One – is like the moon in following the people of this world . . . .*'

And whenever I have urged Sumeit, for heaven's sake, to repair his house before it collapses, he has smiled and quoted: '*A golden palace that is bloodstained can not be an abiding place for the Buddha. A small hut where the moonlight leaks in through the chink in the roof can be transformed into a place where the Buddha will abide, if the mind of its master is pure.*'

'Yes, Sumeit, I assume your mind is more or less pure. But a small hut with a chink in the roof is not the same as a house that has collapsed into a pile of timber in a snake-filled swamp, is it?'

He smiles more widely still and pours me a whisky. I might as well have saved my breath.

Sumeit is one of those simple Thais who love the more decrepit parts of Bangkok like New Road which is actually one of the oldest in the city. Through narrow alleys narrowed further by market stalls, I stumbled with him over the uneven paving stones and drains with broken covers, risking our lives in the petrol fumes. Now and then there are open shops with big circular baskets full of newly hatched ducks covering their floors; shop walls are stacked with coffins, white with brass handles or plain varnished wood; chemists display shelves of bottles of bitter, black Chinese snake wine, and sometimes the live snakes themselves intertwined and beady-eyed in glass cases. Every other shop has a window display of ginseng and deer antlers; expensive, but said to increase potency.

A hundred years ago New Road, with its horse-drawn tramway, ran from one end of the main city to the other – that is from the Grand Palace, through the Sam Peng district with its ginseng and coffin shops and along the river all the way to the next major bend at Bankolem, where Samuel J. Smith, a former missionary, printed the *Siam Advertiser* and the *Siam Repository*. That is quite a long way and, following the road going south, in Conrad's time we would have passed in time the Austrian Consulate, the Portuguese Consulate, the

Hong Kong and Shanghai Bank, the French Consulate, the Custom House and the Oriental Hotel, standing then, as now, next to the fine, colonial-style offices of the East Asiatic Company.

You had to keep your wits about you in New Road. Sam Peng's brothels were in the habit of disgorging raging armies of drunken Chinese hoodlums who had no particular regard for any passers-by, and who were well aware of the incompetence of the police force, such as it was. The *Siam Advertiser* reported:

> Part of New Road in the neighbourhood of Sampeng is becoming rather dangerous to foot passengers after dark . . . . A Mr Lessler and three German military officers were attacked by a party of coolies. Mr Lessler was made the target for quite a number of rocks, and they were thrown evidently by marksmen, and four of them found a resting place on Mr Lessler's anatomy . . . . Where, we wonder, was the European Inspector of Police when these attacks took place, and where were his peons?

Where indeed? It was a question constantly being asked. No wonder that an illustrated catalogue from E. Remington & Sons, New York, 'US of America', attracted great attention.

> Breech-loading Military rifles, Carbines and Pistols, Revolvers from Metallic Cartridges, Breech-loading Pocket Pistols, Double Derringers, Revolving Rifles, Rifle Canes . . . for Private Gentlemen, Siamese Nobles, Princes and Government Officials.

Those words echoed a familiar New England voice in Emmerson's Tiffin Rooms in that other oriental Wild West, Singapore: 'Yes, siree! These Colt pistols I am selling – see? Through and through – like a sieve . . . .'

Was this in the East or in the Wild West? It was a reasonable question that might well be asked. Accounts of foreign sailors brawling ashore filled the newspapers; a horrible Pole named Blitzki was arrested for sending 'disgusting letters' to respectable people. Worse, because it 'let the side down', was the fight outside the British Legation between Mr Westenholz, manager of the Bangkok tramway company, and Mr E. B. Mitchell, legal adviser to the Siamese government (and a habitual scrapper). The two officials went for each other with solid walking sticks so near the creek that ran between the Legation and New Road that both men fell into it, and poor Mr Mitchell was nearly drowned in the mud. They were ignominiously hauled out by some prisoners who had been gleefully watching the whole affair from the British consular jail, and Mr French, the British acting consul, had to give Mr Mitchell a hefty dose of salts to get rid of all the mud he had swallowed.

A number of incidents like this eventually persuaded the British to remove their Legation to somewhere quieter. Another determining factor was the deafening sound of the sirens of steam launches that sounded continually from the river, coupled with the ear-splitting blasts of the hooters of two extremely active rice mills which, when the wind blew eastwards, smothered the whole Legation compound with paddy ash. Add to this the regular clanging of the tramway bells and the rattle of their carriages – and, last but not least, the rowdy bar opposite the Legation in which an Italian lady called Madame Staro and a bevy of young ladies banged away at the piano, attracting a vociferous clientele until all hours of every night – and there seemed reason enough for the British Consul, Sir Robert Schomburgh, to arrange a transfer to a new site. The riverside Legation site became the General Post Office, which it still is; but that happened years after Conrad's time.

Turn left in New Road after leaving the British Legation, keep going for some distance, and the world is wonderfully transformed. It becomes Thailand again. It magically changes into neat arrangements of temples and swooping roofs, chapels and pagodas, compositions of dark gold, dark reds, greens and blues, accentuated by complex golden ornamentations of carved wood as light as filigree work.

The floor of the Wat Pho temple is cluttered with statues: Chinese figures like mandarins; temple guard dogs growling over the terrestrial globes between their paws. An enormous brass buddha fills a whole chapel; candles, purple and white orchids and scarlet gladioli at his feet; his head high up in the rafters. Its huge doors are panelled with mother-of-pearl animals in a forest: squirrels, two copulating monkeys, two cranes peering greedily at a frog and, for a joke, a monkey opening a nut with a pair of nutcrackers. Murals, from floor to ceiling, depict a walled city, temples, *klongs*, boats, trees, a river and bathers.

Two hundred cross-legged buddhas, enthroned, gilded, twice life-size, one hand raised palm outwards, the other draped gracefully over a knee, line an inner compound under a high colonnade of brick and plaster. 'See the buddha from Sukhothai,' Sumeit advised me. 'Look closely. See his face – most beautiful. The body is very suitable, too.' I am not always sure exactly what Sumeit means by 'suitable': if he means 'delicate' he is right. It is curious. At first all the buddhas look identical: the same stately seated poses, the same expressionless golden faces. Yet the Sukhotai buddha's fingers, drooping so casually over a bent knee, are especially well carved; very gently curved, unusually slim and – yes – *delicate*. Also, one has to admit, his face wears a beautifully amiable smile.

Twelve

La vida es sueño. By the side of the Chao Phraya Conrad's phantoms gambolled through his world of dreams in the parts he had written for them.

'*Gottferdam!*' Schomberg was shouting angrily to the universe at large – Schomberg, Conrad's fictional innkeeper, I mean, not Her Britannic Majesty's real-life consul in Bangkok – sitting disconsolately in a cane-bottomed chair on his own riverside verandah.

The imaginary proprietor of the smaller of the two hotels in the Siamese capital was a brawny, hairy Alsatian, an inveterate trouble-maker, irascible, surly, and resentful. People like Falk, Bangkok's 'only tug master' in the story Conrad named after him, felt for him a repulsion some people feel at the sight of a toad. And Schomberg's feelings for Falk were hardly more flattering.

'*Gottferdam!*' Schomberg shouted again, this time, as it happened, to the bearded figure of Falk himself, passing on the bridge of his tug as it foamed down the river to tow a ship waiting beyond the Bar up to Paknam.

A number of things were irking Schomberg to the point where he wondered quite seriously – and out loud to all comers – whether he should shift his hotel with its tiffin and billiard rooms out of Bangkok, out of Siam completely. To Surabaya perhaps. Or Singapore.

'I've another hotel to fight against.' He irritably tinkled the ice in his brandy and soda. 'How can I compete in the squalor of this part of New Road?' His eye fell on an advertisement on the front page of the *Bangkok Times*. 'The Oriental Hotel,' it said. 'Mr Carl Mahlberger having arrived with his well-known Company, will give a concert every evening, commencing at 9 p.m.' The company apparently consisted of seven ladies and seven gentlemen, who 'would render the choicest selections of the latest operas of the day'.

Seven ladies? For some time Schomberg himself had considered bringing over a whole *orchestra* of ladies. But in Bangkok, was that reasonable? His hotel was situated in an area that more and more seemed to invite trouble, and was correspondingly less and less inviting to even moderately respectable women. Foreign sailors, as we have seen, fought regular and determined battles among the dust and cracked paving stones. Howling Chinese continued to carry on their gang wars from one end of the street to the other. Gambling dens proliferated, and nightly from their liquor annexes floated raucous, drunken songs, bawdy in the extreme.

Sam Peng, at the Royal Palace end of New Road, was the city's main 'green light district' – green because Chinese and Thai brothels hung green (not red) lights above their doors. Although a 'green light woman' could be had for the night for no more than a dollar, the madams who owned the establishments became immensely rich and, however prudes might object, respected. One of the richest built an imposing temple, still locally known after her as 'Madam Fang's'; and a son of the notorious Madam Kleep became a much-revered monk, which no doubt gave his mother the feeling that her sin (if it had ever crossed her mind that keeping a 'house' could be said to be a sin) had been atoned for.

Violence worried Schomberg. He hated any kind of row ('fracas' he called it). One such fracas had been the shameful affair already recounted in which Mr Mitchell and Mr Westenholz had to be rescued from the canal by jailbirds. Another was an atrocious incident committed at five o'clock one morning in the tramway shed by twelve men who did unmentionable things to an unfortunate creature who – although this in no way excused such a dreadful act – led an immoral life at the Sampeng end of the street. The men were arrested and sentenced to sixty lashes followed by seven years in the chain gang, but that didn't help Schomberg. Such things were damaging to business.

And things had come closer to home than that as Marlow (or Conrad, if you like) recounted in *Lord Jim*. Schomberg still shivered with anger at the thought of an outrage actually committed on his own premises.

A lodger of Schomberg's had been the culprit, a young English fellow – as a matter of fact the former chief officer so shamefully involved in the *Jeddah* scandal, Jim Something-or-another. He had found a job with Yucker Brothers, the charterers and teak merchants, and had boarded at Schomberg's for six months till Siegmund Yucker had had the good idea of getting rid of him upcountry to the company's teak estates. Then came this absurd pot-house shindy which had put paid to that excellent idea. Yucker did not want anything to do with him after that.

Jim had been playing billiards one evening in Schomberg's saloon, against a Danish lieutenant in the Royal Siamese Navy. The Dane, who was losing, was one of those men who resented being beaten at anything, and he made a remark – probably referring to the *Jeddah* – which Jim immediately resented. It was a lucky thing that the Dane could swim. Schomberg's verandah opened on to the wide, black, fast-flowing Chao Phraya, and a passing boatload of Chinese fished the officer of the King of Siam out before he could be swept down the river and out to sea.

'Well, I mean!' Schomberg fumed to Conrad. 'Jim What's-his-Name was a nice enough young man. But so is the lieutenant, and *he* dines every night at my *table d'hôte*, you know. He might have been drowned.' He thought of another thing: '*And* there's a billiard-cue broken.'

Conrad (or Marlow) didn't blame Jim, although in a small place like Bangkok the incident was certainly regrettable. The Dane, he knew, was not only hopeless at billiards and a thoroughly bad sport, he had had a drink too many, and no doubt made a reference to cowardly ship's officers. But, of course, bar room scuffles wouldn't do; Jim had to be saved from descending into mere loutishness. He had better leave Bangkok. So, a little later – as he relates in *Lord Jim* – when Conrad found Jim back in Singapore lonely, unhappy and bored to death, he thought immediately of Stein.

Stein was very old, very wealthy and a much respected merchant with vast experience in the Malay Archipelago. He had a large inter-island business, and a good many trading posts in the most out-of-the-way places. Intelligent and good-natured, and one of the most trustworthy men alive, Stein was also a naturalist of distinction, world-famous for his collection of beetles and butterflies. So when Jim had parted with Bangkok and Yucker, Conrad (or Marlow) introduced him to Stein. And good old Stein – who knew a romantic when he saw one – found Jim a new place to hide. He sent him off to be his agent up a god-forsaken river, noted for its rattans and its pirates, in eastern Borneo. It was an ideal place for Jim, and he stayed there till he died. Who would have thought Schomberg and a game of billiards would have started that bizarre train of events?

*

Schomberg stared morosely at the clump of weed floating on the river, and wiped sweat from his nose. He could hear the satisfying clack of billiard balls in the room behind him, the shuffle of men's feet, the clink of glasses, but he was not happy.

'Tiffin still going on in here, gentlemen,' he called hopefully across an empty table.

Why should he be comforted in the very least to be told that fracas were to be expected in a seaport like this, or by being told that all hotel-keepers were sure to suffer, one not more than another. Take the case of the Oriental Hotel and Mrs Beatrice Green, a missionary lady, who raged against Siam as a place of white 'men with no scruples and no faith'; Mrs Green's rage was really directed against her own husband who had no scruples whatever, and very little faith in anything except the Oriental Hotel's whisky, payment for which he regularly managed to evade.

'You see,' Conrad said consolingly, 'think how much that costs Andersen. You all suffer equally from charlatans.'

Schomberg's fretful answer was that his rival, Mr Andersen, who had recently bought and remodelled the Oriental Hotel, was a very successful trader and sailor with interests in shipping, teak – oh, lots of things apart from his hotel. What was a trifling loss on whisky to Andersen? It was well known that Andersen had been making a 1000 per cent profit, quite legally, on shipments of teak to Europe and was bringing back Liverpool coal to make a thumping profit on that as well. Andersen owned a soda water factory, and warehouses, and the most valuable land by the river. He was associated with the Siam Electric Company and the Paknam Railway. Schomberg had heard Andersen was looking for someone to buy the Oriental so that he could invest more money in ships, in trade. What were Mr Green's unpaid whisky bills to such a man?

Schomberg spat furiously into the river. All he could do to keep his end up as a simple innkeeper was to attract customers with his special *table d'hôte*: celery soup, chops, curry, pineapples: a give-away for one dollar.

To escape the lonely evening cooped up in *Otago*'s cuddy, while his surly mate made revolting noises 'like a waterlogged trombone' in the cabin next door, Conrad sometimes called at Schomberg's for a meal. It was an escape of sorts. On a ship's deck on the river there are mosquitoes, and on the far side of the river the Chinese theatres were blazing centres of light and howling uproar. It made a change to visit Schomberg – even if you found the bearded Alsatian scowling at the end of the long narrow table with his dreary wife facing him. She was a scraggy little woman with long ringlets and a blue tooth, who smiled stupidly at you when you talked to her and didn't reply. You might find twenty vacant cane-bottomed chairs and two rows of shiny plates waiting for customers under a waggling punkah, and three Chinamen in white jackets loafing about with napkins in their hands; if so, evidently the *table d'hôte* had not been much of a success that day. Schomberg would shout rudely at a Chinese boy to bring back the left-over chops.

'There's little profit in this game,' he would grumble, sadly running a hairy paw through his food-flecked beard. 'The meat is not so good as at home – of course. And dear, too. But I only charge a dollar for tiffin and one dollar and fifty cents for the dinner. Show me anything cheaper.' Looking round the empty chairs, 'And there's first class company always at my table.'

Was Schomberg in the grip of serious hallucinations? Sunstroke could affect a man that way. All this rubbish about a fifth rate *table d'hôte* when Andersen's hotel was entertaining the Lord Mayor of Bangkok, and giving a banquet for dozens in honour of the marriage of England's Duke of York to Princess Mary of Teck of *saumon bouilli concombres*, ox tail, and *ris de veau a là Soubise*, whatever that might be, and the Siamese Naval Band was playing there.

The Oriental suffered like every establishment from the general indiscipline of Bangkok's European community. Both Singapore and Bangkok were eastern versions of the Wild West in those days.

An engineer of some sort named Hitchcock, having 'forgotten' to pay his drink bills, was successfully sued by the Oriental and fined. Having settled his dues at the Oriental bar and seeing Andersen standing there, in true Bangkok style, he drew a pistol and took deliberate aim. This deliberation gave Mr Andersen time to dodge back behind the billiard room entrance so that the bullet glanced off the wall, ricocheting away towards the verandah. Captain Stovell of the ss *Pakshan* gallantly seized the gun, and Hitchcock was carried off to the British consular jail.

Schomberg's troubles were not to end with Andersen's decision to sell the Oriental. Louis, the son of Anna Leonowens of *The King and I*, put on lavish parties which must have put Schomberg's place even more in the social shade.

'A white man should eat meat, dash it all,' one hears Schomberg babbling on in futile self-justification. 'I am not catering for a damned lot of coolies. Have another chop, captain . . . . No? You, boy – take away.' He throws himself back and waits grimly for the curry.

Large areas of shirt under Schomberg's arms are black with sweat. A swarm of flies buzz around. Conrad contemplates the disgusting buffalo chops and while he waits unenthusiastically for his curry and watches Schomberg shovelling spoonfuls of greasy rice into his chomping bearded mouth, thinks of an advertisment he has just read of a recent consignment to Mr Fusco's store of tinned meats, preserved tongues, hams, bacon and cheese from Europe. If only, instead of these infernal chops, Schomberg would serve cold tongue . . . with rice . . . and a piece of cheese. For a dollar and a half – who wouldn't pay half a dollar more?

A moment later Schomberg is railing against his spectral rival the tug master, Falk.

'He never comes in here for the *table d'hôte*, yet he makes ten times the money I do. There are two hotels here. And only one tug. Last year,' said Schomberg, his voice rising, 'I started this *table d'hôte* and sent out cards – you think he had one meal in this house? Not one!'

'He's a vegetarian, perhaps.'

'Bah! He's a miserable miser.' He puts a hand on Conrad's arm as if confiding the greatest secret, and hisses: 'Rice and a little fish he buys for a few cents from the fishing boat alongside, that's what he lives on. You would hardly credit it, eh?' He wipes his lips with indignation. 'And the rows – other day young da Costa, his engineer, got the cook to fry him a turtle steak, and the fat caught or something. Poor da Costa. Is he expected to eat his meat raw? I ask you.'

In his story, *Falk: A Narrative*, it is clear that not even Conrad was devoted to Christian Falk.

In Conrad's imagination, if not in reality, Falk was the only tug master on the Bangkok river, a fact that gave him a dominating position as far as all foreign ocean-going ship's officers were concerned.

The name Falck, with a 'c', was indeed well known in Bangkok a hundred years ago, and the *Siamese Mercantile Gazette* lists a company called Falck and Beidek as agents for Swedish Iron and Steel, and an A. C. Falck as owner of a little steamer decorated jauntily with flags, called *Post*, which regularly waltzed down the river carrying mail, passengers and provisions to ships waiting beyond the Bar, or to his hotel at Paknam. This Falck died of dysentery while on a visit to Singapore and his child was buried in the Anglican cemetery on 26 November 1870.

Conrad's Falk was a Norwegian and a tyrant: the exclusive possession of a marine boiler had given him the whip hand of every ship's master in Bangkok. Every ship needed a *steam* tug to cross the Bar at the mouth of the river.

Conrad said later:

> I don't know how it is now, but at the time I speak of that sandbank was a great nuisance to shipping. One of its consequences was that vessels of a certain draught of water, like mine, could not complete their loading in the river. After taking in as much as possible of their cargo, they had to go outside to fill up. The whole procedure was an unmitigated bore. When you thought you had as much on board as your ship could carry safely over the bar, you went and gave notice to your agents. They, in turn, notified Falk that so-and-so was ready to go out. Then Falk would come along, unsympathetically, glaring at you with his yellow eye from the bridge and would drag you out, with unfeeling haste, as if to execution.

Falk was merciless. He had the gall to charge extra for the obligatory use of his hawser and employed 'the cheekiest gang of lascars anyone had ever seen, whom he allowed to bawl at you insolently, and plucked you out of your berth as if he did not care what he smashed'.

Like him or not, you had to follow him at the end of a wire eighteen miles down the river, and then three more along the coast to the group of islands – I had seen from the *Pegasus Progress*. There – abandoned contemptuously by Falk – you waited staring at nothing but a bare coast, the muddy edge of the brown plain of Siam, and – the one consolation – the lonely, distant mass of the Great Pagoda. Of course if it was night you saw nothing at all, but night or day, you waited fretting for the balance of your cargo. Often you waited for a long, long time. For Falk took every opportunity to return upriver, paddle wheels churning, to spend long hours paying tongue-tied court to the girl he loved.

For Falk was in love with the beautiful, nineteen-year-old niece of Captain Hermann, owner of the *Diana* of Bremen, a curious kind of ship moored by the *Otago*.

The *Diana* had curtained cottage windows and a most innocent look, more a comfortable blunt-nosed barn than an old ship, Conrad thought. On board lived Mrs Hermann and her four children, the youngest of whom had dropped a rag doll on Conrad's head from the rail. Pretty little frocks and pinafores could be seen drying in the mizzen rigging and a row of tiny socks fluttered on the halliards. Conrad was devoted to the Hermanns.

But not to Christian Falk. It was for his friend Hermann's sake that he solved Falk's 'lover's-block'. Night after night Falk sat staring in total silence at Hermann's niece. He did not seem capable of uttering a word. Perhaps only another seaman like Conrad could have dragged Falk's secret from him. For a single secret explained a double puzzle: why did Falk refuse Schomberg's meat and shy away from the very smell of it, and why did he – surely out of character – draw back at the merest thought of asking Hermann's permission to marry his niece? It evidently concerned something dreadful that had happened years ago.

'I have eaten man!' – that was the secret Falk burst out with in the end, and Hermann, excessively shocked, could only murmur idiotically, '*Himmel!* What for?' The short answer to that was 'to keep from starving', but it took longer for Falk to explain and to exonerate himself.

Conrad, the sailor, understood at once. 'Shipwreck?' he asked.

Breakdown, said Falk, was a better word.

An iron steamer called the *Borgmester Dahl*, built in Falk's home town, had set sail for Wellington, New Zealand, loaded with pitch pine; Falk had been her chief officer. Between Good Hope and New Zealand, a long way south, the steamer's tail-shaft broke and the propeller fell off. What sail the ship carried was not enough to keep her head-on, and in exceptionally high winds the main mast soon whipped overboard.

Ships failed to see them. Once there seemed to be a chance of rescue when an English vessel tried to come alongside; but as she did so she lost her own topsail in a sudden squall and soon drew nervously away and disappeared. There were no ships after that. Then gale followed gale driving them south. Mountains of black water broke over the *Borgmester Dahl*, deluging the store rooms and spoiling the provisions. Discipline on board gave way to panic, anger and madness. Some men never left their bunks; some endlessly quarrelled; others wept. An attempt was made to lower the last boat, and the crewmen, maddened by fear, fought each other to get into it. Only two succeeded and they drifted away never to be seen again.

After that, there was only despair. A fireman came up on deck with his throat cut from ear to ear. The captain, a morose sort of man at the best of times, locked himself in the chart room, and next day the cabin door was swinging open, but he had gone. Overboard, Falk supposed.

Whispers of hate began to pass between the languid skeletons drifting about the ship. The carpenter, the 'second-best man on the ship', took a shot at Falk with the captain's pistol; Falk, with his own gun, shot him dead from close range and then threw his weapon overboard.

With the sound of the shots, a band of hungry skeletons crept into view, and he – now the possessor of the only firearm on board – faced them across the body of the carpenter.

Conrad had been listening intently. 'He was eaten, of course.'

Falk nodded. 'I had never any quarrel with that man. But there were our lives at stake.'

At last a whaler returning from the southern cruising grounds nearly ran into their waterlogged hulk. Only three men were left by then. Three men, and Falk.

'They all died,' Falk explained to Conrad. 'All! But I would not die. I was alone. Each man was alone. Was I to give up my revolver? Or throw it into the sea? What would have been the good? Only the best man would survive.' And Falk lived to prove it.

There is no accounting for human emotions. Hermann's gentle niece, Conrad saw to his astonishment, far from being repulsed by this horrendous tale was actually overcome by tears – weeping for Falk, and more in love with him as a man-eater than ever she had been when she thought him a vegetarian. Poor Hermann and his wife couldn't stand the sight of him, but they saw they had no course but to agree to the marriage. If they didn't, the girl was obviously going to spend the rest of her life in floods of tears.

So when Falk came aboard again Hermann made no move to stop him, but sat calmly smoking his pipe on the quarter-deck while Falk and his tear-stained niece clasped hands happily in the Bangkok sunshine, oblivious to everything and everybody.

Talking of *Falk: A Narrative*, Conrad commented that it dealt with

> . . . a little taste of cannibalism – in the past – a long way off – in the South Seas. The idea: contrast of commonplace sentimentality with the uncorrupted point-of-view of an almost primitive man (Falk himself) who regards the preservation of life as the supreme and moral law. I venture to say it is well done.

Perhaps Schomberg, inveterate busybody that he was, somehow got wind of the fact that Conrad and Falk were keeping some scandal of importance from him. However that might be he had his revenge, on Conrad at any rate. His chance came when, needing to replace poor Carlson the cook, Conrad was unwise enough to approach Schomberg. And that troublemaker's candidate for the job was a Chinaman he described as a first class 'boy' – 'Come to Bangkok in the suite of His Excellency Tseng the Commissioner. Lodged with me for three weeks, you know.'

The 'boy' might have been forty or a hundred and forty for all anyone could tell; he had an unprepossessing death's-head type of face. Conrad had his doubts, but he took him on nonetheless. It was only later, Conrad said ruefully, that the Chinese showed himself to be a man of parts: he turned out to be a confirmed opium smoker, a gambler, an audacious thief, and – not least – a first-class sprinter. In that unique sense he was 'first class'.

One day, as Hermann of the *Diana* was extricating his considerable bulk from a gharry on the riverbank, the 'boy' pelted past down the dusty lane behind him with most of Conrad's savings in his pockets. Despite his bulk, Hermann nobly took the lead in the pursuit. Away they dashed, Conrad following close behind the galumphing figure of Hermann and the *Otago's* mate in the rear, whooping like a savage. They galloped down refuse-filled lanes between stretches of decaying masonry, bamboo fences, arcades of brick and plaster, hovels of lath and mud, lofty temple gates of carved timber and huts of rotten mats. They leapt over dead dogs, mounds of refuse and potholes you could be buried alive in. At one point, the *Otago's* new master had got his foot stuck in an empty Australian bully beef tin.

The thief got away in the end, leaving fat Hermann puffing '*Himmel!*' as though he would die and Conrad parted from his money for ever.

Poor Hermann; the account of the chase in the *Bangkok Times* next day quite unfairly left out his part in it altogether.

A Chinese boy employed on the barque *Otago* managed the other day to steal fifteen gold Mohurs from a sailor on board and then to abscond. The Captain and the Mate, however, met the thief a few hours afterwards in Mr Clarke's compound and arrested him. Whilst being conducted to the Bang Rak police station he unfortunately managed to bolt and has not since been seen, but Mr Clarke's cook, a man named Mr Kam Kow, at once offered a cattie of silver if the matter was quashed, and this fact, coupled with his being found in possession of fifteen ticals, raised suspicion so that Kam Kow is now in jail. He appears to have been a friend of the boy, and thus probably knows his present whereabouts.

The result of the brief employment of Schomberg's Chinese 'boy' was threefold. All the money Conrad had saved was gone; the *Otago's* mate went down with fever and almost died; and Conrad learned that Schomberg was the untrustworthy Alsatian humbug that almost everybody else knew him to be.

*

I had to leave Bangkok to follow Conrad to Singapore and the islands of the Malay Archipelago. But first there was something I had to do. Sumeit's son, Nuee, had at last been released from jail, and to celebrate his freedom – Sumeit, his other sons Noi and Ning, and I decided to take him on a boat trip from the Oriental Hotel's jetty through the *klongs* he had not seen for so long. It was an attempt to bring him back to life.

The Oriental was a convenient place to start from. Its handsome old façade is still much as it was when I first came to Bangkok twenty-five years ago. Inside there have been changes: a new lobby gives it an expensive but chilly elegance. There is now a 'Joseph Conrad Suite', the price of which would certainly alarm Conrad's ghost, and there is a vaguely ship-shaped restaurant called 'Lord Jim'. And why not? Perhaps it was not from Schomberg's but from the verandah of the Oriental that Jim had heaved the surly Danish lieutenant into the Chao Phraya. That incident would have been enough to justify naming a fine modern-day tiffin room after almost anyone involved in it.

I suppose that during the sixteen days he spent in Bangkok, Conrad used the Oriental about as much as he said he used Schomberg's. I am not convinced he actually stayed at Andersen's hotel. It would have been irresponsible to have left his new command for long; he had sick men on board and a Bengali dispenser calling daily to treat them, apart from the frequent visits of Dr Willis of the Legation, who had become a friend. There was also cargo to find and load and the need to see that his sailors obeyed strict orders to work under awnings.

The Oriental's jetty was a good place to start Nuee's water tour. The Chao Phraya had for twenty-five years represented peace and serenity when I was chasing wars and revolutions, and when the rest of the world had seemed to me too ugly to be borne. The Past could still be found there: modern buildings stood beside old warehouses teetering on the water's edge; and pillared houses on stilts with fine carved shutters still had families living in them. A little way upstream, the water still mirrored gilded domes and curved temple roofs among the smoking factory chimneys and the new cement warehouses of a naval or customs station. On the left the admonishing finger of the beautiful Wat Arun – the Temple of Dawn – proclaimed the harmony between man's world and the spirit-inhabited earth; on the right, Wat Pho and Wat Sakhet, the sister temples across the river, were reminders in the midst of the modern city's pollution of its serene past.

Klongs barely wide enough for two boats to pass side by side joined the river; houses and little wooden shops clung to their banks, at which Ning and Noi bought cans of Coca-Cola or a sweet fizzy drink called Sprite, and chilled bottles of Kloster beer for Sumeit and myself. Nuee mostly sat gazing, as if drugged, at a river and a city he had half forgotten. In the heat and humidity he took off his shirt and revealed an unexpected sight. Tattoos covered every inch of his back and chest, and they were not the sort you would expect from a prison in Thailand. A head of Ringo Starr, the Beatles drummer, covered his chest, with a sprinkling of sci-fi dragons with smoking fiery tongues and leathery wings. American bald-headed eagles frowned beak-to-beak across his back, and he had a Union Jack on each elbow. A Disney elephant decorated each buttock, he assured us, and every other spare inch was taken up with ET, Garfield the Cat, Snoopy, Bugs Bunny and numerous other cartoon characters.

For how long would he be happy to see in the mirror that pop-tattoo reminder of seven years he would rather forget? I hoped, perhaps vainly, that Nuee would see this outing as a sort of rebirth; a return to life from the spiritual death of prison and a diet of common toads.

Did Wat Arun represent to him 'the Perfectly Enlightened One that is seen, like the moon, in a river, in the depths of a pond, in a jug of water, or in a drop of dew hanging on a leaf?' Did he still have eyes to see it?

*

Our boatman regained the main river and headed towards the Oriental once more. On Schomberg's terrace, it was possible to imagine a corpulent, bearded, Teutonic figure leaning over the water, watching Falk's tug towing with a thud-thud of her paddle wheels a slim, three-masted barque into the main channel to head downstream to the Bar. The last rays of the setting sun shine on the words *Otago* and *Adelaide* across the barque's stern, while on her quarterdeck a short, broad-shouldered man with a pale wide brow stands gazing ahead, his dark-bearded head slightly tilted back, hands clasped behind his back.

In his pocket is a farewell letter.

> I think it is not out of place on my part that I should state, though not asked by you to do so, to prevent any misapprehension hereafter, that the crew of the sailing ship *Otago* has suffered severely whilst in Bangkok from tropical diseases, including fever, dysentery and cholera; and I can speak of my own knowledge, that you have done all in your power in the trying and responsible position of Master of the ship to hasten the departure of your vessel from this unhealthy place and at the same time to save the lives of the men under your command.
>
> Yours faithfully,
> William Willis, MD, FRCSE
> Physician to HM Legation in Siam

The *Otago* moves down the shifting prospect of the river towards the bar. Here, in another kind of rebirth, Captain Korzeniowski is taking his first command down to the health-giving sea.

Part Four

Bugis

It is a common saying amongst the Malay race that to be a successful traveller and trader a man must have some Wajo blood in his veins .... A man who is as ready to intrigue and fight as to buy and sell. Such is the ideal trader of Wajo.

JOSEPH CONRAD, *The Rescue*

I had two distinct objectives from now on. The first was to get to know the Bugis sea-rovers of south Celebes. Conrad had met them up the Berau and Bulungan rivers and Lingard and Almayer (or Olmeijer) had had much to do with them. Singapore had had a Kampong Bugis, and Bugis colonists had settled in Peninsular Malaya, and parts of Sumatra as well. They reached these places in the thoroughbred sailing craft – the praus – they built themselves.

My second objective was the Berau river, where the fictional Almayer and Jim died, and where the real Olmeijer and the real Lingard traded profitably until driven out of business by their Arab rival, Syed Abdullah Al Joofree. The Bulungan river higher up the coast of Borneo than the Berau shared almost as many memories of Lingard, Almayer and Abdullah.

I made two expeditions to the region. The first was in 1977 in the old ketch Fiona. By the time of my second visit in 1988–9, she had been retired to San Francisco Bay, and I went back to the Berau and Bulungan by native boat. Between the two visits few changes had taken place.

thirteen

1977.

With my hair like dripping seaweed in my eyes and spray cascading down my face and inside my sodden shirt, we might as far as I was concerned be anywhere in the Java Sea. I did not have much time to care. I was too busy bracing my feet against the side of *Fiona*'s cockpit to prevent myself being thrown into the water.

The little ketch, butting painfully northwards, seemed to have missed the light on Kangean Island altogether. Either the light was not working or the current had pushed us too far out to sea for us to spot it. At any rate Mac altered course to Pulau Laut and reset the log at zero.

Pulau Laut is an island. Named Samburan by Conrad in *Victory*, it was here that Heyst the Swede, Heyst 'the Enchanted', 'Hard Facts' Heyst (he had many nicknames) started the ill-fated Tropical Belt Coal Company. It was a fair-sized island surrounded by a tepid, shallow sea – the Java Sea – which Conrad described as 'a passionless offshoot' of greater waters; although 'passionless offshoot' was not what I would have called the Java Sea at this moment. Tepid and shallow, yes. But shallow seas have unexpected passions of their own; they can give you hard knocks – not from the huge cliff-like waves that scare the life out of you on the ocean deeps, but from the short, steep furrows, and a high persistent choppiness that throws you about and runs your nerves ragged. Particularly when, like us, you have been buffeted by squalls and lashed by torrential rain for hours.

It had not been by any means an easy passage. We seemed to have been at sea in a sieve. Water had cascaded into the cabin all night. Every match seemed to be wet, so it was impossible to light the oil lamps which swung, rattling, in their gimbals on *Fiona*'s wooden

143

bulkheads. We pulled on oilskins and lurched clumsily about like drunken men in the sound of creaking wood and the slap and gurgle of the sea against the hull. On the bucking deck in the welter of sloshing spray, all I could see was a great whirl of black vapour advancing across our bow as the rain roared down on the sea. Captain McWhirr in *Typhoon* called it 'Dirty weather!'

Visibility down to virtually nil had caused us to miss that light. We missed the next light, too, skirting the island it stood on by what was not much more than the maritime equivalent of a bee's whisker. Why we hadn't banged into it, heaven knows.

Then it was over. The storm passed over us and vanished as suddenly as it had come.

We anchored with relief on the north side of Laut Island at Tanjung Kiwi, and lowered the sails in beautiful cloud-flecked daylight. Two or three praus near us gently bobbed and rolled while their crews stared at us holding fishing lines over the side. Behind them we could see the green, undulating skyline of Pulau Laut with a mountain in the distance, and a tall dead beacon on the shore. A line of hills covered with tangle-headed trees of vivid green looked down on the yellowish-green silky sea and on *Fiona* riding 400 yards from a narrow sandy beach. The storm of the day and night before was a bad dream; the only sound now the quiet slap of waves on a low sand-bar.

We hang out our sopping clothes, blankets and cushions. We swim and dry ourselves in the sun. We have our first meal for hours: fried eggs, potatoes, leeks, Chinese cabbage, Rose's marmalade and biscuits. We sip mugs of tea and watch a prau nose by, large and sleek, with arrogant, upturned bows and the scythe-shaped sail of Java. A large russet-bodied bird with a white neck flaps ponderously over the sea near us, back and forth. We cannot be blamed for feeling contented.

I scribble in my notebook what we all feel:

'Kalimantan! We have stepped into Lingard and Almayer country!'

There were four of us on the *Fiona* that day in early August 1977, and I suppose only two of us were there because of Conrad. Brian McGarry ('Mac') was there because he was part owner of the boat, an expert navigator, and had agreed to take me round Conrad's Eastern World in her; Murray Moncrieff, my nineteen-year-old godson, was there mainly because he thought he liked boats and sailing, and had nothing else to do; and Wilfred Thesiger, the oldest of us at sixty-seven, who

144

was certainly no sailor having been an Arabian explorer most of his life, had accepted my offer to show him the river where Jim died because, he said, *Lord Jim* had always been one of his favourite books. I wanted to give him a small return for having introduced me years before to the magical world of the Marsh Arabs of Iraq – the descendants of the old Babylonians.

Fiona was just the right sort of craft to take sailing in these waters. I am sure Conrad would have approved of her. After all, she was a product of his era; built in 1912, when Conrad was fifty-six, by a firm called Newmans in Poole in Dorset, *Fiona* was a 20-ton 42-footer with a 6-foot draught. Some years before, a friend of mine, Jo Menell, had been sailing the Mediterranean in quite another craft and had run into Brian McGarry, who was earning a living sailing people's yachts for them. They got on well and sailed together a good bit for fun. Quite soon Jo decided to find a better boat and looking around England he found *Fiona*. He asked Mac's opinion.

'Buy her,' Mac said, 'she's great.'

'What was it you liked about her at first sight?' I asked him.

'Just the look of her. Her marvellous shape.' We took her out on the Solent on a wild sail; it was very, very windy. And Jo said to me again, "It's up to you. What do you think?" And I said, "Go ahead. Take her." She *felt* right: the solid wood and the big bowsprit. Just the right boat, well, to sail just to anywhere on earth.' When Jo signed the cheque, he said, 'This is *our* boat, Mac. And don't you ever forget it.' They sailed *Fiona* twice around the world and then Jo lent *Fiona* to Mac and suggested he should pilot me round Conrad's islands. Mac was pleased to do so. He wrote to me, mentioning a possible starting date, fortunately far ahead. 'Meet you in Bali. Benoa Harbour. Please arrange Indonesian Sailing Permit.'

An immensely long time elapsed between my receipt of Mac's message and my eventual appearance in Bali with the permit. Regulations governing the freedom of foreigners to sail their boats around the islands were far stricter then than they are now. Knowing things moved slowly, I immediately applied for our Sailing Permit at the Indonesian Embassy in London. Telegrams to Jakarta flew thick and fast week after week for six months or more, and thick and fast (though not *quite* so fast) came renewed requests for detailed information. Where *exactly* were we going? Give dates. Conrad's name was not one to open doors in Indonesia; no one there had heard of him.

At last – at last – I felt I could fly to Jakarta to pick up that Sailing

Permit. It was not ready, and I was forced to spend day after interminable day listening to the Barcarolle from 'Tales of Hoffmann' piped into the bar of Jakarta's Sheraton Hotel, where at intervals friendly waiters brought me pink gins instead of hope. Not a bad way to spend one's time, you might think – ah, but not when the fate of our expedition depended on being able to leave as soon as possible. Would Mac get tired of waiting and sail off somewhere else? Again and again I cabled Mac sitting impatiently on *Fiona* in Bali: 'Permit expected soon.' I soon ceased to believe in those cables myself.

From time to time I sweated to the Directorate General of Sea Communications, a heavy-looking Dutch building of circa 1923, where the Permit would be issued, if ever, from the office of the Director-General, an admiral. I remember 15-foot high double doors of carved wood with brass handles, and there was an anteroom prettily decorated with blue and white tiles with a moulded ceiling at least 30 feet high. Some of the tiles showed wintry scenes in Holland, windmills and people skating, others seventeenth century warships and sailing-barges under full canvas in what might have been the mouth of the Scheldt.

I got to know those pretty Dutch scenes quite well as the days went by, and in the end I was shown in to see the admiral himself. He sat at a large desk, a tall, good-looking man with thick grey hair, obviously benign. We talked briefly about this and that. And at last he said, 'Your permit,' and I stopped breathing. 'I hope you will get it in about a week's time. Maybe two weeks.'

Two weeks! That, in reality, could mean anything up to a month. Struggling to keep calm, I told him about the many months I had already waited for this confounded permit, the number of forms I had filled in. I shall never know why I came out with what I said next.

'Admiral,' I heard myself announce, 'I am going out now to buy a gun.'

He looked up with a startled smile. 'To kill me?'

'To kill myself. On that carpet outside your door.'

'Oh. No need for that.'

I returned to my hotel in cold despair, to the 'Barcarolle' and the pink gins.

The next morning, the admiral's secretary called the hotel to say I could pick up the Sailing Permit at his office that afternoon.

I arrived at Benoa Harbour to find Mac, Murray, Wilfred and *Fiona* all looking at me in disbelief; I think they had given me up. I remember racing with Mac round the stalls of an open market where helpful girls carried the ton of food we bought in open-weave baskets balanced on the crowns of their heads. There was time for a brisk walk to a temple in a rice field where the wind surged and died in clumps of bamboo like spirit music in a Balinese elfland.

Then we sailed. First, east along the Balinese coast, through the Lombok Strait (in an unwelcoming sea that had us on our beam-ends) and into the Java Sea.

A day later we missed, as I have said, the light at Kangean Island.

As we groped our way in *Fiona* towards Pulau Laut through the rain squalls of the Java Sea, half my mind had been preoccupied by a portly, heavily bearded, Teutonic figure obsessed with his *tables d'hôte*. For in *Victory* Conrad tells us Schomberg had set up shop in the port of Surabaya in East Java, not far south of us now.

In Bangkok Schomberg had planned to move his business out of the violence of New Road. He did move, twice – first to Singapore, and then to Surabaya where he continued to spread malicious gossip at the expense of his customers. That would have been in '93 or '94.

Schomberg's new pet hate, (replacing Falk) was a Swedish baron, a loner called Axel Heyst. An Eastern Hand of almost saintly properties, well known in the islands, where for years he had mooned about doing no one any harm, and a number of people great good.

He had, for example, rescued poor Captain Morrison from destitution when his brig was seized on some pretext by the Portuguese authorities in Dilli in Timor. Heyst happened to wander by and found Morrison almost out of his mind. The Swede paid his fine and so saved him from ruin – out of the sheer goodness of his heart. That's what Heyst was like. 'Heyst's a ut-uto-utopist,' said a disreputable white man, who himself owed something to the Swede.

But Schomberg had taken it into his head to detest Swedes – particularly Heyst. Heaven knew why, but as Conrad commented, fools are good haters. Perhaps Heyst had turned up his nose at the *table d'hôte*.

At that time Heyst became the unlikely manager of a coaling station in Pulau Laut (Samburan, Conrad calls it in *Victory*) belonging to the Tropical Belt Coal Company. He recruited clerks and engineers and coolies, and Morrison as well, thinking he was doing him another good turn. It was not Heyst's fault that the company went bust, nor that Morrison caught a bad cold and died in England while pushing the company's affairs there. But in Schomberg's hate-obsessed mind,

Heyst had deliberately destroyed the TBCC and robbed Morrison of his last farthing. He said so to anyone who would listen. 'Watch out for that Swede,' he growled to all and sundry.

Schomberg's Surabaya hotel stood back in a large tree-lined enclosure that contained a garden, and even a private 'concert hall'. 'Concerts Every Night' said signs in heavy red letters on each side of the enclosure's brick gateway. He had achieved his dream of a ladies' orchestra – Zangiacomo's 'Eastern Tour' orchestra composed of eighteen females. They had had the honour, a programme note claimed, of playing before 'various colonial excellencies, also before pashas, sheiks, chiefs, HM the Sultan of Mascate etc., etc.' None of them was young and they came from a variety of nationalities. Even the *Konzertmeister*, Zangiacomo, was not a real Italian despite his name; he was a skinny German who dyed his hair and beard black. His wife, a raw-boned harridan, with ugly elbows, controlled his flock with punches, slaps and pinches. The poor 'girls' sat staring stony-eyed at their music stands, bare arms sawing away mechanically in the terrific heat usually at 'some more or less' Hungarian dance music, not so much making music as murdering silence, while above them the appalling Zangiacomo wielded his baton with as much feeling as if he was beating a rug.

The one genuine 'girl' among those tone-deaf musical slaves was called Lena. She attracted Heyst's attention because he happened to see Mrs Zangiacomo giving her a particularly vicious pinch. His kind heart was outraged and he decided at once to rescue her and fly with her to the bungalow he had built on the godforsaken island of Samburan, or Pulau Laut, his retreat from the wicked world.

*

The Strait of Laut is narrow and divides itself like a wishbone round a small island called Suwangi. With a good breeze behind, Mac put us round the island under full sail to where a pretty Makassar ketch lay at anchor just before the old coaling-station whose pier – or what is left of it – pushes unimpressively out into the water just below Setagin village. 'Coal is found,' the *Pilot* said, 'in the Northern parts of the island, but the mines are now closed.' We anchored here for a while, but the look of the place, oily and smelly, was decidedly unattractive.

Here Heyst, after the collapse of the coal company, had continued to live alone. Even by then it was difficult to imagine that a large coaling-station had stood on this spot. Captain Davidson, sailing in to visit his friend Heyst from time to time, could see nothing but decay – vague roofs lost in low vegetation, broken bamboo fences in long grass, an overgrown piece of road, an inky mound of abandoned coal near the jetty where a gigantic blackboard announced: 'T.B.C. Co.' in peeling white letters two feet high. The company's engineers, clerks, coolies, had all long gone. Everything had gone – except Heyst, who had settled into one of three or four abandoned bungalows.

Schomberg was the last man on earth to understand Heyst's self-exile. To Davidson he said, winking and leering with immense malice: 'What I want to know is what he gets to eat there. A piece of dried fish now and then – what? That's coming down pretty low for a man who turned up his nose at my *table d'hôte*!'

In the Laut Strait we saw our first Bugis prau. A small launch approached *Fiona*, and when it came alongside a man and a boy, smiling, held up a basket of prawns. Murray threw them a line and the two boats moved together, and Mac bought a small basinful. By then a large prau whose sails towered above *Fiona* had skimmed up behind us silently, almost menacingly like a footpad on tiptoe.

It was inexpressibly beautiful. The prau's foresail was pale blue striped with white; its huge mainsail was a third deep purple verging on black and two-thirds green with a strip of ivory white. It had the beauty of a strangely plumed kingfisher soaring over blue water. Dark, grinning faces and half-naked figures in sarongs lined its low rail, peering at us smiling through hair that hung to their shoulders. When we waved they waved enthusiastically back.

In the nineteenth century, I suppose, at this moment we would have heard the fearful sound – like the sharp hissing intake of breath – of krisses slithering from their sheaths, and the click of cocked muzzle-loaders. Bronze, muscular legs would have edged over the prau's

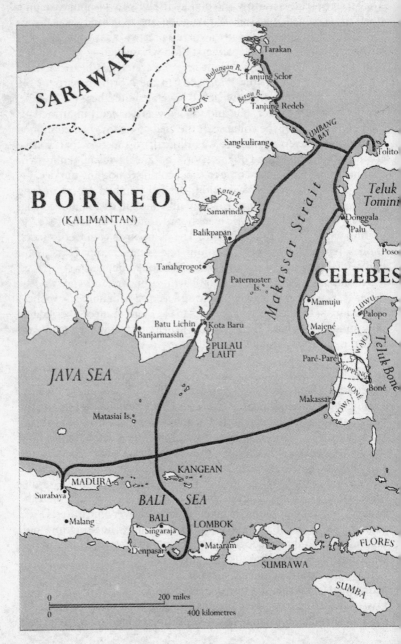

gunwales: and we would have prepared for boarders, slavery and death. *Mandar Baru*: the name of the vessel was painted on her bows. She maintained her course 20 feet away, while her toffee-skinned ragamuffin crew continued to smile at us: not murderous, but cheerful human smiles.

The spectral grimaces of skeletal Mr Jones had meant nothing except some horrid form of death.

Mr Jones had no doubt he was a match for Schomberg. He and his two henchmen – his 'secretary' Martin Ricardo and the inarticulate Caliban of a Colombian 'alligator-hunter' called Pedro – were the most ruthless kind of peripatetic cardsharpers and treasure-seekers you could have found in the eastern seas just then. They turned up at Wilhelm Schomberg's hotel in Surabaya on the mailboat from Makassar – though where they had been before that heaven alone knew. So Nemesis came to poor harmless Axel Heyst by a roundabout route. 'The world is a bad dog,' he had remarked to Davidson. 'It will bite you if you give it a chance.' His delusion was that you could escape Nemesis by hiding from it.

Schomberg picked up Mr Jones and his entourage and shipped them gladly back to his hotel. He discovered his mistake too late. When he and his idiot wife searched the trio's bags, they found them full of weapons.

Jones was a born villain; in his sunken eyes was a 'spectral intensity' that chilled Schomberg to the bone. A brilliant cardsharper, he was ready to murder at any minute any number of people he took against. Touching the knife strapped to his ankle, he leered at Schomberg, 'You wouldn't believe the damage a bloke with a knife can do under a table . . . .' Schomberg of course wanted to get rid of him; Jones could see that in his stupid face.

'Try to put us out?' he said with indescribable insolence. 'You couldn't do it without getting hurt – very badly hurt. We can promise him that, can't we, Martin?' and Martin Ricardo, the 'secretary', looked at Schomberg as if dying to leap upon him there and then. Schomberg's strategy turned on finishing off Heyst and the Jones trio at one and the same time.

Naturally everyone who knew Heyst, accepted that his 'abduction-elopement' of Lena was a praiseworthy rescue of a deeply distressed human being. Originally, Schomberg's plan had been to elope with Lena himself, but his new plan was to convince Jones and Ricardo that

Heyst had fled to Samburan not with a girl but with a cache of stolen money.

Why, he suggested, didn't they go and take it off him? It would be child's play. Amazingly Jones believed him. But where was this island? How did one get there?

They could lie up, Schomberg said, in a plantation in Madura and set sail in a small boat after dark. Fifty hours steering northeast, and they would reach Heyst's island. What could be more simple?

'Steer northeast for fifty hours, eh?' objected Ricardo. 'That's not much of a sailing direction.'

Nobody could miss the island, insisted Schomberg. There was a volcano on it, like a beacon – 'a pillar of smoke by day and a loom of fire at night'. And with the thought of gold in their heads the three villains actually set sail, with little more on the boat for the fifty-hour voyage, than two barrels of water, one of which Schomberg had contrived to fill with salt water.

The sea route to Pulau Laut from Madura Island, across a narrow strait east of Surabaya, skirts the western tip of Kangean Island. We had missed the light there as we came up from Lombok in *Fiona*. In 1894 there was probably no light of any kind there at all.

It had taken *Fiona* forty-eight hours or more to traverse the Java Sea from Kangean to Tanjung Kiwi on Pulau Laut, and we had sails and an engine. Jones, Ricardo and Pedro reached the island in the ultimate extremity of thirst and exhaustion because Schomberg had not mentioned currents. They had had to pull at 18-foot oars for thirty hours in the sun.

They recovered on the island, and Heyst, who had deliberately isolated himself from a world he thought of as a bad dog that bit, found himself playing host to a mad one called Jones. From the deck of *Fiona*, we could see where Jones had begun to try to wheedle out of the saintly Swede the hiding place of a treasure which, in fact, existed nowhere except in Schomberg's imagination.

'I am the world itself,' said Jones, baring his teeth at the man who had deliberately fled from it, 'come to pay you a visit.' Few more chilling remarks ever fell on human ears.

Jones never found out that Heyst had no treasure on his paradise island. What he did soon discover was that the girl, Lena, was with him, and he discovered it to his horror, for Jones had a pathological hatred of women. On the other hand, Ricardo, his 'secretary', couldn't be trusted a second with them; Ricardo would kill his own master,

Jones, if he thought he could get away with the treasure and the girl. Suddenly Jones was in greater danger than Heyst.

Heyst soon understood that it was Schomberg who had lied about the treasure.

'Fooled by a silly, rascally innkeeper! Talked over like a pair of children with a promise of sweets!' he taunted Jones. But very soon the lies of that rascally innkeeper succeeded in killing them all.

In 1977, *Fiona* lay close to the slopes of Pulau Laut in an immense silence and the gentle sound of waves on the shore. A hundred years ago Davidson had called here and found a shambles. The bungalows of the Tropical Belt Coal Company had gone up in smoke, and Davidson had found the remains of Heyst and the girl in their embers. Ricardo, shot through the heart by Jones, lay sprawled on the shore to swell and rot in the sun, and Jones himself lay huddled in the water by the wharf, a genuine skeleton at last. Pedro-Caliban, too, was as dead as one of his Colombian alligators.

I gazed at the shore. Related as fiction by Conrad in *Victory*, such a tragedy might easily have happened on this silent, tropical place. Why should it not have? There was the island; we could see it plainly before our eyes. There had once been coal on it; the *Pilot* confirmed that. Who could be sure that deep under *Fiona*'s keel, the long, lean bones of Mr Jones were not buried in the sandy bottom of Laut Sound?

'Hey, come on. They're hoisting sail. They want a race.'

That is what it looked like. The *Mandar Baru*'s crew were waving their arms, grinning, shouting and making various vigorous and encouraging signs. Sail after sail flickered up the prau's towering masts like white, purple and green flames. Yes, they wanted to race.

There were only two sailors on board *Fiona*, Mac and Murray; Wilfred and I, the landlubbers, barely knew a stay from a halliard. If there was one thing which would guarantee to lose us this race (and races have to be taken at least moderately seriously) it was any attempt on the part of either of us to lend a hand in the raising of sails or any other aspect of seamanship. Wilfred, who had once spent weeks on the back of a camel in the wastes of Arabia, wisely lay back in the stern, peering ahead with his deep-set big game hunter's eyes protected from the sun by an old linen cabbage-leaf hat of the kind that old ladies wear to prune rosebushes in.

The prau moved up the waterway like a gorgeous moth swarming with energetic fleas – her crew. They shinned up her masts and raced from one end of her deck to another, shouting gleefully at the unaccustomed prospect of a race. Australian or American 'gin palaces', gleaming with chrome and aluminium, passed from time to time down the Strait of Makassar, but *Fiona* was different. For one thing, she was over sixty years old and looked it. She had never had a square centimetre of chrome laid on her, and she carried the original masts fitted in her by the old boat builders in Poole. Her six sails were certainly not in anything like their first youth – a warm rust brown, slightly stained here and there. Her white hull had a quite old-fashioned sweep to it. I could see why Mac had felt she was 'right'.

Fiona and the *Mandar Baru* flew into the anchorage of Kota Baru, bow waves curling, with *Fiona* leading by about two lengths. The prau's sailors' pleasure was undiminished by the narrow defeat, they whooped with joy, long hair flopping round their bare shoulders. We hoped we were going to see them again, although in Kota Baru the *Mandar Baru* joined the prau harbour and port officials waved us to a place alongside the wharf.

Kota Baru was a friendly town of about ten thousand people, where old wooden buildings lined the streets and a good market pushed out over the water of the strait. No doubt it had seen better days when it was a regular port of call in the days of the sailing ships from Singapore and Surabaya. Lingard came here in the *Coeran* and the *Rajah Laut*, and Syed Mohsin Al Joofree's *Vidar* had bunkered here in 1887 on her way to Donggala and the Berau when Conrad was her chief officer.

The next day we were allowed to move up to join the praus. The jolly crew of the *Mandar Baru* came pouring aboard, shouting friendly salaams, looking round *Fiona* intently and excitedly, pointing out to each other this or that feature; it was almost as if they were thinking of buying her.

They were Bugis from the port of Paré-Paré north of Makassar, the first of all the Bugis people I was to meet later in Celebes. Dark-skinned like all seamen in the tropics who labour daily half-naked under the sun, they wore checkered sarongs of brown and green, and one or two had small decorative tattoos on wrists or forearms. I remember especially one called Udin, the *serang*, or bosun. He was tall above the average with strikingly high cheekbones and large eyes that slanted wickedly upwards at the outer corners and which would have put the fear of death into one had one been his prisoner. These Bugis simply wanted to make friends. They sat down in *Fiona's* cockpit and passing

154

our English-Indonesian phrasebook back and forth, we found communication was just possible.

On the whole the Bugis preferred to talk to us in gestures. They slapped our shoulders, pointing enthusiastically here and there. They tumbled down into the main cabin like puppies whenever something caught their eye – a pair of sunglasses, a slide rule, a packet of foreign cigarettes. It is worth recording that nothing was missing when they left us; the Bugis took nothing we did not give them; it was not part of their code to steal from friends. That they considered us friends was soon very obvious. At intervals they demonstrated their affection with platonic Bugis kisses: laying splayed noses against one's cheek with a quick intake of breath – a sort of sniffing.

They brought presents – bunches of small golden bananas and a big fish which must have weighed a kilo. Local men on board offered to swap two chickens for my watch, and others wanted to buy my shirt – a book – my pen – *Fiona*'s hosepipe – the stuffed monkey in the cabin – anything. But the Bugis felt protective; they shooed interlopers away, telling them we had come all the way from Bali and must rest.

They welcomed us aboard the *Mandar Baru*, as in the old days they might have welcomed their own rajahs. It was our turn to examine the prau's thick ropes, her unexpectedly coarse and heavy beams of wood and her huge buttressed masts, and take a closer look at her beautiful coloured sails. Their cargo was prosaic enough: instant noodles from Surabaya.

When it was time to part – we were eager to be off up the Strait of Makassar and across to Donggala – there were prolonged and affectionate goodbyes. Bugis noses snuffled sadly against our cheeks. Udin and one of his shipmates wrote their names in my notebook, not dreaming we would meet again.

When *Fiona* pulled away into the Strait of Makassar, the mosques of Kota Baru were still calling the faithful to the dawn-prayer. During the night I had taken down my copy of Alfred Russel Wallace's *Malay Archipelago* and marked with a pencil what he had written in 1869 about the Bugis:

> Often in former years, when strolling along Campong Glam in Singapore, I have thought how wild and ferocious the Bugis sailors looked, and how little I should like to trust myself among them. But now I find them to be very decent, well– behaved fellows . . . .

The sun had not risen. Bugis voices from the *Mandar Baru* were calling to us across the water:

'*Selamat jalan, selamat jalan!* Happy voyage! Happy sailing!'

Donggala (which he spelled 'Dongola') stuck in Conrad's memory for two main reasons. First, because of its exceptionally deep harbour, and second – and more importantly – because it was in Donggala that the name Almayer first began to stamp itself on his brain. If it had not done so and if he had not got to know Almayer pretty well, Conrad said later, 'it is almost certain there would never have been a line of mine in print.'

It was not the first time Conrad had heard the name Almayer (or Olmeijer as he was in real life). 'I had heard of him in Singapore. I had heard of him in a place called Pulau Laut from a half-caste gentleman there, who described himself as the manager of a coal-mine; which sounded civilised and progressive till you heard that the mine could not be worked at present because it was haunted by some particularly atrocious ghosts.'

And he heard of him in Donggala, 'in the Island of Celebes, when the Rajah of that little seaport (you can get no anchorage there in less than fifteen fathoms which is extremely inconvenient) came on board in a friendly way with only two attendants, and drank bottle after bottle of soda water in the after skylight with my good friend and commander, Captain C.' That meant Captain Craig of the *Vidar*, of which Conrad was first mate. There in Donggala, above the snap and fizz of the soda water on the steamer *Vidar*, Almayer's name emerged distinctly several times in a lot of Malay talk. 'Almayer . . . Almayer.' He saw Captain Craig smile and the fat, dingy Rajah laughed outright.

The *Vidar* was on her way to the Berau carrying cargo to Almayer in the shape of a very small pony, which Conrad says came from Bali. Just then it was tied up forward by the galley and irritating the Chinese cook by flicking its tail at him through the door. Two pretty little

Celebes cows had been loaded at Donggala in addition to the pony, and they whisked their tails at the cook through the other door of the galley. These cows were not for Almayer (or Olmeijer); they were destined for Syed Abdullah, his enemy.

Fiona left the Strait of Makassar at dawn, accompanied by a bodyguard or welcoming committee of the most amiable dolphins I have ever seen. They sped out far out under water to meet us, and, mile after mile to the entrance of the deep 'pocket' of the bay which shelters the little port, they played in the phosphorescence round *Fiona*'s bows. They might have been waiting for our arrival. They plunged and dived, and like cats rubbed their bodies on our wooden bows; quartets of them raced towards us, arching out of the water like steeplechasers in some aquatic Grand National; and as a finale gave a galvanic leap like a Polaris missile leaving a submarine. It was a stunning performance for which they might have been trained.

Donggala was a sprawl of houses on the right of a deep yet narrow bay resembling on the map the little finger of a glove. It crouched under a ring of hills within a higher ring that encircled the bay as Scottish highlands enfold a loch. A few roofs and the tiny metal domes of mosques poked up above the trees, and domestic fires laid a smokescreen horizontally across the town.

Just off and alongside a diminutive jetty a number of praus formed a cluster of masts and spars – small, local praus, outriggers balanced on outrigs of slim tree trunks or bamboos fastened with nylon cord, and much larger vessels, with towering masts and heavy furled sails. I counted twenty-four of these, but there may have been twice that number because vessels were continuously moving in and out and new arrivals charged round the headland and had lowered their sails almost before you had time to turn your head. The seas of the Archipelago were full of sailing ships in those days.

We tied up with the praus and went ashore. The little town had few cars or jeeps; you got about in carts drawn by pretty little Celebes ponies that clip-clopped down narrow streets. Small shops and stalls sold rice, biscuits, cigarettes, eggs, condensed milk, chocolate, whisky, Bintang beer, coffee, 7-Up, and the people of Donggala were as welcoming as the dolphins. To our question, 'How much?' a Chinese shop owner replied, 'As you like.'

And the Depot 39 coffee shop – *warung* – nearest the wharf was a cosy place with shuttered doors opening onto the street. Posters of Charles Bronson movies, Chinese operas, Japanese girls advertising motorbikes, and the remains of Christmas decorations were pinned to the walls. The tables had friendly red checked plastic covers and there were comfortable wicker chairs.

Depot 39 became our home from home. Sailors from the praus patronised the *warung* in the evening; they helped themselves to *air*

massak, boiled water, from the jugs of it on each table, and ate a cheap *table d'hôte* that was much more appetising than anything Schomberg would have considered 'fit for white men'. *Nasi campur ayam* – chicken, rice, hard-boiled eggs and hot chilli – was far better than 'buffalo steaks'. It was the sort of meal we had come to prefer.

I remember Donggala as the perfect Indonesian harbour with its shops, its friendly people, the cosy *warung* and the waterside market selling (I scribbled a list one morning, but it is incomplete) pineapples, aubergines, yams, potatoes, crisp cabbages, mung beans, tomatoes, spring onions, runner beans, carrots, oranges . . . .

Even the *shahbandar*, the harbour master, a man with a face like a friendly, sun-darkened crab apple, made none of the difficulties officials seem to delight in creating – for reasons of self-esteem, no doubt. He was only too glad to be taken to the *warung* and given a warming slug from an unusual bottle labelled, 'Fine Pure Whisky. Guaranteed made of finest flavour and other whiskies'. He said he preferred it to the 'Grand Brandy from France'.

It was not long before prau crews came tumbling aboard *Fiona*, with many cries of 'Hallo, misterr!', and inevitably they at once set about examining *Fiona*'s ropes and sails, winches, and brass fittings. '*Bagus*. Good,' they told each other, and tapping our old wooden beams they whistled appreciatively and gave us and each other the thumbs up sign. Peering into the cabin through the glass of the skylight, they exclaimed in wonder at the little kitchen, the cowskin rug on the deck, the painting from Bali on a bulkhead. It was a purely professional examination. They picked up nothing they were not invited to; there was no tinkering; certainly no question of theft. Even the dockside children, the 'Artful Dodgers' of every port in the Eastern Islands, who think nothing of taking the watch off your wrist, were subdued in Donggala.

We learned a good deal about the so-called 'brotherhood of the sea' from these Bugis *orang laut*. Before leaving Bali Mac had bought a dugout canoe from some local fishermen. This was now lashed to *Fiona*'s deck and it immediately attracted the attention of the crew of a large prau from Lombok which had moored alongside us. They looked it over with professional eyes, discussed it, and were obviously scornful. How much had we paid for such a thing, they asked Mac.

'What *should* we have paid?'

'Five thousand rupiahs!'

We had paid five times as much. Twenty-five thousand rupiahs! They were outraged. It was a fortune.

In a mixture of *bahasa Indonesia* and garbled but impassioned English from our phrasebook they told us what they proposed to do.

'That boat is not properly finished. The bow needs rounding. It needs an inch off the bottom; it needs smoothing off.'

They asked for an adze. A slender bush-knife, the nearest implement we had to one, was discarded in disgust.

With a monstrous blade of their own and a fistful of sandpaper, there and then they went to work.

For three days the crew of the *Sumber Karya Jaya* took it in turns to work at our dugout. They squatted hour after hour in the sun on *Fiona*'s deck, sarongs hitched up, muscular legs tucked under them, wholly absorbed in what they were doing. Their hand work was solely for our benefit and involved most of the prau's crew: the *nakhoda*, or captain, called Kardy; the *jura masar*, cook, Ngatiji; the helmsman, Nago Sunardy, and above all the prau's little carpenter with the pixie face and curious name which he wrote in my notebook, The S. Adyos. I never discovered what the 'S' stood for.

Wilfred became *Fiona*'s tea-maker; Adyos drank mugs of it between his bouts of carving and scraping. Wilfred's big sunburned nose fascinated Adyos. This was not surprising: it was a famous nose in its way. Several generations of Bedouin Arabs had hero worshipped it, murmuring '*Ma'ashallah*! Wonder of God!'

'My cousin Ernest, the actor, had his nose insured for £20,000,' Wilfred informed Adyos in Old Etonian English, and Adyos nodded politely as though he understood every word. When the Bugis asked, as they always did, permission to board *Fiona* Wilfred bellowed, 'Step aboard!', and it did not seem to matter to the crew of the *Sumber Karya Jaya* that he addressed them as if they were members of his London club.

Once, when Adyos brandished a parang, he drawled, 'I say, mind my nose with that thing. You'll have it off in a moment.' And Adyos nodded solemnly, silently promising to be more careful.

The *Sumber Karya Jaya*, 58.5 metres long and weighing a little over 20 tons, was not the biggest prau in Indonesia by a long chalk. She was owned by Kardy's father and had been built in Kota Baru on Pulau Laut where we had raced the *Mandar Baru*.

Kardy and Adyos were Bugis, but for convenience they lived at a friend's *warung* in Gillimanuk, a village at the extreme western end of Bali across from East Java. Nago Sunardy, from the small town of Sragen near Solo, was the only Javanese aboard the *Sumber Karya Jaya*. He had been born on a plain in sight of a row of volcanoes that cool their heads in the clouds a long way from the sea.

As our dugout gradually took on a more suitable shape, the Bugis brought bamboo poles and lashed them to two wooden cross pieces on each side of the body of the boat, so the dugout became an outrigger. Sometimes they came with us to the Depot 39 *warung* – they liked the *arrak*, the palm or rice liquor; and after a few *arraks* and water they stumbled tipsily back to their boat singing and mumbling incoherently to each other. Their *bonhomie* knew no bounds. Each day they brought us presents: a sack of peanuts, eggs, bananas, and one day they carried aboard a whole stack of hot banana fritters from the *warung,* sealed in banana leaves.

Such generosity had to be repaid, and luckily we didn't have to look far for presents for them. Kardy had told us he ran the gauntlet of those lethal reefs and shoals of this long Celebes coastline by trusting to his memory of them. Actually, he said, reefs were not the most serious problem. Praus were lost on them, of course – in fact, recently one had been reported stranded on a reef somewhere between Surabaya and Makassar. But even more dangerous than reefs were the huge tree trunks, escaped from logging camp sites, that floated free, propelled by tide, wind and current down the coast – massive waterlogged battering rams, capable of breaking apart the timbers of a prau, and which, half submerged in the water, were almost impossible for any lookout to spot.

There was no mistaking Kardy's delight when Mac gave him a detailed chart of the waters from Bali to East Kalimantan and the Makassar Strait. He took it away, hugging it to him as if it were a secret map of buried treasure, and I came across him on a quiet part of the deck, wholly absorbed, poring over its finely engraved depictions of islands, reefs, beacons and offshore oil flares.

Adyos was primarily responsible for refashioning the dugout in outrigger form, and we gave him two shirts that Mac found in the bottom of a locker; they carried a label that said, 'Laura Ashley, Wales', and luckily they both fitted him.

A Lombok prau made a great spectacle of herself. She must have weighed 100 tons. Her masts were thick and her timbers unusually solid, and she carried twin rudders, rectangles of wood so massive that four men at least would be needed to control them. She came storming into the packed prau harbour with all sails flying, and the question suddenly seemed to be: would she be able to pull up before smashing into the jam of vessels at anchor? But we were watching experts. With

161

no audible commands from her *nakhoda*, the prau's sails came down in a flash, the anchor rattled into the water, ropes snaked to the jetty. In no time at all the prau's sailors were looking round them like a record-breaking British or American crew after a victorious ocean-race, hands on hips, as if to say, 'See that – pretty good, eh?'

We learned something of praus one way and another. Kardy and Adyos told us that two-masted Bugis praus – called *pinisis* – could weigh as much as 300 tons or as little as 40 tons, and carried a crew of twelve men. *Orang laut* had a hard life. They spent a great deal of most voyages lying on the jib-boom or huddled high in the stern with their sarongs around their shoulders, drenched by the waves that swept across the decks, while the prau rolled and wallowed in the troughs of the sea.

Sailing was a traditional way of life – son followed father – but it was not a particularly desirable one. The pay was small: you got as much rice as you could eat, with a small percentage of the profits. The *nakhoda* received a salary as well as his percentage of the profits; but he had to work for it; his job was a responsible one, and *nakhodas* were picked for their honesty as much as their seamanship. Sailing praus, one could see, were doomed. An owner fitted an engine into his prau as soon as he could afford to, and this meant that sooner or later sailing praus like the *Sumber Karya Jaya* would be things of the past in Indonesia.

'They are a thing of the past in Malaysia already,' I said.

'I have heard so,' Kardy said, without regret or pleasure.

Would the traditions of the prau world disappear too – for example, the rooster *nakhodas* kept on to give warning with loud 'cock-a-doodle-doo' if there was a hidden obstruction in the water ahead? Probably not; and cargoes would remain the same: salt from Surabaya; oil and batik cloth from Java; wood from southern Kalimantan and Celebes; copra from Donggala; cloves from Ternate and Ceram; dried fish, coral and lava from practically everywhere. And the Berau river would remain the source of rattans, gutta-percha and birds' nests that it had been in the days of Conrad and Lingard.

When the time came to leave Donggala, it was not a happy moment. It meant saying goodbye for ever to the devoted crew of the *Sumber Karya Jaya* who had finished their work on the dugout.

We pulled away one windless morning on the engine, and Mac blew blast after blast on our 'foghorn', a strange flask-shaped trumpet. Its flatulent blasts echoed round the little harbour, and the men of the *Sumber Karya Jaya* stood on deck waving and calling. Indeed, throughout the harbour all the praus seemed to be lined with men watching and waving.

The forest of masts, the *warung*, the steep slopes with their ranks of palm trees grew smaller. Soon a breeze got up, we turned the point of the bay, and Donggala vanished. Mac set our course in the direction of Makassar, south to the Bugis lands of Wajo and Boné.

It was to be twelve years before I visited Donggala again, this time in the *Kerinci*, a passenger steamer belonging to the national shipping line.

The little port looked as inviting as ever, huddled behind its low headland with the encircling hillsides covered by ranks of copra palms. But as I stared at the wharf through my glasses I could only see one or two sailing ships. Steamers went alongside a jetty on the opposite side of the bay at Pantoloan, so I did not even have a chance to see what decorations had replaced the Charles Bronson posters in the Depot 39 *warung*.

On the *Kerinci*'s deck, Daniel, a talkative, pleasant fellow passenger of about sixty, with a Red Indian cast of face and grey stubbly hair, turned out to be a senior customs officer from Donggala, accompanying his friend, the *shahbandar*, the harbour master, of Toli-Toli, a small port further up the coast.

We leaned over the ship's rail looking at the coastline of hills – threadbare hills now. The thickly wooded slopes I remembered had a patchy look as though they had been nibbled away by rats.

'There's no wood left anywhere in the world,' Daniel said sadly.

'I sailed to Donggala in 1977 in a yacht,' I told him, 'and then we were surrounded by ships with big sails.'

'Yes, I remember that. Just big sails,' he said. 'That's a long time ago.'

In recent visits to Indonesia I have done my best to find the *Sumber Karya Jaya*. I have questioned *shahbandars*, officials responsible for registers of shipping, prau crews in numerous harbours, anyone likely to have news of her.

Finally in Surabaya, at last, I ran to earth the prau's helmsman, the only Javanese in the crew, Nago Sunardy. From him I learned that a few years ago the *Sumber Karya Jaya* sank in a storm off the coast of Bali, and he added quickly, 'Ooah, mister, the crew has been saved.' He had lost touch with his former shipmates since he had joined a new ship registered in Samarang. Kardy and The S. Adyos, I thought, could have settled anywhere from Goram to Samarinda. It could take me years of searching to find them. So I suppose I have seen the last of our unforgettable Bugis friends.

Fifteen

Perched on a tiny coconut shell bobbing in the calm, blue sea, a large tern with a rakish demeanour and a sleek black head gave us a beady look.

The shore *Fiona* was passing at that moment seemed untouched since Conrad's day – even since the time when Alfred Russel Wallace, zoologist, botanist and explorer, passed here in the 1860s. Now in 1977 I saw a beach and a barrier of palms through which peeped occasional small houses, and now and again among the palms the tiny lead-coloured onion-shaped dome of a mosque. Behind the palms, there were endless ridges of mountain and the tops of vast forest trees dappled by the changing shapes of cloud made tossing, frothing, outlines of dark foliage, a green tidal wave for ever on the point of breaking.

The sight of Celebes from the sea was magnificent. When I saw the same shoreline twelve years later from the *Kerinci* only part of it remained as I have just described. Then we steamed past mile after mile of treeless ridges that were as extravagantly bald as sand dunes.

It took us ten days and nights in *Fiona* to reach Makassar from Donggala, including stops for expeditions ashore and the odd stranding. It seemed far less. Joseph Conrad had observed that 'nowhere else than upon the sea do the days, weeks, and months fall away quicker into the past. They seem to be left astern as easily as the light air-bubbles in the swirl of the ship's wake.' He probably needed to add 'if you are part of the crew of a smallish vessel.' Speaking for myself, the boredom of a long cruise in a big passenger liner can lead me to the edge of suicide in next to no time. I cannot remember that

165

our sail down the west coast of the extraordinary island of Celebes – or Sulawesi as it is now called – contained one minute of boredom.

I remember the nights possibly best of all. I liked to spend hours in the darkness, sitting up in the bows, leaning my back against the anchor winch, watching the luminous waves rearing up under *Fiona*'s bows beneath me, feeling the cool, fresh breeze from the shore, hearing the great moonlit billow of sail over my head booming great guns. I could lay my hand on the triangular corner of the sail by my head and feel it quiver as a racehorse quivers with tension and excitement; or on the stays themselves and feel them shivering with the tremors pulsing through them from the straining 45-foot mainmast, reeling back and forth against the stars.

I had never seen stars so big. Shooting stars arced across the perfect sky, falling impossibly far and glowing impossibly brightly, some of them with a greenish tinge like signal flares. They fell so far towards the horizon that you almost expected a splash, a fizzle and an immense cloud of steam, and the sea was full of dancing globes of phosphorus as if the waves were lit by a thousand muddled reflections of the stars overhead.

Conrad wrote that a ship is not a slave: 'you must never forget that you owe her the fullest share of your thought, your skill, or your self-love.' If you remember that, he said, she will sail, stay, run for you as long as she is able. A sailor's romantic exaggeration, I had thought, but on this passage to Makassar, I learned something. It was curious. *Fiona* in a dead calm could become almost human. She seemed to 'smell' an approaching wind, for example – to sense its approach. Long before I felt the faintest breath of it, she would begin to shift restlessly, her rigging would stir impatiently and she would utter little squeaks of excitement and anticipation. Part of the simple mechanics of sails and rigging, no doubt; but odd all the same.

Of course that had nothing to do with the voice that came to me on deck at night. That was even odder. On deck I more than once felt a certainty that I was not alone – although Mac and the others, I knew, were below. One night I heard a voice in my ear, male, quite pleasant, saying distinctly, 'Come on, come on. Come on, then.' Mac told me he had had the same kind of experience from time to time. There is no explanation, as far as I know. It was not *Fiona* whispering words of love. Nor was it seductive chatter from her sails and rigging.

The competition between Sail and Machine, long over in most of the world, even now continues in these eastern islands.

There is something to be said for both. During the long haul down the coast of Celebes (and later to Borneo) we were to have days and nights of pure sailing; perfect days with breeze enough to allow us to cut the engine and silently skim our way southwards. On other days the wind failed completely, and rather than dawdle for hours in sticky heat we were obliged to motor. Then we were glad to have an engine – it meant that at least we were never becalmed as engineless sailing boats can be, stopped in our tracks for hours on end. On the other hand, all of us on *Fiona* felt a delight with the pure sailing, when there was only the lap of water against the hull, the rustle and murmur of the sails, the crying of the sea birds around us. They seemed like the happy sounds and sighs of life itself. Sailing was the way to see the East as Conrad had preferred to see it.

Conrad remained basically a sailing ship man although he covered this shoreline several times, and each time in an 800-ton steamer. The *Vidar*, by the time he joined her, had been owned by the Singapore Arab trader, Syed Mohsin Al Joofree, for fifteen years. When he first saw Donggala as first mate of the *Vidar* he arrived there in an iron vessel that came clanking in from the Strait, belching smoke and tearing up the water of the little bay with a single mechanical screw.

Sail versus Steam was still a worldwide battle then. Before the opening of the Suez Canal in 1869, old clippers like the *Cutty Sark* bound for China from England, took the long route round the Cape of Good Hope. Crossing the Indian Ocean, they made for the Sunda Strait and, without stopping, proceeded directly to the China coast. With the opening of the Canal distances were reduced, and steamers could make a beeline for the Strait of Malacca, and take on coals at Singapore for the remainder of the voyage.

This may have been 'progress', but it was not something Conrad applauded. He was a 'sail man' to the depths of his seagoing soul. When he presented himself at the Marine Department of the Board of Trade to be examined for Master, the examiner who passed him, an easy-going sort of man, with a round, soft face and 'loquacious lips', felt he was expressing a foregone conclusion when he said, 'You will go into steam presently. Everybody goes into steam.'

There, says Conrad, he was wrong. 'I never went into steam – not really. If I only live long enough I shall become a bizarre relic of a dead barbarism, a sort of monstrous antiquity, the only seaman of the dark ages who had never gone into steam – not really.'

The examiner tried again.

'You are of Polish extraction.'

'Born there, sir.'

'Not many of your nationality in our service, I should think. An inland people, aren't you?'

'Very much so.'

'I don't know what may be your plans but you ought to go into steam. When a man has got his Master's Certificate it's the proper time. If I were you I would go into steam.'

Conrad thanked him, and remained a sail man. If there had to be a first unforgettable experience, one which fixes the moment when a man realises irrevocably that sails are for him and steam is not, that moment came for Conrad as a very young man off Marseilles as a member of the crew of a sailing boat. In a great moonlit silence the islets of Monte Cristo and the Château d'If seemed to float towards him. 'My fingers itched for the tiller, and in due course my friend the *patron* surrendered it to me in the same spirit in which the family coachman lets a boy hold the reins on an easy bit of road.' There in a magical moment, in the open water of the *avant-port* with 'a quick rattle of blocks and one silky swish' the boat's sail was filled, and young Conrad heard the *patron*'s voice: 'Keep her in the furrow of the moon.'

It is easy to see what drew Conrad to Captain William Lingard. Lingard was a 'sail man' *par excellence*. Even though Conrad may not have met him in life there were more than enough stories about Lingard's exploits circulating around Emmerson's in Singapore and in every other tiffin room in the Archipelago for Conrad to feel that in an important sense he knew him.

In *An Outcast of the Islands*, Conrad describes how Lingard tells Willems, 'Pah! There's only one place for an honest man. The sea, my boy, the sea.' And goes on:

> Lingard was a master, a lover, a servant of the sea. Generously it gave him his absurd faith in himself, his universal love of creation, his straightforward simplicity of motive and honesty of aim. Lingard grew rich on the sea and by the sea . . . he made light of it with the assurance of perfect mastery, he feared it with the wise fear of a brave man. His greatest pride lay in his profound conviction of its faithfulness – in the deep sense of his unerring knowledge of its treachery.

Lingard's little sailing brig was the instrument of his fortune. They had come north together – Conrad said – out of an Australian port, and after a few years there was not a white man in the islands, from

168

Palembang to Ternate, from Sumbawa to Palawan, that did not know Captain Lingard and his lucky craft.

Lingard himself was liked for his generosity and his honesty, and he prospered greatly. He fought successfully with pirates and his great popularity began, growing greater as the years went by.

Lingard acquired mystique among Malay *orang laut* as much as European seamen. By visiting out-of-the-way places in search of new markets for his cargoes, and by successfully tackling the murderous sea-rovers from Sulu and the Philippines, he established the terror of his name and soon became so well known to the Malays that they would address him half seriously as 'Rajah Laut' – the King of the Sea.

That 'dismal but profitable ditch', Conrad called the Canal. Lingard would have enthusiastically echoed Conrad's view that from the moment of its opening 'the hand of the engineer began to tear down the veil of a terrible beauty in order that greedy and faithless landlubbers might pocket dividends.' It was as if the sea's devoted servants had become a calculating crowd of cold and exacting masters. After that the sea, Conrad thought, became 'a used-up drudge, wrinkled and defaced by the churned-up wakes of brutal propellers, stripped of its beauty, of its promise'. Harsh words. Lucky for Conrad that he did not live to see the mechanised container fleets of today struggling to keep up with their computerised schedules.

The *Vidar* was as near as Conrad got to steam; and it was the *Vidar* – and steam – that did for the Rajah Laut.

The loss of Tom Lingard's brig the *Flash* in *An Outcast of the Islands* – 'Wasn't she a sweet craft? Could make her do anything but talk. Hey, Almayer?' – was Conrad's metaphor for William Lingard's ultimate failure. With his sailing ship planted firmly and for ever on a ledge of rock at the north end of the Gaspar Strait, he was never the same man again.

In the region of Berau and Bulungan, the rivers that Lingard liked to say he had 'discovered' – '*his rivers!*' – he lost his commercial supremacy to Syed Abdullah Al Joofree because Syed Abdullah's father owned steamers. It was as simple as that. The steamers passed through the Carimata Strait, to Banjarmassin and Pulau Laut (where they coaled), to Donggala and from there to Berau and Bulungan – with perhaps a detour to Makassar, Samarang and Surabaya – and were back in Singapore in something like thirty days. And in the Eighties, their heyday, the Al Joofrees' house flag – a white crescent and star on a red background framed in green – fluttered over not the *Vidar* alone, but three other steamers, the *Emily*, the *Tiang Wat Seng* and the *Eastern Isles*, as well. Sail – the love of Lingard's life – became, like the *Flash*, a thing of the past, a past which Conrad compared to an old cemetery full of the neglected graves of dead hopes that never return.

Rajah Laut

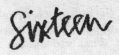

Sixteen

Sometimes, in the daytime, when the sunlight was scattered on the water in hundreds of golden fragments, shoals of diminutive fish – thousands of them – suddenly began to churn up the sea ahead of *Fiona*, as if tiny waves were breaking against a sand bar.

Terns began diving out of the sky, white, streamlined and ruthless, pouncing on the tiny fish like German Stuka bombers dive-bombing a concentration of enemy troops. Frigate birds' cruel, piratical shapes looked down jealously on the commotion as they floated high overhead on rigid, angular wings, their short, stiff tails like the extended blades of flick-knives. But they left the fish to the terns.

Mac said: 'I've seen frigate birds in their breeding grounds in the Galapagos. Thousands of them. They lay their eggs in low bushes on big nests of twigs some of which they steal from the nests of other birds. They'll go for you if you go too near them. I've never seen one land on water. They're sea birds, of course, but I've never seen one actually on the sea. Strange.'

Two days from Donggala came what I always think of as the Incident of the Rectangular Eggs. I have several times described the incident in England or America and it has not gone down well. The response to my account has often been the sort of faint, half-amused smile that means, 'You can do better than that. Surely.'

Yet the fact was that, two days from Donggala, an old man and a boy paddled in a canoe slowly towards *Fiona* as we lay dozing on deck one relaxed afternoon. We were anchored in a wide bay partly bordered by a village in a line of trees behind a shallow beach. The chart named the village Kambunong.

It was a small canoe, barely big enough for the old man and the boy. They bumped gently alongside, smiled and pointed to something on the bottom of the canoe. There, in a banana leaf 'nest', lay two eggs, about 4 inches long and almost rectangular. Our first question was, 'What bird laid these?'

The old man held up his hands like an angler describing the fish that got away. He seemed to be outlining something roughly the size of a chicken. '*Burung*,' he said.

I said to Mac, '*Burung* means bird in Indonesian. It can mean anything from a sparrow to an emu. Not much help.' We had a bird book on board, with pictures. We opened it under the old man's nose at a coloured plate of a turkey.

The man at once ruled out the turkey and, after a solemn scrutiny, dismissed the bustard as well. Fluttering through a few pages – 'There,' he said, and jabbed his finger down hard on a magnificent pheasant. Not even an ordinary pheasant. It was an Imperial Pheasant – an extraordinarily exotic fowl which the book said was only found (but rarely) in Annam and Laos. Not in Celebes.

'If those eggs were laid by a pheasant,' Wilfred Thesiger said in disbelief, 'I am an ostrich!'

'Perhaps I should get you a bucket of sand, then?' Murray asked cheekily.

'Not necessary.'

The boy handed both the eggs to me, and I laid them carefully on a towel on the deck and asked Mac for a tape measure. The eggs measured exactly 4 inches by 2¼ inches and they had light brown shells. They were not absolutely rectangular – I mean their corners were not as sharp as the corners on bricks you usually see in a house. How could any bird lay a brick? But even so, what bird could lay a brick with vaguely rounded corners?

Among many incomprehensible remarks, the old man seemed more than once to mention a word that sounded like 'Maleyo' or 'Maleo'.

'Do you think "maleyo" or "maleo" means a bird hereabouts?' I suggested. 'The old man seems very insistent.'

'I'll look it up in Wallace,' said Mac. And in *The Malay Archipelago* under 'Birds (see Maleo)', Alfred Russel Wallace gave us the answer:

Among the birds my hunters got me were the rare forest Kingfisher (*Crittura cyanotis*), a small new species of megapodius, and one specimen of the large and interesting Maleo (*Megacephalon rubripes*), to obtain which was one of my chief reasons for visiting this district . . .
I found here Mr Goldmann, the eldest son of the Governor of the Moluccas, who was superintending the establishment of some Government salt works. I obtained some fine butterflies and very good birds,

among which was one more specimen of the rare ground dove (*Phlegaenas tristigmata*), which I had first obtained near the Maros waterfall in South Celebes . . . .

Mr Goldmann kindly offered to make a hunting-party to the place where the 'Maleos' are most abundant . . . . The place is situated on a large bay, and consists of a steep beach and deep loose and coarse black volcanic sand or rather gravel, very fascinating to walk over.

It is in this loose, hot black sand that those singular birds the 'Maleos' deposit their eggs. In the months of August and September when there is little or no rain, they come down in pairs from the interior, and scratch holes three or four feet deep, just above high-water mark, where the female deposits a single large egg, which she covers over with about a foot of sand, and then returns to the forest. At the end of ten or twelve days she comes again to the same spot to lay another egg, and each female bird is supposed to lay six or eight eggs during the season. The male assists the female in making the hole, coming down and returning with her. The appearance of the bird when walking on the beach is very handsome. The glossy black and rosy white of the plumage, the helmeted head and elevated tail, like that of the common fowl, give a striking character, which their stately and somewhat sedate walk renders still more remarkable.

They run quickly, but when shot at or suddenly disturbed, take wing with a heavy noisy flight to some neighbouring tree, where they settle on a low branch . . . . Many birds lay in the same hole, for a dozen eggs are often found together; and these are so large that it is not possible for the body of the bird to contain more than one fully-developed egg at the same time.

Every year the natives come for fifty miles around to obtain these eggs, which are esteemed a great delicacy, and when quite fresh are indeed delicious. They are richer than hens' eggs and of a finer flavour, and each one completely fills an ordinary tea cup, and forms with bread or rice a very good meal. The colour of the shell is a pale brick red . . . . They are elongated and very slightly smaller at one end, from one to four and half inches long by two and a quarter or two and a half wide.

It was satisfying to find that my measurements were not at fault, but the most extraordinary detail of the birth of maleo birds was yet to come:

After the eggs are deposited in the sand they are no further cared for by the mother. The young birds on breaking the shell, work their way up through the sand and run off at once to the forest; and I was assured by Mr Duivenboden of Ternate that they can fly the very day they are hatched. He had taken some eggs on board his schooner which hatched during the night, and in the morning the little birds flew readily acoss the cabin.

We did not hatch the eggs we had bought. Wilfred and I ate them, scrambled, for dinner, and were relieved to find Wallace had had no compunction about doing the same. As he said, cooked, they were delicious.

Perhaps the inhabitants of Kambunong mistook us for a delayed boatload of potential Alfred Russel Wallaces, because as soon as the old man and the boy who sold us the maleo eggs had paddled back to the village, two young men came briskly alongside with what looked like a sort of large black-haired bush-baby glaring out from a wicker cage. Woolly, male, with huge appealing eyes, little four-fingered hands and a prehensile tail, it moved in a bemused sort of way, looking half asleep. Its fur was as thick as a well knitted rug.

'Buy it,' urged the men. 'It doesn't bite. It eats coconut and pineapple.' It was called a *cus-cus* in Malay, and Wallace's book informed us that the English for *cus-cus* was 'Eastern opossum': a curious genus. The local people of Kambunong eat them. We didn't want to do that; nor did we want a woolly pet swinging about *Fiona*'s cabin. We were sorry, we told the young men, but we didn't want to buy it.

I remember Kambunong for the maleos, the *cus-cus* – and also for the simple charm of its untouched simplicity. No one could reach the village by road, the only access to it was from the sea. Mac launched *Fiona Kecil* – Little Fiona – there for the first time. The little outrigger the Bugis had built turned out to be perfectly balanced; the bamboo outrigs sat on the water perfectly. We were met on the shore by a man called Sako, who took us round the village and into his house, which was perched on stilts and could only be entered by climbing a steep bamboo ladder. The house had an elastic split bamboo floor and walls of wood through the chinks of which the sea breeze entered to cool the hot humid air.

At Sako's I was offered a lump of rock embedded with crystalline substances that sparkled – it may have been a kind of quartz – and a small white cockatoo on a branch. When, with thanks, I refused both,

174

the subject of their sale was immediately dropped as if it had never been mentioned.

It was cool in Sako's house. A baby lay in a cradle made of a sarong suspended from the roof; two women gossiping sat on the floor; the clucking of chickens rose from the open space under the floor. Sako's wife brought us sweet condensed milk in hot water, and powdery cakes which Sako said were made from maleo eggs.

The main and only street was dusty but cool, shaded by trees and lined by neat wooden cottages with sarongs and blankets hanging out to dry on their garden fences like coloured flags at a festival. People waved and offered us mugs of *air putih* from a well inside the mosque – fresh water with a pleasant mineral taste, a rare thing where water is invariably boiled. Every man wore a sarong and a songkok and nobody said, 'Misterr'. Here we were addressed as *tuan*.

With Sako I walked round a rocky point of land that fell abruptly into the sea. Here were deep, dark caves where hundreds of bats swirled and screamed and disappeared into impenetrable shadow, and rocks on the edge of the sea embraced by mangrove roots as remorseless as the tentacles of a monstrous squid. Wild pigs had stabbed staccato tracks in the wet sand; on the water's rim a flock of storks pecked up grubs; and heron stood in the shallows motionless as pewter statues. Behind the beach large butterflies hovered in clusters over bushes of small, flame-coloured chillis and shrubs with saffron and scarlet flowers. It was inexpressibly beautiful.

Round the next headland the landscape was different – something like Wales: shallow, sunlit valleys, and rolling hills green and dappled by the shifting clouds, like good grazing land. But there were no cows or sheep here; only a few goats tethered close to scattered houses. Great plumes of smoke sometimes enveloped a hillside and at night strips of flame. There were no timber company camps here, so these bush-fires were the work of local cultivators clearing land. The resulting green, pasture-like appearance of the hills is pretty, but 500 years of tree-forest growth was gone for ever. 'It is the same in Kenya,' Wilfred said. 'I recognise the symptoms immediately.'

Prau-land! The sea swarms with praus, like great winged insects – pale green, dark green, dark blue streaks, brown, white-and-pink. Every shape and combination, except spots. Where else in the world could Mac have counted eighty-one sails this morning – at *one time*?

To be anchored in a remote bay with only praus for company is wonderful, almost unearthly. The praus lie, sails furled, white and ghostly in the silent darkening water. There are no other boats. No yachts. No engines.

Near sunset small, light outriggers skim noiselessly into the bay from the sea, with men standing on the outrigs to keep them flat on the water. The prau-men have erected fish traps – elaborate six-foot wooden rigs with platforms where they can perch and keep watch high above the surface of the bay. The sun sinks into a veil of grey behind the circle of uneven mountains turning a deeper and deeper mauve, until its last rays have disappeared behind them. After sunset the stars come out, matching the dancing phosphorescent blobs in the water,

and between the trees small household fires begin to gleam like glow-worms. The silence is so intense there that it seems to invest every sound with a mysterious significance. The surf sighs on a sand bar. You hear the plop of fish, a dog barking, and the passionate chant, rising and falling, from an invisible mosque, calling the world to prayer. A slender five-day-old moon rises through the tousled heads of palm trees on a low headland and, silhouetted against it, a boy in a prau calls 'Hello!' We might be the first people ever to visit this bay.

In that intense silence, *Fiona* rocking at anchor makes almost imperceptible sounds. It is as though, very gently, she is breathing.

Two old men come aboard, squat down on the deck, smile and are silent. One of them brings from the folds of his sarong a long tusk; hollowed out, it makes a six-inch cigarette holder. A whale's tooth? A wild boar's?

'Dugong!' the old men say. They catch dugong in this bay; the strange, rare creatures come to the shallows to feed on sea-grasses. *Animals of Malaysia* says the male dugong has two tusks like upper incisors. They are mammals and very rare.

A day or two later, we find a small prau becalmed on a sandbank. Its crew – three men – shout and wave, wanting a tow, and throw us a rope. We make it fast and away we go, and after two and a half hours we have saved them almost a day's sail. In return they pass us a bucket containing three large hunks of whitish, corpse-like meat in it, smelling strange.

'Dugong, dugong!' they shout. From its picture the dugong, which resembles a snub-nosed, densely whiskered sea lion, is ugly enough alive. It is difficult to believe stories that ancient mariners once took

these grotesque mammals for 'mermaids', and its meat as unappealing as its appearance. Even drowned in Amoy Oyster Sauce and hot Kerala Pickle made in Bangalore, it is revolting. Wilfred and I tip the whitish mass on our plates overboard at the first opportunity. Why die prematurely of rare dugong poisoning?

Another landfall. Another village.

We are invited ashore to a Mandarese wedding. The reception is held in the open space under a small village house whose wooden stilts are covered with coconut fronds and the floor above, now our ceiling, is disguised with a sheet. Hissing pressure lamps give out a fierce heat and harsh, steely light.

The women are dressed smartly in gold and red sarongs and short-sleeved, loose jackets of some material so light it is almost transparent. The men, disappointingly, wear ugly western suits in checkered green and brown, loud shirts and pin-on ties. Some wear white jackets like waiters.

The groom is in a dark suit, white gloves, and a white shirt with a black full-length tie. On the fingers of his left hand he wears three enormous rings with black and brown convex stones. On his head, the traditional songkok. The bride wears a familiar long white dress and a crown of white artificial flowers and a veil. Flashing in the light of the pressure lamps, under her impassive little doll's face, is a necklace of – I should say – semi-precious stones. She carries a white bouquet in her tiny doll's hand. It is a pity, in a way. I know from pictures that the traditional Mandarese dress, shirt and sarong is full of magical colours and beautifully shot through with thin glistening threads of gold.

I shake hands with these human waxworks, and then sit on one of the metal chairs they have brought for us. 'Good evening,' we say politely to everyone in turn. We eat rice and sautéed beef and fried vegetables. We drink warm boiled water. It is all very solemn for what should surely be a jolly occasion. I wish our Bugis seamen were here to liven things up.

There may be three hundred people crowded in under the house, and others unable to get in look in at us over the wooden planks like railway sleepers that form impromptu walls. Everybody loves a wedding. Among Muslims celibacy is not only unknown, it is incomprehensible.

I can hardly help noticing the best man. He is tall, white-jacketed with a trim Adolphe Menjou moustache, above large teeth which he bares in an alarming manner while he rolls his eyes round the room as though demented. He behaves like an outrageous caricature of a top-hatted villain in a Victorian melodrama. Has he been at something stronger than the *air massak*?

Leaving the coast at Majené, we can see ninety-four praus this morning! Ninety-four in the immediate circle of our vision. Ninety-four single-winged moths loitering on the surface of the Strait!

Off the coast under sail near Makassar, Fate takes a hand. A *pinisi* speeding up the Strait under full sail almost bumps into us. She is a big, seagoing two-masted vessel and she sweeps up fiercely; her bows, ploughing deep into the choppy water, make a wave that sweeps back over the nearside gunwale in a cascade of spray. She sways towards us, close to our port side, and all of a sudden I see a tall man in a checkered sarong under her foresail, waving dementedly.

I hear a shout, 'Gavin! Hello, Gavin!'

Not only one man. I can see a whole crew waving and shouting – their dark skins glistening, teeth and eyes flashing under the great billow of a sail part purple so deep it is nearly black, part green and white. A designer's dream that we had heard was in Surabaya. The *Mandar Baru*.

Udin was standing there. An arm above his head, his pirate's eyes with the dangerous slant wide now with excitement, shouting across the water between the two vessels as they converged, lay parallel, drew apart again. We too are all on deck, shouting and waving back. Someone calls, 'Where you go?'

'To Palanro . . . to Makassar.'

'Ah, Palanro. We go to Majené.'

That was all there was time for. But it was strangely moving – one's name shouted by *orang laut* across such a remote stretch of water.

Once more, as it had that early morning at Kota Baru, the cry of '*Selamat jalan! Selamat!*' followed us down the Strait, and the waving continued until our arms were tired. By then our friends had dwindled to vague, tiny figures dwarfed by the coloured square of sail, and their voices, hoarse and frenzied across the water but unforgettable, had slowly died away little by little . . . died away . . . for ever. At least, from our ears.

The long run into Makassar from Mandar Bay is made extraordinarily hazardous by the reefs – constellations of reefs, lying in ambush under the water like killer submarines. You can look at the chart and wonder where all those fly-specks came from that clutter up that part of it – and all at once realise that those 'fly-specks' were engraved there with great precision by some old hydrographer. They are reefs, waiting to rip the bottom out of your boat.

Conrad wrote:

> 'Stranded' stands for a more or less excusable mistake. A ship may be 'driven ashore' by stress of weather. It is a catastrophe, a defeat. Your strandings are for the most part unexpected . . . except those heralded by some short glimpse of the danger, full of agitation and excitement, like an awakening from a dream of incredible folly. The cry of 'Broken water ahead!' is raised, and the heart-searing experience of your ship's keel scraping and scrunching over, say, a coral reef. It is a sound, for its size, far more terrific to your soul than that of a world coming violently to an end. You ask yourself, Where on earth did I get to? How on earth did I get there? with a conviction that the charts are all wrong, and if the charts are not all wrong, that land and sea have changed their places . . . .

Alfred Russel Wallace ran into several reefs in two days, and was lucky to survive.

> At about ten o'clock we ran full onto a coral reef, which alarmed us a good deal, but luckily got safely off again . . . . At night we did not know what to do, as no one on board could tell us where we were or what dangers might surround us. We therefore took in all sail and allowed ourselves to drift. A light breeze, however, sprang up, and about midnight we found ourselves again bumping over a coral reef . . . . Had there been a little more wind we might have been knocked to pieces. Soon after daylight on the next day . . . we sailed on with uncertain winds and squalls, threading our way among islands and reefs, and guided only by a small map, which was very incorrect and quite useless, and by a general notion of the direction we ought to take.

In the afternoon they found a tolerable anchorage; Wallace shot a large fruit-pigeon new to him and shot at a rare white-headed kingfisher without killing it.

> Next day we ran full on to a coral reef with the mainsail up, and luckily the wind had almost died away, and with a good deal of exertion we managed to get off.

Wallace spent eight years wandering by foot or native boat round the islands. He obviously had a charmed life, for when he died in 1913 he was ninety years old.

How can I describe the lethal beauty of these strips of coral? Take a tiny island in the sun – the ideal Desert Island – perhaps 300 square yards covered with a top-knot of palms and ringed by a yellow beach. (There are dozens, scores, of them.) On either side, for perhaps one mile each way, is the reef. It is not hidden. On the contrary, it is not only visible, it is eye-catching. The sun makes of it a brilliant, glowing bar of underwater light – a subaqueous neon strip, turquoise and beautiful. Yet deadly, too, because as soon as the merest cloud covers the sun, that bright light in the water disappears totally – it is as if a switch has been pulled. Suddenly in the unknown, you are feeling your way, as it were, blindfolded through a pit of cobras.

Reefs glowing under the sun make a spectacular lane through which, with a good look-out, you can sail without difficulty or danger. From a point west of Palanro southwards, with the sun behind us, we accordingly found ourselves sailing between two glorious spotlit lines of blue-green jade. But imagine what it would be like having to negotiate that avenue of coral at night – with perhaps a squall on its way.

From time to time we could see those squalls sweeping towards the coast, dense curtains of rain that in seconds blotted everything from sight. Other seas have other hazards. The waters of the Strait of Makassar were not like those Pacific or Indian Ocean deeps in which huge creatures move like drowned islands and from which emerge gigantic squids like the monster that was said in 1874 to have grappled, boarded and sunk the 180-ton schooner *Pearl* between Rangoon and Mauritius. Yet reefs in shallow water could in their way be just as dangerous.

From time to time the chart said 'beacon', and sometimes we peered in vain. Off the coast of Celebes 'beacon' is – or was – a euphemism for what could turn out to be nothing more eye-catching than a black and white pole only six inches across and easily lost in tossing waves or in low-lying, thick mist.

One unofficial 'beacon' – nearly invisible – was an excellent reminder of dangers ahead. This was a wreck – a ribbed, rusty shaft of metal, thrusting up to the surface of the water. It was marked on our old chart as the wreck of a ship called the *Bromo*, although what sort of vessel the *Bromo* had been and how it had come to rest for ever on that reef our *Pilot* did not tell us.

The newest edition of the *Indonesia Pilot* says of this part of the Makassar Strait: 'The new entrance to the North channel [to Makassar] lies between a number of reefs extending 1.5 miles West from Pulau Panikiang, a low wooded island, 1.25 West of Karang Tomisa.' Tomisa Reef!

The name Tomisa (Tamissa, he spelled it) Reef meant a great deal to

Conrad. Old Jörgenson (late of the *Wild Rose*), leaning one night over the balustrade of the Cavenagh Bridge in Singapore in *The Rescue*, warns Lingard to drop his plans to restore the prince to the usurped throne of Wajo. And he adds (always in *The Rescue*):

> Suppose the Dutch want the things just so – did you ever hear of Dawson? Cut his throat on the beach below Fort Rotterdam. Yes. He broke some trade regulation or other and talked big about law courts and legal trials to the lieutenant of the *Komet*. 'Certainly,' says the hound. 'Jurisdiction of Makassar, I will take your schooner there.' Then coming into the roads he tows her full tilt on a ledge of rocks on the north side – smash! When she was half full of water he takes his hat off to Dawson. 'There's the shore,' says he – 'go and get your legal trial, you – Englishman – .' All was lost. Poor Dawson walked the streets for months barefooted and in rags. Then one day he begged a knife from some charitable soul, went down to take a last look at the wreck, and – .

That is Jörgenson's version of a deliberate wrecking here. Conrad described a similarly contrived wrecking on this very spot to mark the end of Jasper Allen, the swashbuckling privateer who loved Freya of the Seven Isles so much that he regularly risked his pretty little brig *Bonito* simply for the pleasure of tying her up virtually under the window in old Nelson's (or Nielsen's) bungalow while Freya pounded away at Wagner.

The 'cudgel-play of Fate' did for Allen, as well as his beautiful brig with her white paint that shone 'like a satin robe'. The jealous hands of his rival, Lieutenant Heemskirk of the Dutch Navy, put paid to both of them. For Heemskirk, like the lieutenant of the gunboat *Kismet*, found a spurious reason at last to arrest his hated rival.

'The courts will have to decide on the legality of this,' said Jasper.

'Oh, yes, the courts! Certainly. I am going to take her to Makassar in tow. I shall keep you on board here with me.'

And he did, towing the *Bonito* 'at great speed as if for a wager'. Until after a time 'the deep-toned blast of the gunboat's steam whistle made Allen shudder by its unexpectedness. He leaped from where he stood. "You will be on Tamissa Reef!" he yelled.' But there was nothing he could do to stop the *Bonito*'s destruction. The tow-line had been let go at the blast of the whistle, and the brig was 'cast adrift, shooting across the gunboat's stern with the impetus of her speed'.

> She ran upright in a terrible display of her gift of speed, with an incomparable air of life and grace. She ran on till the smooth level of water in front of her bows seemed to sink down suddenly as if sucked away; and, with a strange, violent tremor of her mastheads she stopped, inclined her lofty spars a little, and lay still . . . already lonely, already desolate . . . .

For a little while Allen could not take in the full, irreversible horror of what had happened. The *Komet* had reached Makassar and Heemskirk had called a sampan to take himself ashore, when at last Jasper came to himself and looked up.

> 'Gone on the reef!' he said, in an astounded tone. 'On-the-reef!'
> 'On the very top of high-water spring tides,' Heemskirk struck in, with vindictive, exulting violence. 'On the very top. And now you may go ashore to the courts, you damned Englishman!'

On that long stretch of water from Palanro, the sea around *Fiona* was like a rolling expanse of peacock-coloured shot silk. In the galley, Wilfred sliced limes, boiled water, added tea from a green plastic bowl and sugar from a red one, careful not to waste a grain, and then called, 'Tea ready!' Was it here that Lieutenant Heemskirk had revelled in his obscene triumph? Murray had put up the awning over the cockpit and had begun washing the decks.

We ourselves were nearly on 'the very top' of Tomisa Reef, but there was no sign of it. Tomisa was covered by the tide. I could only imagine I heard the deep-toned blast of the *Komet*'s steam-whistle in the roaring of *Fiona*'s sails. The mountains of Celebes looked placidly across the peaceful Strait. Even the ghost of the pretty *Bonito* was no more.

Before reaching Makassar we made a tally. Since leaving Donggala we had lost, through theft: one big clasp knife, a dinghy pump, a pair of sail-repair scissors, a fishing line, the lead line, a pair of dividers and

12,000 rupiahs. All these things had disappeared during visits to *Fiona* of marine policemen and port officials. It was significant, we thought, that without exception they chose to come aboard after dark. They seemed to prefer 11 p.m. or three in the morning. Earlier experience had told them, no doubt, that people were less alert at those hours.

Seventeen

A sort of rowdy Feydeau farce was being acted out on two twin-tiered passenger motor boats in the Makassar prau harbour. Both of the large, ugly, ramshackle wooden craft kept their generators pounding away long after dark, and pop music – thudding drums and guitars like electric saws – screamed late into the night. Cabin doors opened and banged shut and men slammed in and out, and their laughing and shouting resounded around the stone harbour walls as if it were an echo chamber.

The prau harbour was old and high but not wide. We had tied *Fiona* up alongside stone steps that led to the wharf by the *shahbandar*'s office, among an assortment of tugs, harbour launches, a tender and three large *pinisi*s that could not have been less than 100 tons each, and whose wonderful white masts towered over the other vessels, even over the roofs of the dockside houses and godowns. Outside, behind a line of derricks, longer wharves were reserved for ocean-going steamers, and evidently the *shahbandar* was out on one of them. A note stuck to his door with tape said: 'Come tomorrow at 9.'

The music, heat and the biggest mosquitoes we had ever seen repelled sleep. Anti-mosquito coils, which had worked perfectly against flying insects in Singapore, seemed merely to stimulate the local variety. I slept for an hour or two on deck, and next day my cheeks and eyelids were swollen with bites. I went ashore as soon as the sun was well up and booked two rooms in an hotel – the Grand – for the next night. I wanted to see Makassar, and apart from noise and insects the prau harbour was too enclosed by gates and guards who made things difficult going in and out.

The Grand was an old Dutch hotel built, I suppose, in the 1920s or 1930s, which stood four-square and imposing in the centre of the town. It was a magnificent colonial pile. Somerset Maugham had stayed there. My room was huge and contained three beds under a wooden-framed mosquito net, each equipped with a Dutch wife – which is not a buxom and obliging blonde from Utrecht or Eindhoven, but a long bolster which you hug to your overheated body in order to absorb the sweat. I wondered if Maugham had suffered from insect bites as I did. Despite the net, a good number of mosquitoes clung to the wall, sleeping by day, no doubt to work up an appetite for the busy night ahead. They had to be beaten out of the net with a towel or done to death with an insecticide spray before you could think of sleep.

The Grand's dining room had outstandingly high ceilings, from which two twirling fans hung down and wobbled about threateningly on long metal stalks as though about to crash down and decapitate the guests in the middle of their heavy Dutch breakfast of fried eggs, cheese, tea, jam, bread and incongruous dishes of hundreds and thousands. The walls carried huge and vivid murals of exaggeratedly muscular, saronged Malays hauling praus through shallow water against a background of exotic Douanier Rousseau jungle and exaggeratedly swirling clouds. Another favourite scene showed moustached Bugis rajahs on horseback hunting deer with bows and arrows.

Once ashore, the first thing Wilfred wanted was sweets. Not drinking or smoking, he guzzled instead handfuls of candy, and now the great Arabist and the hunter of lion and wild boar said greedily,

'Well, I'm going out to look for some licorice allsorts or bull's eyes.'

'Bull's eyes?' said Murray. 'I thought a great Arab trekker like you would go in more for sheep's eyes.'

'Hmm.'

Murray may have been impertinent, but more important he had a fever and a temperature of 102°F. As soon as we could we took him in a pedicab to a doctor recommended by the hotel who we found sitting at a desk in his bungalow almost invisible behind a humming cloud of mosquitoes, wearing a dilapidated Panama hat and puffing cigarette smoke in all directions to keep them off.

'Don't worry. Not much malaria here,' he said to soothe Murray, flapping his hand at the insects. 'But cholera is endemic, of course. Have you blood in your stool by chance?'

Murray had not; nor had he got cholera. In a day or two, after a good few pills of different colours, he was cured.

*

Makassar – saddled these days for some official, and maybe officious, reason with the unmemorable name Ujung Pandang – is still called Makassar by many people living thereabouts. It is the major port of Celebes and was universally known under that name since at least the sixteenth century, when it was dominated by the nearby kingdom of Gowa. Malays, Portuguese, English, Danes, French, Manila Spanish and finally the Dutch found it a most convenient trading centre, placed as it was in the middle of the Malay Archipelago, halfway between the western islands of Sumatra and Singapore, and the islands east of Bali and all the way to Ambon, Ternate and Ceram.

Alfred Russel Wallace found Makassar prettier and cleaner than any town he had yet seen in the East. The houses were whitewashed, and by order of the Governor the roads in front of them had to be watered by each householder at four o'clock sharp every afternoon. Visitors noted the lack of refuse on the mile-long street of Dutch and Chinese offices that ran along the seafront. Several square-rigged trading vessels and a 42-gun frigate lay in the harbour the day Wallace arrived, surrounded by gunboats and cutters the Dutch Navy used to chase pirates or catch European gun-runners sneaking arms and powder to bellicose natives. Lieutenant Heemskirk, the Nemesis of poor Jasper Allen, was in charge of one of them at a later date, waiting for the *Bonito* to fall into his net.

The *Bonito* incident created a sensation in little Makassar. A sailing vessel on the reef? Why was that? Even Europeans rose from their desks to go to the window to peer up the coast at the unexplained wreck. They peered at poor, ruined Jasper Allen, too. The day Heemskirk dropped him ashore, Allen – shipless, bereft – staggered into the Orange House, an hotel in which he was well known, with a set face, ignoring everyone, as if under the influence of drugs. He was never to recover. Day by day he shambled down the seafront, past the great seventeenth century walls of Fort Rotterdam, its garrison buildings and its church, to a point opposite the remains of his pretty brig. Daily he watched her deteriorate into matchwood – that little craft Freya had so sweetly described as 'a perfect darling of a ship' and in which Jasper had dreamed of carrying her away to 'ever after' happiness.

Olmeijer's (or Almayer's) Makassar was quite another matter. Looking back from Berau on his time there twenty years before Lingard took him off to Borneo and made him his agent up that remote river, he saw himself young, slim and confident in a white suit, expecting to make a fortune. In the fiction of *Almayer's Folly* he recollected he had thought it was the beginning of a new existence for him. His father, a subordinate official employed in the Botanical Gardens of Buitenzorg, was no doubt delighted to place his son in such a firm. The young man himself too was nothing loth to leave the poisonous shores of Java, and the meagre comforts of the parental bungalow, where the father grumbled all day at the stupidity of native gardeners, and the mother from the depths of her long easy chair bewailed the lost glories of Amsterdam, where she had been brought up, and of her position as the daughter of a cigar dealer there.

Charles Olmeijer might have shared exactly similar thoughts, for the original of 'Kaspar Almayer' was also a Eurasian who was born in Surabaya in 1848 and was to die there in 1900, and he, like Kaspar, had started out as a storekeeper in Makassar before William Lingard took a fancy to him and posted him to Berau in 1870.

Makassar in 1977 had not changed so much that I could not visualise it then,

> the image of Hudig's lofty warehouses with their long straight avenues of gin cases and bales of Manchester goods; the big door swinging noiselessly; the dim light of the place, so delightful after the glare of the streets; the little railed off spaces among the piles of merchandise where the Chinese clerks, neat, cool and sad-eyed, wrote rapidly and in silence amidst the din of the working gangs . . . .

Almayer worked at a table not far from a little green painted door by which a Malay in a red sash and turban pulled at a string as regularly as a machine. The string worked a punkah on the other side of the door where old Hudig – the Master – sat enthroned, holding noisy receptions with visiting ships' masters, particularly with Lingard.

'Velcome, Captain!' Hudig would roar. 'Ver' you gome vrom? Bali, eh? Got bonies? I vant bonies. Gome in!'

Makassar is a sleepy place now; attractively situated on the rim of a clear blue sea where the big ships come and go as they always did; and commercial aircraft fly in and out, too. It still has life; it is still the centre of the Islands. But recently it has lost something of its maritime importance, and of course – at least on the map, if not on the tongues of men – it has lost its world-famous name. Conrad described the Makassar of a hundred years ago as 'teeming with life and commerce', peopled by

> bold spirits in search of money and adventure. Bold, reckless, keen on business, not disinclined for a brush with the pirates that were to be found on many a coast as yet. The Dutch merchants called those men English pedlars; some of them were undoubtedly gentlemen for whom

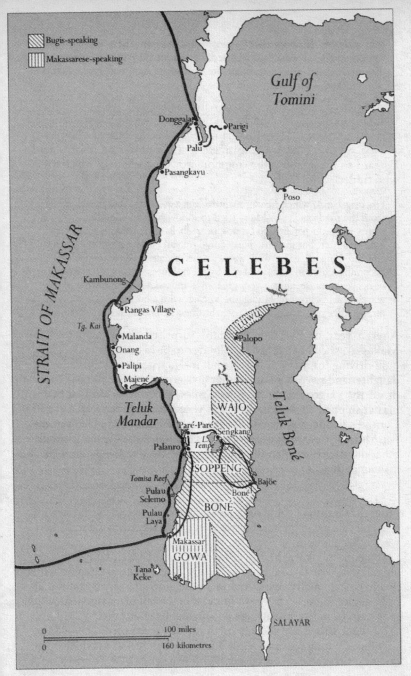

that kind of life had a charm; most were seamen; the acknowledged king of them all was Tom Lingard, he whom the Malays, honest or dishonest, quiet fishermen or desperate cut-throats, recognised as the 'Rajah Laut' – the King of the Sea.

Tom Lingard – like his original, William Lingard – was a rich man. 'Captain Lingard,' Mr Vinck, Hudig's cashier, would say solemnly, 'has lots of money. More than Hudig! *He has discovered a river.*'

That was it! That was the single fact, Conrad said, that placed Lingard so much above the common crowd of seagoing adventurers who traded with Hudig.

His brig *Flash*, which he commanded himself, would disappear quietly from the roadstead . . . . Many tried to follow him and find that land of plenty for gutta-percha and rattans, pearl shells and birds' nests, wax and gum-dammar, but the little *Flash* could outsail every craft in those seas. And so Lingard came and went on his secret or open expeditions, becoming a hero in Almayer's eyes by the boldness and enormous profits of his ventures, seeming a very great man indeed as he marched into the warehouse . . . greeting Hudig, the Master, with a boisterous, 'Hallo, old pirate! Alive yet?' as a preliminary to business behind the little green door.

After a year or two Tom Lingard surprised many onlookers in Makassar when he snapped up Almayer to be his clerk – 'to do all my quill-driving for me' was how he put it – married him to his adopted daughter and swept him off up that mysterious river, to keep account of all the cargoes of brass gongs, rifles, gunpowder and cloth his master shipped up there in the *Flash*. One difference between fact and Conrad's fiction was that *William* Lingard's ship was called not the *Flash* but the *Coeran*, the first of three sailing ships he owned. The only other difference was that the quill-driver he took up the Berau spelled his name Olmeijer.

From the Grand we could see a park and a curious Dutch church with a steeple like a witch's hat. But we were some way from the sea. There were other things to investigate.

Someone in Jakarta had given me the name of a well-known marine animal collector in Makassar called Dr Carl Bundt, a German who had lived here many years. And in a bungalow in a street that ran at right angles to the seafront we found him – a tall man, stooped, with grey hair, of indeterminate age. He invited us in at once.

'You want to see my orchids or the shells, gentlemen?' He led the way down a long passage beside a line of small offices in which open doorways revealed tables covered with seashells.

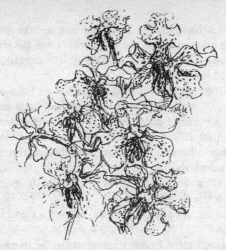

We followed him to a small garden at the back of the house where orchids in earthenware pots stood in rows climbing up slim bamboo poles. They were of many colours, principally white and purple.

As we admired them, Dr Bundt shook his heavy head sadly. '*Ja, ja,* but the orchids are dying with the forests. You cut trees, you destroy orchids, *nicht wahr?*' He smiled. 'Some of these flowers are sick. Sometimes I must travel. If the boss is not there, the boys forget to water them, to look after them . . . .'

The doctor had been born here before the First World War. In the Second he had taken to the hills when the Japanese invaded Celebes. Makassar had been badly bombed. I thought I had heard that his wife had died then.

'I have had heart trouble,' he was saying now. 'And blood pressure. Well, I am not so young. I have to be careful. Yet I worked four hours today already.'

We walked slowly through the lines of orchids, followed by a troop of yapping dachshunds of various ages and lengths of hair.

'It is difficult now to collect new specimens,' said Bundt, ignoring them. 'It is forbidden by the government to collect orchids in the forests.' His voice took on an ironic tone. 'Of course, gentlemen, it is not forbidden to cut down, destroy the trees. Oh no! You are allowed to burn hundreds, thousands of hectares.' He shrugged his heavy shoulders. 'The forests, you know, will never come back. Never.'

He waved a big hand vaguely towards the street.

'My neighbour across the way has bought 50,000 hectares. And what – ?'

He raised his hands palm upwards like a high priest offering, without much hope, a gift to the gods and shook his shaggy head.

'He cut down *all*,' he said with a heavy sigh of despair. Alfred Russel Wallace should have heard all this.

Pursued by the yelping train of dachshunds we followed Bundt into a room full of shells. Huge conches lay side by side in open boxes; yellow-lipped mother-of-pearl, like grotesquely enlarged oysters, and giant pink-lipped clams like grinning man-traps, jostled ginger-coloured sponges the size of my fist and strange dumpy shells that looked extraordinarily like cakes covered with pink icing sugar. All around us lay an amazing variety of shells: fragile sea urchins, stringing shells, the dangerous cones.

Wilfred, picking up a cone shell the size of a thimble, asked, 'Do these harm you?'

'You'd be dead,' cried Bundt triumphantly, 'in five hours.'

'And where do you find them?'

'Mind your feet on any reef. You would have only five hours.'

The cone shells may have been deadly but they were exquisite. They were covered with tiny delicate markings like regularly spaced bird's feet or the minute cuneiform etchings you find on Babylonian seals.

In separate boxes were long knobbly sprays of black coral like carbonised wooden filigree work. Looking at it, Bundt sighed again.

'If the government could stop people bombing the reefs for fish. The coral is all destroyed.'

Drinking tea in Bundt's sitting room, talk of destruction continued.

Wilfred said, 'I've known places in Africa where you could once have seen four hundred or more elephants. Now you wouldn't see one.'

'The same here with the antelopes,' sighed Bundt. 'They kill them for their antlers. The crocodiles, huge devils, four or five metres – killed for their skins. The people here claim their medicine men can "call" crocodiles and that when they call they come.'

'I've seen that in Ethiopia,' said Wilfred. 'I was there when the crocs came across the river. Leopards are doomed, too; killed for women's coats. The trouble is that no one protects anything any more.'

'Protect – hah!' shouted Bundt scornfully. 'They protect the pocket. *Ja?* Protect only the pocket! Do you know the Bugis saying about a corrupt man – "Someone who eats like a bird and shits like a buffalo." How's that, eh?'

We told Bundt how we had been offered dugong meat by the crew of a prau and had had to throw it overboard.

'*Ach*, don't eat!' Bundt said in disgust, and went on, 'Did you know about dugong tears? You would never kill one if you saw that. Well, a dugong keeps its eyes open under water – in the liddle bit murky water of the shallows, you see. Above water, it makes tears to wet the eyes to clean them. And people say, "Ooh, ooh – the dugong is crying!"'

Dugongs are mammals or, as Bundt put it, 'Real cows. They swim very fast, which is their protection from sharks. The dugong's tooth is very high up inside the head. You have to cut open the head to get the huge root out.' I was glad I had not bought that cigarette holder.

'I tell you,' Bundt continued, 'one evening I am in my canoe, I look for a dugong. When there's just a liddle bit light and my paddle is making no noise, suddenly I hear "Phew, phew" and there it is, the dugong, floating and going down to feed on the seaweed. What a strange animal! They are so quick and sometimes four metres long.'

Bundt waved us goodbye amid a furious cacophony of barking.

Makassar profited greatly from Singapore's rise in importance as the halfway trading station between West and East. Trade boomed in every island commodity from pearls and sea slugs to copra, sandalwood and the famous macassar oil which Victorian gentlemen plastered on their hair, obliging their wives to protect the backs of their armchairs with white cloths called antimacassars.

The town had been dominated since time immemorial by the ancient kingdom of Gowa, which was endlessly at loggerheads with the untameable Bugis rajahdoms further inland and had its capital a few miles south of Makassar.

Alfred Russel Wallace visited it:

> Before I could move to any more promising district it was necessary to obtain permission from the Rajah of Goa, whose territories approach to within two miles of the town of Makassar . . . . My friend Mr Mesman accompanied me on my visit to the Rajah with whom he was great friends. We found his Majesty seated out of doors, watching the erection of a house. He was naked from the waist up, wearing only the usual short trousers and sarong. Two chairs were brought out for us, but all the chiefs and other natives were seated on the ground . . . . Permission was immediately granted me to go where I liked . . . . Some wine was brought us, and afterwards some detestable coffee.

Thanks to Dr Bundt we had the name and address of the son-in-law of the last rajah of Gowa – 'last' because, Indonesia having become an independent republic in 1950, there was no longer a rajah. His son-in-law's name was Andi Ma'mun; 'Andi' being a noble title, Bundt said.

Andi Ma'mun lived in a low tile-floored bungalow on a narrow tree-lined street on the way south, and was welcoming in a shy, reserved sort of way. He would like to show us the old capital of Gowa, he said, and the royal regalia there. The walls of his own sitting room were decorated with faded photographs of former rajahs; one was dressed in some sort of hussar uniform with gold facings, and carried a shako under one arm.

Gowa was less than an hour's drive away. More than a hundred years ago Alfred Russel Wallace had seen it like this:

> I went to Goa again, accompanied by Mr Mesman, to beg the Rajah's assistance in getting a small house built for me near the forest. We found him at a cock fight in a shed near his palace, which however he immediately left to receive us, and walked with us up an inclined plane of boards which serves for stairs to his house. This was large, well built, and lofty, with bamboo floors and glass windows. The greater part of it seemed to be to be one large hall divided by the supporting posts. Near a window sat the Queen squatting on a rough wooden armchair, chewing her everlasting sirih and betel-nut, while a brass spittoon by her side and sirih-box in front were ready to administer to her wants. The Rajah seated himself opposite to her in a similar chair, as a similar spittoon and sirih-box were held by a little boy squatting at his side. Two other chairs were brought for us. Several young women, some of them the Rajah's daughters, others slaves, were standing about; a few were working at frames making sarongs . . . . The princesses were, it is true, sufficiently good-looking, yet neither their persons nor their garments had that appearance of freshness and cleanliness without which no other charms can be contemplated with pleasure. Everything had a dingy and faded appearance, very disagreeable and unroyal to a European eye. The only thing that excited some degree of admiration was the quiet and dignified manner of the Rajah, and the great respect always paid to him. None can stand here in his presence and when he sits on a chair, all present (Europeans of course excepted) squat upon the ground. The highest seat is literally, with these people, the place of honour and the sign of rank. So unbending are the rules in this respect that when an English carriage which the Rajah of Lombok had sent for arrived, it was found impossible to use because the driver's seat was the highest, and it had to be kept as a show in its coach-house.

At Sunggunimasa, the old capital, the palace was very like the one Wallace had described: a pleasant wooden structure with steep wooden steps to its door. It had been built as recently as 1936, and had been used by the last of the rajahs. Now it was a museum.

Scarlet and silver ceremonial umbrellas – and a grander one in royal yellow – filled one small wooden-floored room in the museum. Glass cases of elaborate costumes in green velvet with silk sarongs and gold-ringed sleeves lined the walls of others. There were drums of wood-bark, with heavy thongs that enabled drummers to sling them across their bodies and beat them by hand; there were flutes, and golden cymbals. In glass cases thick bracelets like golden snakes lay beside heavy gold ear-rings. A museum assistant reverently unwrapped krisses with shining blades two and a half feet long, whose ornate buffalo-horn handles winked with semiprecious jewels.

A brass plaque dated 1818 had an inscription to say it was a gift from the British government

to
Krain Lemban Parang Rajah of Gowa
in testimony of his attachment
and faithful services

'As the last rajah's son-in-law,' I said to Andi Ma'mun, 'why not bring this plaque the British gave your great-great-grandfather and show it to the Queen?'

'Oh, I wish I could.'

The crown of Gowa glinted in a glass case like a golden fire – it was fat and round; a shining, pudding-shaped crown; gold with a scattering of red and green stones set into it. The most unusual thing about it was a curious sort of brim formed by a circle of golden spokes.

Two golden ceremonial umbrellas guarded the museum's entrance. They were shaped vaguely in the form of palm trees. 'The sugar palm,' Andi Ma'mun said. 'Very common in Gowa. The palm water is very like wine and we call it *tuak*.' He laughed. 'All the people like it. It makes you strong and you are not afraid to die. In your mouth, it dances.' Later I tried *tuak*. It was cool, packed a punch, and it *did* 'dance' in your mouth. No doubt, given a pint of *tuak* the most timid of warriors would believe the Bugis saying: *'Death among friends is but a festival.'*

On the green outside the palace a football match was in progress. Shouts of what sounded like battle cries punctuated the hot and steamy air. I pressed forward, hoping we had come across a replay of some old battle between Gowa and its Bugis rival Boné, recreated between two goal posts. But this was a friendly match between two local secondary schools; there was not a kriss to be seen.

Andi Ma'mun wanted to show us the coronation ground of Gowa. It stood near an ancient mosque, a gloomy pyramidical structure darkened by years of damp and with a strange tunnel-like entrance. The sacred stone on which for centuries the rajahs of Gowa had been crowned was confined behind an iron railing. Descending from Heaven, so legend said, the first Queen of Gowa had sat on that stone, and every king since her time had followed suit, bowing his head to receive the crown from the hands of a religious judge, until the last *hakim* had placed the pudding-shaped crown on the head of the last rajah of all, whose coronation five-year-old Andi Ma'mun had witnessed in 1946.

Among a grim, rather chilling collection of tombs lay buried the rajah of Gowa in Conrad's time: Kumala, Sultan Abdul Kadir, crowned as a boy just before Victoria became Queen of England, and rajah until 1893. We felt our way through its cavernous entrance into a high-domed place whose walls, mildewed and cobwebbed, lost themselves in shadow and peered about through dank air that smelled vaguely of bat droppings and death. Dracula may have been lurking there. It was no place to loiter in.

Fiona sailed in a day or two. Mac pointed her bows towards the gap in the reefs and then due west on a course that would take us south of Pulau Laut and on to Carimata and Sarawak.

Looking back, I saw the low, elegant line of Makassar and the church spire like a witch's hat. Heavy clouds lay like a thick scarf across the barrier of mountains of the lands of the Bugis. Occasional flashes of lightning illuminated the clouds, and now and again a peal of thunder rolled down to us muffled by the distance.

Wilfred was reading *The Rescue* in *Fiona*'s cockpit. He laid it down after a while and said, 'I've given up *The Rescue*. I can't excuse Lingard's appalling conduct in abandoning to their deaths his Wajo friends and allies for those Europeans in their wretched yacht. They should have been left to fend for themselves. How can Conrad have allowed Lingard to behave like that? Do you agree?'

I had worried about that, too. Had not Lingard, for the sake of an infatuation with Mrs Travers – the wife of a man whose 'life and thought', as Conrad put it, 'ignorant of human passion, were devoted to extracting the greatest possible amount of personal advantage from human institutions' – broken his word to Prince Hassim and his sister Immada, knowing that in doing so he had condemned them to death?

With the thunder of Wajo at our back the matter seemed of supreme importance.

'Yes. I do,' I answered. 'I agree very much.'

Eighteen

Twelve years later I returned to Makassar.

The same thick scarf of grey cloud lay across the mountain barrier on the eastern horizon, and as before, lightning flickered like cannon flashes among the hilltops of Bugis-land. Nothing much seemed to have changed.

In the town the Grand Hotel was gone, and although I tried to find its former site I was unable to; I think a shopping centre had replaced it. So presumably the fine dining room murals of prau-men with their boats and the moustached rajahs out hunting were rubble now.

I came by steamer this time – a modern, well-conducted Indonesian government ship on a regular run from Jakarta, with a wheelhouse full of officers in crisp white uniforms, gold bars of rank on their shoulders and a good deal of 'scrambled egg' on their uniform caps. Outside Makassar the ship took on a pilot, and despite our radar we reduced speed to edge through the reefs as carefully as Mac had done in little *Fiona*.

This time I had only one companion: a Dutch professor and resident of Jakarta, Jacob Vredenbregt, linguist, writer, entomologist, art collector, the representative in South-East Asia of Leiden University, and general *bon vivant*. I don't know how long Jacob has spent in different capacities in Indonesia – not much less than forty years, I should judge, and I can't see him ever leaving it. He speaks *bahasa Indonesia* like a native, and a few other local dialects besides. In his youth he lived and worked on coffee plantations in East Java and he writes stories about that colonial time. He collects butterflies, too, so that whenever I visit his house outside Jakarta I think of Stein in *Lord Jim*, Stein, the old Bavarian butterfly collector, and the wealthy and respected island trader who thought he could help Jim's incurable romanticism by sending him to represent him on the Berau. The Stein described by Captain Marlow, who introduced him to Jim, was

> . . . tall and stooping, he stood alone in the middle of the room between the rows of butterfly cases. '*Ach*! Is it you, my friend?' he said, sadly peering through his glasses. A drab sack of alpaca hung, unbuttoned down to his knees. He had a Panama hat on his head, and there were deep furrows on his pale cheeks . . . .

Jacob Vredenbregt is not stooped, nor have I ever seen him in a Panama hat or a drab sack of alpaca. He does, however, share other attributes with Stein. For example he has the, sometimes deceptively, 'innocent smile which makes him appear benevolently ready to lend his ear', and his spectacles, like Stein's, certainly have a tendency to ride up over a massive forehead and thick, bushy eyebrows.

Yet there are other likenesses. When it comes to houses, Stein's and Jacob's seem surprisingly similar. In *Lord Jim* Marlow says:

> You know Stein's house and the two immense reception rooms, uninhabited and uninhabitable, clean, full of solitude and of shining things that look as if never beheld by the eye of man?

One difference lies in the fact that Jacob's reception rooms are immensely habitable. Another difference is that Jacob has never, like Stein, gone in for *Buprestidae* and *Longicorns* – 'beetles all – horrible miniature monsters', so his interior walls are not catacombs of beetle corpses. Jacob favours moths.

Jacob's house outside Jakarta is spacious and surrounded by extensive gardens. Like Stein, he lives with a magnificent collection of books, which fill numerous long shelves on his library walls, leaving little wall space for his glass-fronted cases of ceramics and statuettes of wood or stone from all over the islands.

Behind Jacob's house is a large ornamental fish pond, covered with a dense blanket of lotus plants. Now and again a snake slides out of it and menaces Jacob's tame deer, the guinea fowl, the peacocks and the white-backed pheasant with a long silvery tail. At one time Jacob bought four superb and immense eagles. They glared morosely at visitors through the bars of their cages until Jacob took pity on them and released them and sadly watched them flap away towards the hills of Java.

The centrepiece of the living room is a large seated buddha lit by a spotlight. Old Javanese portraits and fine gilded antique screens adorn other parts of the room round a wide wooden staircase which leads to a collection of Indonesian paintings. A passage is lined with caged birds – cockatoos, blackcapped bulbuls, a golden oriole and red and purple macaws.

Jacob had taught linguistics at the University of Makassar for five years. He volunteered to go there with me partly to make an expedition to Boné, the capital of Bugis rajahdom. I was delighted. Jacob's perfect Indonesian and his knowledge of Celebes were an invaluable bonus and, besides, he had one other mission – to arrange for the student son of a friend, a Buginese teacher, to supervise the construction of a model of his Jakarta house in silver by a colony of expert Malay silversmiths living on an island off Makassar. The student, who spoke English, would become my translator when Jacob returned to Jakarta.

Now that the Grand was no more, Jacob recommended an hotel on the seafront; a place with fluctuating electricity and an erratic water system, but clean. Sometimes water, ice-cold or scalding, came into one's room by the bathroom pipes, and at others cascaded in through the ceiling; one was kept on one's toes. The wonderful view made up for everything; that and the hotel's sympathetic and diminutive manager who, it seemed, was related to an important personage in the government of the town.

The hotel looked out on an immense sweep of sea and islands. Immediately under my window was a narrow road and a low sea wall from which small boys fished, and beyond that nothing but the bay and the emerald islands running out to the Strait of Makassar.

Makassar is a great place for fish. Night and day fishing boats scattered themselves across the bay and among the islands surrounding it – small sailing craft with upswept prows, whose crews, when they were not fishing, sat languidly cleaning their nets, chatting and smoking, or dousing themselves with water from buckets they lowered into the bay. I spent hours watching the little vessels with their pale green and white hulls, their sometimes royal blue masts, and their sails like gaily coloured sharks' fins moving through the water. Some had gracefully curved sails, Arab-style, and I could see the crews haul them up opposite my window as they moved out to the fishing grounds. Launches – the taxis of the people who lived beside the sea – scurried continuously to and fro over the water, trailing their frothing wakes beyond the islands or towards the harbour.

In the rainy season the weather was erratic. Squalls swept out of the Strait without warning, and heavy colonnades of rain forced all sailing vessels to head as swiftly as they could for the safety of the islands, barely visible by then in the mist thrown up on the surface of the bay by raindrops the size of bullets. But on clear nights the fishermen hoisted pressure lamps to their mastheads or hung them over the side on bamboo poles to attract the fish, and then a whole fleet of little boats lay out there glowing in the darkness like a bobbing constellation of waterborne stars.

The first evening Shafaat, the Bugis student son of Jacob's friend, came to the hotel and said of course he was ready to come with us to Boné, and would also arrange Jacob's silver house with the people of the island. And he assured me that after Jacob's return to Jakarta – he could spare only a limited time in Makassar – he would accompany me wherever I wanted to go and would translate for me. This was good news, because, of course, Shafaat knew Bugis as well as he knew *bahasa Indonesia*.

I wondered what had happened to Andi Ma'mun and, before anything else, we went to call on him. He lived in the same house in the same leafy street leading south from the town, and after twelve years recognised me at once. His wife had died a year ago, he said, but, never mind, he was not alone; he had eight children. He was still in charge of the Gowa museum.

'We had twelve visitors last month,' he said proudly. 'Mostly German and Dutch, but British and French as well.' He gave us tea in the room I remembered so well with the pictures of the old rajahs still on the walls.

I did not remember having seen before a large imposing house that stood across the street from Andi Ma'mun's bungalow. It was a well-kept and well-built two-storey house; its tall windows had elegant white shutters with green-painted frames, and it was set back in a garden of trees and clipped hedges. It was so imposing that Jacob stopped a passer-by to ask him who lived there. The passer-by, an oldish man walking under an open umbrella to keep the sun off his bald head, smiled and said: 'The King of Boné lives here.'

'I've never heard of a king of Boné living here,' Shafaat said in a puzzled voice.

Nevertheless a sign on the gate said, 'B. S. Mappanyukki, ex-Rajah of Boné'. And as we walked boldly past it towards the front door, a small boy emerged. 'Come in,' he said as if he had been waiting for us. He sat us down and offered us tea in a big room, high-ceilinged and well furnished with sofas, tables and several easy chairs. A wide open staircase led out of it to rooms above.

After a minute or two a man came in. He was wearing a songkok, a checkered sarong and short-sleeved shirt with green geometrical patterns on a white background. He had rather long black hair, was short and stocky, and might have been anything from forty-five to fifty years old. He smiled, perched himself jauntily on the edge of an armchair upholstered in imitation leather and looked at us curiously but with no sign of surprise.

'The Rajah of Boné?' Jacob asked him tentatively.

'I am the Rajah,' he said with a gracious nod of his head. 'Let me show you something.' He skipped to a wall and beckoned us to look at a photograph of the late President Sukarno. He was standing with a group of men in songkoks and sarongs.

'Those are,' said the Rajah, pointing at them, 'the former rajahs of Boné and Luwu. Luwu is the older one.'

Well, Jacob explained, as it happened, our intention was to go to Boné.

That excited the Rajah. 'Let's go, yes. Good idea. I'll come with you,' he cried, springing up. 'Which day? Wednesday? Tomorrow? As the King of Boné, you know, I have duties there.'

He added inconsequentially, 'We might go to Luwu at the same time.'

Luwu was a long way north of Boné; I knew that from the map I had just bought.

'From the distances on the map, we would never make Boné *and* Luwu,' I suggested. 'And this is the rainy season. The roads – '

The Rajah rolled his eyes and waved a dismissive hand. 'Well, never mind . . . .'

He scribbled something on a scrap of paper and I took it. 'My name,' he said.

'Bau Sawa Mappanyukki,' I read.

The Rajah fitted a cigarette into a holder. 'I am the thirty-fourth king, you know.'

In a gloomy silence a servant brought cups of cocoa and set them down on tables beside us.

'The Sultan of Brunei is a relative,' the Rajah continued apropos of nothing at all. 'He is very rich. *Very* rich,' he repeated. 'One night I thought: Islam is part of the state philosophy; Islam is also the word of Allah, and Boné is the heart of Islam. So if the Sultan of Brunei . . . will . . . .' His chin sank to his chest and he closed his eyes.

To my relief Jacob got up and headed for the door.

'Goodbye! We will let you know which day we leave for Boné,'

Jacob called. In the street he breathed a sigh of relief. 'Phew!' he said, mopping his brow. 'The bloody man's crazy. Crazy!'

A few miles beyond Gowa is a large farm belonging to an old *daeng*, a Gowanese nobleman and friend of Jacob's.

The old *daeng* may have money but he does not show it; he prefers it to appear that he is down to his last rupiah. His house is woebegone: a wooden structure of uncertain solidity standing at the end of a muddy lane that is almost impassable in the rains, in a copse of areca palms and the broad-leafed *nangka* or jackfruit, a football-sized object with a rough skin and sweetish, creamy flesh covering a stone the size of a bantam's egg. There is a store-shed and nearby a cockeyed 'summer house' looking down a wide vista of rice fields. Clouds of mosquitoes infest the house and the trees, making it difficult to sit or stand without slapping or scratching.

The nobleman spoke faultless Dutch with Jacob and hesitant English with me; he was something of an intellectual. A good many books and papers were scattered higgledy-piggledy about the house – most of those I saw being about Gowanese and Bugis history and politics. He was happy in his poverty – if indeed it was poverty. He was one of those men who are born with a sunny nature: he smiled a lot, exhaling a not unpleasant aura of whisky or *tuak*. We sat under his trees and drank his coffee, perhaps the most delicious I have ever tasted, quite unlike the 'detestable' stuff Wallace had put up with at the court of the Rajah of Gowa.

The *daeng* liked the simple things in life. He talked about his farm, saying he earned enough to support thirty-two families on his land. He was quite rich, he acknowledged, but he would never use tractors.

'Water buffalo are better. They don't need expensive spare parts,' he laughed.

When Jacob told him about our encounter with Bau Sawa Mappanyukki, he laughed again.

'He is *not* the Rajah of Boné,' he protested. 'If he says so, he is crazy.'

'Ah-ha! I thought so – he *is* crazy!' said Jacob.

'The real Rajah of Boné is living in Jakarta or Surabaya. So I tell you, if you go to Boné with this man you'll be with a lunatic.'

'We shall not,' Jacob assured him.

'Better not,' commented the old man, and he took us for a stroll round his farm. Ducks, rice fields, butterflies, buffaloes, clumps of bamboo – this was a corner of the old Gowa that Alfred Russel

Wallace would have found virtually unchanged. The charming *daeng* might have stepped out of an old print.

The rains continued to fall on the mountains. Next day several bridges were down, 'Wait a day or two,' Shafaat advised us. 'Wait for them to be repaired.'

'Let's go and see the bishop,' said Jacob.

The bishop was Jacob's old friend Monsignor Dr Frans van Roessel, the Archbishop of Makassar, whose house was in a dark, leafy street near the steeple in the shape of a witch's hat.

We found him waiting for us in his study, a bucket of ice and a full bottle of Red Label whisky on the table before him. 'Bless you, my son,' he said, laughing, as Jacob placed a bottle of old Dutch gin beside them. Dressed in a loose short-sleeved cotton shirt which he wore over his trousers, and at seventy-one, short and wide-shouldered, his thinning hair still fair and his eyes brightly benign behind gold-rimmed spectacles, he looked at least ten years younger than his age; tough and alert.

'So you're going to Boné tomorrow, Jacob,' he said. 'And will pass the night there?'

'Is there an hotel? With air conditioning?'

'Oh dear, oh dear,' the Archbishop looked at his old friend sadly. 'You expect air conditioning? I shall pray for you!'

The bishop had fourteen European priests to look after in southern Celebes. It was a big diocese and he got about it by car, even by ship. Preaching the Word of God in the Islands was not always easy, particularly when he sometimes found himself at odds with the Pope over things like celibacy, for example. Celibacy was very difficult for Indonesians to understand – it is unknown to them.

Celibacy ... Catholicism. There were Christian Torajas in central Celebes, the Archbishop said, but none at all in Bugis-land. He was an excellent man but clearly he had his work cut out here where Islam had been universally accepted in the early seventeenth century.

And with the Bugis, one was in deeper spiritual waters. Pre-Islamic Bugis chronicles tell of kings and queens descending from heaven. And an epic Bugis cycle, *La Galigo*, a massive work written on the leaves of the *lontara* palm, describes how, at the creation, the rulers of Earth, Heaven, Undersea, Sea and Underworld chose a king for this world and how he descended to earth by means of a golden bamboo, to marry the eldest daughter of the king of the Underworld. From this mystical union sprang successive Bugis royal dynasties.

After a period of anarchy future kings by common consent were bound by contracts insisting on their responsibilities as much as on their rights. 'The rights of freedom of the Wajo people will be maintained and defended by the ruler,' a proclamation affirmed. Prince Hassim used words very close to the proclamation to Lingard in *The Rescue*: 'Wajo where every man is free and wears a kriss.' The people of Wajo are proud of their liberal constitution, since among Malays such a thing did not exist outside South Celebes.

Even so, life in Wajo was regularly disrupted by false pretenders to the rajahdom, by treachery of all kinds, and by merciless invasions from other Bugis states – sometimes with Dutch participation. 'We burn our powder amongst ourselves and blunt our weapons upon one another,' Hassim admitted to Lingard.

Defeat, oddly enough, made Wajo's name. A ruthless invasion by the seventeenth century Bugis hero Aru Palakka of Boné destroyed Wajo, and the men of Wajo fled their country in what amounted to a Bugis diaspora. The Wajo Bugis became the region's most intrepid sailors, energetic colonists and active traders; they set up settlements up the Mahakam river in Kalimantan, Selangor, Acheh, Singapore, Johore and other places. Wajo traders were soon renowned and feared throughout the Eastern world. By the time of Conrad and Lingard the common saying among Malays was that a true trader was he who had a properly adventurous spirit, the fearlessness of youth and the sagacity of age. In short, people said, 'Such a man is the ideal trader of Wajo.'

Hassim's mother had been a great princess in Wajo – and almost as soon as the old rajah drew his last breath, a typical Wajo civil war broke out. It was a war, Conrad said, 'of jungle and river, of assaulted stockades and forest ambushes'. Hassim's was a lost cause. It was a question of numbers. Hassim's outnumbered party retreated to the sea; and there as the massacre was about to begin a great thunderstorm descended, and suddenly a ship 'resembling the ships of white men' appeared – so the later legend went – 'as though she had sailed down from the clouds'. When the storm cleared, the ship was gone – God knew where – and Rajah Hassim and Mas Immada, his sister, had disappeared, too.

The truth was that Jaffir, Hassim's faithful servant, had seen Lingard's brig and had risked drowning to swim out to report the desperate state of things. Lingard, true to his solemn promise, had sent his boat to the beach to rescue Hassim, the man who had saved his own life. In the end it took a white woman, Mrs Travers, to make Lingard break his word to the Bugis Hassim.

Lingard's rescue of Hassim had not taken place on the coast of the Makassar Strait we had sailed down in *Fiona*. The Wajo coast ran down the Gulf of Boné, south of Luwu and north of Boné itself.

Boné was where we were headed now. The morning after our dinner with the Archbishop, when Shafaat came to the hotel with a taxi to take us there, thunder still rolled among the hills like the lingering echoes of Aru Palakka's cannon.

'Let's hope the bridges have been mended,' said Jacob.

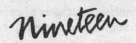

The rain suddenly stopped and the cloud layer over the hills evaporated. By the time we had left Makassar and driven along the shore past the Tomisa reef and the invisible wreck of the *Bromo*, Paré-Paré was bathed in sunlight.

Turning inland, we climbed into a landscape designed by warriors in a fairy story. White limestone ridges lay one behind the other, ramparts enclosing a long, wide rice plain: rocky bastions hundreds of feet high and brown isolated shafts of rock like dragons' teeth pushed out of the soil. This mountainous world was as different from the plain we had left as Heaven from the Empty Earth.

We turned south this time across the face of Wajo: paddy fields, men ploughing with water buffaloes, and marshes bordered with clumps of sedge. Now and again a narrow part of the road was blocked by a string of horses loaded with cylindrical panniers that bulged with sacks of rice or coconuts. The bridges, flimsy things at the best of times, had been repaired but they were slippery with mud and it was a tricky business crossing them. The landscape, flat, green, melancholy, stretched away seemingly for ever, interrupted here and there by copses of bamboo or banana plantations, and the big, shady trees of the Equator.

Further south, the road pushed its way into the mountains, edging round the debris of landslides of the recent past. Slowing down at untrustworthy bridges, we surmounted pass after pass, at last plunging steeply down to the plain beside the grey expanse of the Bay of Boné. The mountains made a formidable natural wall, guarding the old rajahdom from its enemies further inland.

Boné was not, as I had believed, a port; it stood back about three or four miles from the sea. The port itself was called Bajoë, and was inhabited largely by people known as Baju, who lived by and from the sea, had never been pirates and have a harmless reputation as small traders. Belonging to no state of their own, they were called sea-gypsies.

The long road from Boné to the coast ended at the jetty in Bajoë. The coast curved away northwards, barely populated by the look of it. Several small vessels lay alongside the jetty that ran out far into the shallow waters of a wide coastal shelf. By the gangplank of one of the biggest of them, an ungainly double-decked wooden passenger-cargo ferry, a young sailor, dark as a Malay but with the light hair of many Bajos, told us it would set sail soon with a couple of hundred passengers and a cargo of rattans round the cape to Makassar. She looked a top-heavy old tub to me. Could she really carry two hundred passengers as well as a full cargo?

I put on a nice smile, 'Do you lose many ships like this?' I asked.

And he replied, 'Regularly, if the wind gets up.' He said it quite calmly with the fatalism, I suppose, of all true *orang laut*.

This was where Lingard, edging his brig through the reefs that ran all the way up this shore, had anchored in the middle of the thunderstorm. He, too, had seen far off the immense sombre wall of forest-clad hills we had descended only an hour or two before. Hassim's native land, Wajo, lay 20 miles up the coast.

The search for an hotel took time, but the one we eventually stayed in made me think that perhaps the bishop's prayers had been answered. It was clean and cheap. It was not air-conditioned – prayers had their limits evidently – but once the young couple who ran the hotel had dislodged a swarm of sleeping mosquitoes from the furniture and found three fans that worked our rooms were habitable. After dinner of prawns and rice, Jacob poured a glass of 'Glenmorangie – 10 Years Old' whisky, and sent Shafaat to find the curator of the museum. 'Tell him we've heard the regalia of Boné far surpasses that of Gowa,' he called encouragingly after him.

The curator of the Boné museum was a courteous middle-aged man with glasses and two prominent front teeth. To be a museum curator in Celebes evidently required royal blood; this one was called Andi Mappasissi, and he was the nephew of the last rajah.

He laughed and said it was a good thing we had come without the 'Rajah of Boné'. 'The last rajah,' he assured us, 'died in 1968. There are four sons: one a quarter crazy, one half crazy, one three-quarters crazy.'

The museum was larger than that of Gowa and much more modern: a new brick building in which – first things first – you were confronted at once with an artist's impression of Aru Palakka, Boné's warrior hero and despoiler of Makassar and Wajo. The Boné champion was shown with his flag and the strange quotation attributed to him: 'As long as sun and moon endure, so will friendship between Boné and Holland.'

It was not a remark to endear him to present-day nationalists, I thought. A photograph on another wall no doubt gave pleasure to visitors from Wajo and Gowa. It showed smiling, bearded Dutch officers in crumpled uniforms and slouch hats two hundred years after the burial of Aru Palakka. They had just conquered Boné, the subjugation of which, despite the 'enduring' friendship, had cost the Bugis a thousand lives; Boné's rajah (no collaborating Palakka) had been captured after four months of bloody pursuit and guerrilla war.

I asked Andi Mappasissi if rivalry still existed between Waju, Gowa and Boné and he replied, 'Oh, no!'

'Only battles on the football field.'

'Oh, football. Yes.'

A hint of nationalism surfaced in him only momentarily, when I asked him what difference there was in character between the Bugis of Wajo and Boné. He could not resist it: 'The people of Boné,' he replied, 'are pure, typical Bugis. The people of Wajo are rougher, coarser than Boné people. We in Boné are the real Buginese.' If all *orang* Boné, like Andi Mappasissi, insisted on the unique purity of Bugis blood of Boné, I thought, those football matches might still generate some blood-letting.

I had heard already of a superb bejewelled and antique kriss full – it

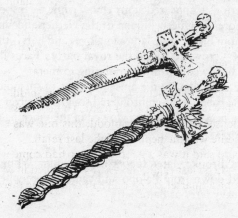

209

was rumoured – of the most powerful Bugis magic; the *pièce de résistance* in the royal Bugis regalia. In a barred room we could see numerous krisses – gold krisses with what looked like dragon-head handles encrusted with diamonds; krisses with handles of silver and carved wood; krisses with sinuous blades that seemed to wriggle like snakes; krisses with smooth, straight, silky blades that looked as if they would slip down behind the collarbone – the standard way of inserting them – and reach the heart as easily as a surgeon's knife. As in Gowa, there was case after case of earrings, some as big as coffee saucers, and anklets and bracelets shaped like golden serpents. 'The *bissus* keep everything clean,' Andi Mappasissi said, referring to the court retinues of transvestite priests whose job it still was.

But the famous kriss of Boné was missing.

'The *bupati* [governor] has taken the kriss to his house.' Andi Mappasissi looked embarrassed, and there was an edge of bitterness in his voice. 'He says it might be stolen here.'

'It *has* been stolen,' remarked Jacob with meaning, fingering the bars and the padlock. The plain fact was that the governor from Java wanted to boast to his guests that the jewel in the museum's crown, the royal kriss of Boné, was hanging over his mantelpiece. No wonder that museum curators like Andi Mappasissi and Andi Ma'mun live in constant fear that the most valuable pieces in their royal collections may be 'borrowed', ostensibly for some exhibition in Jakarta. If this happens, the chances are that those rare pieces will never be seen on Bugis territory again.

Andi Mappasissi had a room at the back of the museum, where we sat in modern armchairs looking at his albums of old photographs. Glasses of tea and fried banana cakes were passed around; a brass spittoon mysteriously appeared at my elbow while we inspected black and white pictures of Queen Juliana of the Netherlands meeting the Dutch Resident in Boné; large ladies in gloves and hats – the wives of Dutch officials – crowded round the royal party. 'Faces like bloody horses,' Jacob bellowed scornfully, pointing to them.

Through the open door to the museum, cases of splendid gold and scarlet Buginese robes, gold-embroidered songkoks, silver boxes and vases sprouting peacocks' feathers glowed in the morning light.

In 1846 James Brooke, later to become the first White Rajah of Sarawak, sailed down from Palopo and came ashore where we had seen the top-heavy ferry at Bajoë jetty.

He noted: 'The hills are peopled with wild tribes. The entire country is wretchedly poor, and both rice and salt are transported from Boni to Makasser.' Riding up to Boné, which was 'as yet small', he was told that the cargoes of Bugis praus were in part procured from the eastward. 'Tortoise shells, gold, mother-of-pearl, etc., come from the eastern islands or the north extremity of Celebes.'

Boné, in Brooke's time, was now the most powerful region in Celebes, the king being chosen by eleven nobles. But 'the people are greatly oppressed and life and wealth is as insecure as in any other Malayan state. A popular assembly shows there is some check upon public acts, though private wrongs may be committed with impunity.'

The Bugis script, Brooke was surprised to see, is quite unlike that of European languages, and bears no resemblance to Chinese characters, or Arabic or Javanese script. To me it looks like arrangements of more or less straight lines of different lengths; the sort of writing birds might try to invent out of a haphazard collection of twigs.

Brooke arrived at the court of Boné in the presence of the ruler and his council.

> There were 3,000–4,000 men in the courtyard in skull caps and blue sarongs over the kriss. The ruler, seated at a table in a moderate-sized hall, is about 50 years of age, dark complexioned, with a good-tempered expression and pleasant manners. He was above middle height and corpulent, and wore a plain long robe of English chintz fastened with a number of gold studs at the throat and wrists. He wore also a plain kris and a black skull cap.

The coffee he served would have been considered good in Stamboul or Paris, Brooke considered, and the tea fit to drink even in Canton.

The ruler, in Brooke's opinion, was a despot whatever sort of 'constitution' he was meant to respect, and his councillors so absurdly servile that 'should he fall from his horse, all about him must fall from their horses likewise'. Should he suddenly decide to bathe, his retainers threw themselves in the water in whatever clothes they happened to be wearing at the time. It sounded to me like the Red Queen and the gardeners in *Alice in Wonderland*, and strange behaviour for people who, Jacob had told me, were obsessed with a kind of congenital machismo.

'Two important things unite Bugis,' Jacob explained. '*Siri*, a concept of honour which can lead to violence in the face of the mildest slights; and *pacce* – more subtle, meaning loyalty and solidarity through thick and thin. That's the clue to the Bugis. They think it is better to die in defence of *siri* – honour – than to live without it. Bugis

211

men walk around like roosters. Their legends are full of stories of kings with penises as big as houses – that sort of thing. That's the *siri* in them. I can't see them plunging into the sea after some mad monarch, but Brooke should have known.'

Back in Makassar, Jacob was due to return to Jakarta. We sat on the balcony of the hotel gazing out at the bay, drinking cold Bols Genever. Relaxing on his last night, Jacob was wearing what he called 'colonial garb', which to him meant what he called 'pay-yamas' – loose-fitting garments, white with wide blue stripes.

I was going to stay to visit Wajo, and later I would look for a ship to take me to Berau. Shafaat, who had to supervise the building of Jacob's silver house, would translate for me until I left.

That last evening with Jacob the sunset was as spectacular as always. The sun, veiled lightly in cloud, was beginning to sink, a deep glowing mass so like a red-hot coal you expected a cloud of steam when it met the sea's horizon. Below us, men, up to their necks in water, were arranging fishing nets; and closer inshore men and women were rootling in the mud for crabs or fishing-bait. The high white hull of a freighter with a blue funnel was passing out of the breakwater, beginning its turn south-west towards Surabaya. And as usual the fishing fleet was crossing the bay on its way to work, showing off the wonderful colours of its sails.

That afternoon, Jacob and I had driven with Shafaat a few miles north of Makassar to the waterfall at Maros – a famous place for butterflies, where the gorgeous creatures flap about you in the sun like chips of jade, sea-green and purple, red and brown. The water thunders down a cliff and all around chalk-white clefts and fissures in the limestone are draped with trailing creepers, bushes and ferns. It is like a scene in a Romantic poem about Xanadu.

It had enchanted Wallace. Tempted to go further and explore the rocky mountains beyond, he reluctantly decided not to: 'I had no guide, and no permission to enter the Bugis territories.' He was satisfied to stand where we stood while 'the gay butterflies – orange, yellow, white, blue and green – rose into the air by hundreds'. Now, among the live butterflies, boys sold dead ones in cellophane packets – all monstrous; some with coffee stripes on dark brown; others with dark wings marked with light green ovals the colour of a sunlit reef, flecked with crimson – all imaginable, and many unimaginable, colours and shades.

Knowing Jacob had begun to collect moths again in recent years, I took out my copy of *Lord Jim* to read out loud what old Stein had had to say about butterflies.

Look! The beauty – but that is nothing – look at the accuracy, the harmony. And so fragile! And so strong! And so exact! This is nature – the balance of colossal forces. Every star is so – and the mighty Kosmos in perfect equilibrium produces – this. This wonder; this masterpiece of Nature – the great artists . . . .

I captured this very rare specimen myself one very fine morning. And I had a very big emotion. You don't know what it is for a collector to capture such a rare specimen. You can't know . . . .

Flop! I got him! When I got up I shook like a leaf with excitement, and when I opened these beautiful wings, my head went round and my legs became so weak with emotion I had to sit on the ground . . . I had dreamed of him in my sleep, and here suddenly I had him in my fingers – for myself. In the words of the poet –

So halt' ich's endlich denn in meinen Händen,
Und nenn' es in gewissem Sinne mein.'

'"At last I hold it in my hands and call it assuredly mine",' Jacob
translated. 'Goethe, of course.'

He went on: 'Do you know the difference between butterflies and
moths? I like moths more and more. At my age I can't go chasing about
in the sun for hours after butterflies. But moths fly mostly at night. You
put a little honey on the trees, the moths become a little bit drunk, and
you can catch them easily. Moths are interesting. If a bird attacks them
they draw up their hands in quite a fearsome way to defend themselves
– quite frightening, really. Butterflies and moths are equally beautiful.
And here in Indonesia, it is true, some of the biggest butterflies are to
be found. Their caterpillars are sometimes huge. You can see tens of
them, even hundreds maybe, all together. If you are silent, you can
even hear them eating. Yes – I tell you, *eating*!'

The sun was halfway below the horizon and a fan of fiery rays was
turning the underside of slim horizontal clouds to crimson. A
magnificent evening. A prau was coming towards us between the two
nearest islands.

Jacob continued: 'You see, a caterpillar is an ugly thing. It eats all
day and all night; it never stops. But a delicate butterfly or a moth
cannot eat; it only sips. He touches his food, so *gently* – with his legs –
to see if it is worth sipping. And then merely sips.'

He broke off to say, pointing to the bay: 'Watch that prau.'

Then he continued, 'What is it about butterflies? Beauty, of course.
And innocence; a butterfly is so completely harmless. I've spent weeks
in the mountains collecting them. What excitement it is to discover a
species you've only read about in literature. In Wallace, perhaps.
There's nothing like it.'

The prau had turned sharply, exposing all at once the full glory of
her sails. Half her mainsail was a rich, shiny bronze, the other half
satiny yellow with white stripes, while her foresail was a pure fiery
orange. Her hull, ivory white, had a broad crimson strip from prow to
stern. She moved across our vision, mirrored in the water, as the red-
hot coal of the sun sank in the haze behind her. It was an extraordinary
sight.

'Who designed those colours?' asked Jacob, staring at it. 'God
designed a butterfly, we know. Who designed that prau?'

'Perhaps prau-men are butterfly watchers,' I said. All that Stein had
said about butterflies – their apparent fragility, their strength, the

harmony in their structure and the beauty of their appearance — seemed to apply to these little vessels, too.

Jacob laughed. 'You may be right. Or maybe they are all born artists. A miracle, I think.'

I think it was the diminutive, hospitable manager of my hotel in Makassar who told me about Princess What-for. Waving his hands with their enormous rings, he urged me to stay in her small hotel in Sengkang and passed me one of her cards. 'Hotel A: Pada, Sengkang, Wajo,' it said. Of course, it led me to her.

The Hajja Petta Ballasari, the very epitome of Wajo Bugis culture – or at least a self-appointed repository of it – groped around in a crumbling old box and brought out a family tree drawn on a large, swiftly disintegrating piece of paper. It had, I noticed, an interestingly early date written on it: 1573.

'You should get that treated, princess, lined perhaps with canvas or something. In a year or two it will have fallen apart.'

'Repair it?' she asked testily. 'What for?' It seemed a strange question, but even after only a day or two I knew that her '*Untuk apa*?' – 'What for?' – was meaningless, a curious kind of nervous tic. It was the reason I had come to call her 'Princess What-for'. She giggled, rather liking that. I had already discovered her sense of humour.

She dipped again into the box and fished out more yellow and crumbling pages wrapped in a faded yellow silk sarong. 'These are *lontara* belonging to my family,' she said. 'History . . . stories. All Bugis. These pages are called *Silasa* which means Religious Instructions. Of course, the writings have been taken from the old *lontara* leaf inscriptions and put on to paper.'

The painstaking scratches were in a deep brown ink and made with seaweed stalks, and the writing was in the twig-like Bugis language – as I have said, the sort of writing birds might invent for themselves –

216

with an occasional word in twirling Arabic or Javanese script. I could only decipher one word of the Arabic: 'Emir', which means 'prince'.

Princess What-for's mother had been a Queen of Tempé, a tiny state on a large lake not far from Sengkang, the capital of Wajo, where we now sat in the princess's house. Small, antique-filled, her house is half museum, half hotel. She had moved here when her father, who had been an important rajah of this region, died – he had been related in some way to a Makassarese rajah of Gowa.

In spite of her assumed indifference to the fate of these old family *lontara*, the princess had every intention of holding on to them.

'We used to have a big house with servants.' She was referring to the days before the declaration of the Republic of Indonesia. 'Now we are poor. But I don't mind that. My elder brother wanted to burn everything – the old *lontara*, everything. He said, "Why not? What is all this? It is all over." But I said, "What nonsense! It is *not* finished. It is *ours*. We are Bugis. If this is destroyed, we Bugis are destroyed."'

She looked at me fiercely; in a Victorian drawing room no doubt she would have stamped her foot. As it was, she continued, 'I know that all Indonesia is one place now. And that these days the only culture considered important is Javanese. It's all Java, Java, Java.' Another fierce look. 'But still . . . .'

After a pause to recover her breath she went on, 'I have a young niece. She has just married an *orang* Java. That is the first time anyone in my family has married a Java man.'

'He is probably very nice and will look after her very well,' I said diplomatically.

'Humph!'

When James Brooke wrote of the Wajo Bugis: 'No people are more tenacious of their descent. They are as careful of their blood as we are of that of our racehorses,' he might have had Princess What-for in mind.

Petta Ballasari, the princess, was a diminutive and imperious lady of between fifty and sixty. If the true Bugis warrior spirit lived on in her, the Bugis culture had gone to ground in her house. Her small hotel was filled with old furniture, ceramics in glass cases, masks, rings, old books. Two or three ladies much older than her sat perpetually absorbed in sewing in various corners of the main room, the double glass doors of which opened out into a small, tiered garden of brilliant flowering shrubs and singing birds. One could eat out there in the fresh air, although in the evenings this neat garden was as infested with whining mosquitoes as the crumbling house of the old *daeng* near Gowa had been. The princess served Bugis food in little dishes – beef, vegetables, soups and rice; and in the evening a troupe of handsome girls in rainbow dresses and glittering if false jewellery – well-born relations of the princess, I think – gave displays of Bugis dancing to music from a record player. 'We are too poor to have a live orchestra,' explained the princess, giving me a poignant look.

A sort of infant Sam Weller kept the garden watered and the house meticulously clean – a twelve-year-old gnat of a boy called Hasbi, whom the princess had adopted from poverty-stricken parents in a village in Tempé and intended to educate. A self-possessed little Bugis 'cockney', Hasbi went about briskly sweeping and watering, singing quietly to himself, and when occasion arose he showed himself capable of mending everything from a fuse to the hotel's shaky plumbing. The lights of Sengkang went out quite regularly, but that was due to an inadequate power station and not anything that Hasbi could control.

There was also an older servant – a born butterfingers. Serving at table he repeatedly dropped fistfuls of knives and forks on to the floor with a hideous clatter. When this happened the princess – whom I expected to explode with anger – would look at him gravely, murmuring '*matongko*' (stupid) in a sad tone of voice; and the boy would grin back toothily, and later on drop something else. The greatest hullabaloo took place one evening when this gormless boy climbed into a tall and brittle tree in the garden in an effort to retrieve a large rooster apparently stuck in the topmost branches. The boy took hours bringing it down, grabbing it by its tail feathers on a cracking branch, getting his sarong entangled on a twig while the demented fowl flapped and screeched, cascading feathers and droppings on to the princess below as she stood with her arms raised ready to catch it. The rooster eventually plummeted head downward, still screeching and beating its wings, on to a table set for dinner in the garden, scattering glasses, plates and cups. The princess, covered in feathers as though she had been in a pillow fight, looked at the boy, and again I waited for an explosion. She shook her head sadly, but '*matongko*,' was all she said. She has a kind heart.

Knowing that I was interested in Bugis affairs, the princess asked me one morning what I would like to see. I replied immediately,

'Tesora, princess, if it's not too far.'

'What for?' she predictably demanded.

'Because it is the old capital of Wajo.'

James Brooke wrote that when he arrived there in 1846 Tesora was 'a large straggling city, generally in decay' having been 'razed by Aru Palakka and the Dutch', but still the capital of Wajo. The description 'large, straggling' is ludicrously – tragically – unreal now.

Tesora is about 40 kilometres from Sengkang. Now that the rains had stopped, at least temporarily Wajo's small bridges were all under urgent repair; their spindly iron supports spanning narrow but dangerously deep riverbeds were being hurriedly replaced by stout sections of tree-trunk reinforced by the meccano-like sections of sheet-iron often used to construct makeshift aircraft runways in swamps or jungles. We bumped over potholes past gardens still awash with floodwater and houses decorated with the high Bugis horn-shaped gables, perched on stilts – the need for which was now evident. The rainfall had been dire. Ducks waddled and quacked in mud pools that had been vegetable gardens, and the small, long-maned ponies plodded along, head-down between the shafts of their carts like so many dismal Eeyores.

In Tesora we seemed very remote in place and time. Instead of the sprawling city it once had been the old capital was now no more than a small village off the main roads – such as they were – of Wajo. The arrival there of the princess was quite an event. It brought out an excited village headman and his wife, and we walked with them around the sad remains of the city that once the great Aru Palakka had thought fit to destroy. He would not have bothered with it now.

The old graveyard contained one or two beautifully carved headstones about a hundred years old under a colossal tamarind tree, and other graves of various kings lay in a special enclosure that I had an idea might sometimes be used as a football field. The oldest ruin there was that of a sixteenth century mosque; but all that was left of it was the arched alcove, the *mihrab*, which showed worshippers the direction of Mecca. It was nearly completely overgrown by trees and hidden by a patch of banana plants.

'Many graves long ago were simply pots full of ashes and bones of famous kings. In the pre-Islamic times,' the princess said, 'it was more like Bali here. They burned the dead as Buddhists do, or Hindus, or animists.'

It was strange to think that only a century and a half ago in this pathetic relic of a glorious age Brooke and his party had been welcomed by a mob of Bugis horsemen, 'yelling and firing as quick as they could load and as near to us as possible'. In the rajah's house they had eaten sweetmeats and drunk hot water among clouds of mosquitoes. A dense mob gazed at them hour after hour as they ate, which maddened Brooke. But the food Brooke found to be excellent: rice and forcemeat balls of fowl or fish, broiled vegetables, buffalo, minced and richly cooked with coconut milk, and eggs prepared in various ways including omelettes .... 'Nothing,' he noted, 'will exceed the kindness of these people.'

In the village headman's office near the ruined mosque a servant brought six coconuts, freshly cut, and deftly lopped off their tops with a parang. A cool breeze played in and out of the panelled windows, but it was still humid.

'Ladies first,' I said to the princess.

She smiled demurely, tipping up her decapitated coconut shell to drink from it. 'Ladies first, thank you.'

Brooke had noted that high-ranking Bugis men wore tight trousers that came halfway down the knee, a sarong, a *baju* and a belt with a richly embroidered kriss. They all wore rings of rough – not precious – stones. The headman with us, who normally cultivated rice and mace, wore a flowery shirt in blue and grey, and white trousers, while his wife wore a one-piece long blue dress and an embroidered skullcap on her head. Neither wore rings; perhaps they could not afford them.

The princess, in a yellow and blue flowered jacket and calf-length skirt that day, was certainly well-dressed, but I had come to notice that she usually was, in a quiet, understated way. She wore several fine rings with delicate gold settings, although I had no idea of the quality of the stones.

Driving back to Sengkang we bumped, swayed and sometimes skidded over the potholes and ridges of mud, and I began to worry about the tyres.

'*Hati-hati*,' I murmured to the Gowanese driver. 'Careful.'

He looked at me, 'Racing Parees-to-Dakar!' he cried, and burst into peals of laughter, joined by the princess. Attracted by the greyish white colour of a string of buffaloes wallowing knee-deep in a paddy field, she immediately launched into a story.

'Once,' she said, 'a princess of Luwu was a leper. So she was expelled and came to Wajo from Palopo. Here the buffaloes approached her and began licking her in a friendly way. Which is why many buffaloes in Wajo are born white, and why people avoid eating the meat of white buffaloes. Is it contaminated?' She added, 'Naturally in Makassar no one knows if buffalo meat comes from a white buffalo or a black one.' She laughed. 'But don't worry, it's only a fairy story.'

Brooke had been impressed by the unusually 'progressive' government of old Wajo: most foreigners were.

> It is feudal and comprised of numerous rajahs, independent or nearly so, living in their own districts, possessing the power of life and death, and each surrounded by a body of slaves, retainers or serfs.

But the head of state was an elective monarch, and a council of nobles of inferior rank could veto the appointment of any rajah and even, like the American Congress, veto a decision of the monarch to go to war. 'The Bugis of Wajo', Brooke wrote admiringly, 'alone have arrived at the threshold of recognised rights of all the people of the Mahomaten religion from Turkey to China.' Four out of the six great chiefs of Wajo when he got there were females. 'They appear in public, riding, ruling and even visiting foreigners.' Had she been living then, I have no doubt that Princess What-for would have been one of them.

The one drawback to the princess's delightful garden-hotel came from the cluster of mosques nearby which seemed to direct their much-amplified religious exhortations straight into one's window with pinpoint accuracy. Morning after morning, starting at four o'clock, first one, then half a minute later another of, I think, five local muezzins came to the five different microphones and let rip. Religious exhortation one can take or leave as one likes; noise one cannot dismiss. Not only was the noise shattering – I have never heard anything approaching that decibel-level in thirty-five years in and out of Muslim countries – it continued full-blast for about two hours on end. The usual Muslim call to prayer is quite brief and unexceptionable, but Sengkang went in for a whole series – the call to prayer, the prayers themselves, a sermon and I don't know what else. Wajo is an especially religious place. But that is no consolation to the exhausted traveller, who can forget about sleep from that early hour until well past daybreak.

Bleary-eyed, irritated almost beyond endurance by the noise, eyes puffed up by innumerable mosquito bites (the princess had as yet no air conditioning and only inadequate mosquito nets), I even found myself snapping over breakfast at poor Shafaat, whose prayers in the room next door had seemed to me deliberately ostentatious, his great grunts of 'Allah!' purposely exaggerated to annoy me.

The princess, whose sharp eyes missed nothing, ordered Hasbi to hurry along my breakfast as soon as I appeared – thinking, rightly, that a papaya and a cup of tea would calm me down.

In the evenings I read passages from Brooke to the princess who was highly amused by such Brookiana as: 'The Wajo women are not handsome, but playful and good-tempered – not modest, though very *chaste*,' and, 'Bugis minds, like Bugis manners, are shrewd but simple; cunning but not acute.'

I read her Brooke's observations about effeminate men – which I suppose, though he did not say so, related to the *bissus*, the transvestite priests of the Bugis.

> Some men dress like women, and some women like men; not occasionally, but all their lives, devoting themselves to the occupations and pursuits of their adopted sex. In the case of males, it seems that the parents of a boy, upon perceiving in him effeminacies of habit and appearance, are induced thereby to present him to one of the rajahs, by whom he is received.

This provoked loud laughter from the princess and, as I expected, a piercing cry of 'What for?'

The day we went to Masseppe, the kriss-making centre of old Wajo, we were directed to a series of small smithies behind the main street of a small village in the middle of the vast, soggy plain. The main street was called Jalan Air Panas or Hot Water Street, and the crack-crack-clunk-clunk of hammers on anvils could be heard long before we turned in among a line of houses on stilts and found our first smith.

Three men – two in shorts and soft straw hats and the third with a wide headband tied round his head pirate-fashion – were squatting in a lean-to by a charcoal fire making a parang, a farmer's machete, and shaping its point to look like the head of a serpent.

Between rounds of hammering they told us that Masseppe was still full of smithies; the business was passed down from son to son and from generation to generation. The metal they used came from ships' plates, perhaps from the iron girder of an old bridge, antique pistons from third-hand cars, broken spring-leaves and short sections of discarded railway line.

The making of Bugis parangs was a money-making business now. The Bugis parang is short, about a foot and a half long including the handle, and its head is like the beak of a hornbill. There was much skill in all this ironwork – just how much you were able to appreciate when two men split a piece of glowing red-hot iron into two slices, as one splits a piece of bread, deftly insert a sliver of steel like ham in a sandwich, and returning the iron sandwich to the fire, heating and beating it into one blade.

It was ten years since these smiths had made a kriss. It is illegal to wear one; but the skill persists. Rising from the fire of his smithy, an old man with skinny legs threw away his cigarette, pushed his hat to the back of his head, and made me an offer. 'Order as many as you like, *tuan*,' he said. 'We'll make them for you, as good as any krisses you will find.'

Brooke had commented that 'the Bugis are a manly and spirited race. Their vices are the vices of their condition and state of society, amongst which laziness and the use of the kriss are the most frequent.' No wonder krisses are forbidden.

'Music there is none in Wajo; a common tom-tom or drum, and a small gong, were the only instruments I heard as accompaniments to four dancing women.' When I read this piece of Brooke to the princess it stimulated her to mild fury. 'Here,' she snapped, 'the government gives no money for our culture, although in Java the *ramayana* performances draw thousands of rupiahs. What for?'

It seemed to me that Wajo, with its 'invention' of constitutional monarchy, its reputation for courage, commercial skill and intrepid exploration, its sailing and boat-building expertise, besides growing some of the best coffee in Indonesia, had enough to be proud of. What did it matter if artistically it went little further than four graceful ladies dancing in a beautiful garden to music from a record player? That music, incidentally, had had a good deal more to it than the White Rajah's 'common tom-tom and gong' might lead one to believe.

If one contrasts its different landscapes, Wajo could almost be two different countries. On its rim stand the mountains, the forests, the valleys and soaring eagles. In a basin flat as a plate, where buffaloes plough rice fields white with flocks of egrets, is the great gloomy lake of Tempé. There had been crocodiles in the lake in Brooke's time and then it had been known as *Tapar-ke-Rajah*, the Lake of the King, at a time when Tempé was ruled by the infamous Rajah Karain. He had turned it into a nest of thieves and plunderers. One could imagine the courageous communities of villagers, enduring the extremities of sun and rain, haunted after nightfall by armies of malicious spirits.

The lake dominates the very middle of Wajo and anyone crossing the rajahdom cannot possibly ignore it.

The princess insisted on driving me there; we arrived at the river that joins it to the town and embarked in the cool late afternoon on a narrow dugout canoe with an outboard motor. Sitting on bamboo strips, cross-legged to maintain a delicate balance, we watched the houses and now and again a mosque slowly move past us on the banks. When the houses gave out, the sky, a threatening grey that day, seemed to flatten down on top of us in a curiously sinister way, while the featureless landscape offered nothing to the eye except endless fields of beans or maize, the occasional isolated hump of an attap-roofed house and a very few unhealthy-looking trees. Sedges tufted up on the river banks, and then the lake itself stretched away around us like a dull metal shield. It might have been the lake in *Morte d'Arthur* – but no Excalibur would rise from those sombre waters. The dark wall of the cordillera was a distant shadow on the horizon; the only moving things were egrets slowly flapping overhead, or smaller wading birds that moved swiftly against the grey sky uttering doleful little cries that emphasised the gloomy silence of the lake.

The mountains, so often wrapped in thunder and lightning, summoned up thrilling images of titanic battles between mythical heroes, but that evening the grim face of Lake Tempé reminded me of *La Belle Dame Sans Merci*. It was a relief to return to the town at sunset and find it was 'rush hour' on the river, with people bustling back home with their shopping, riding home in the crowded canoes that were their commuter buses, laughing, waving and cheerfully shouting, 'Where you go?' when they saw us. It was a relief to see and to smell the smoke of evening fires that lay in horizontal strips across the rooftops. There were evidently two sorts of magic in Wajo: one full of exuberant life, a lust for adventure, war and travel; the other disturbing and full of melancholy.

Shafaat and I gave the jolly princess a lift to Makassar, and dropped her there at her brother's house. Next morning, in pouring rain, she appeared in her brother's Japanese jeep at my hotel. Smartly dressed – she never forgot she was a Bugis aristocrat – in a cotton jacket and skirt patterned with zig-zags of mauve and black, she was on her way back to Sengkang. 'Thank you for bringing me yesterday,' she said. 'You must come again to Wajo.' I promised I would. She took a plastic bag from her driver, and handed it to me. 'A memento of the Bugis,' she smiled. It contained five fresh mangoes from her brother's garden.

The time was approaching for me to leave Wajo – to leave Bugis-land, completely – and cross to Kalimantan and the last stage of my pilgrimage, that would culminate in the 'secret' river that Lingard had discovered. The river on which Almayer and Lord Jim had met their very different destinies; the river that Joseph Conrad himself had immortalised as Sambir and Patusan.

To get there by sea, I had been recommended to the operations manager of a shipping company in Makassar, Captain Tomasoa, whose office, in the jumble of narrow lanes near the port, was not far from the mosquito-haunted prau harbour in which *Fiona* had once tied up. Captain Tomasoa turned out to be a most helpful man: a charming, and experienced, seaman turned office-wallah.

When I walked in out of the blue and introduced myself at his desk – a desk barely visible behind a phalanx of clerks, a layer of files and an out tray full to bursting – the captain at once stood up, shook my hand, shooed the clerks away, asked his assistant to take any incoming calls on the telephone, ordered coffee from a passing boy and said, 'Sit down, Mr Young. Sit down, please.' Captain Tomasoa was a large man, dark-skinned, probably I thought from Ambon, with a cheerful, helpful-looking face over a crisp white shirt. And when coffee, thick, dark and sweet, came in tall glasses with little metal lids to keep it warm, he told me in the best English I had heard in Makassar that he had been born in the distant eastern island of Nusa Laut, one of the Ceram group.

He shook his head sadly. 'I never go back. Actually they only have cloves there. Only cloves. It's a very small island. Now then –' He raised his coffee glass, 'Cheers, Mr Young. What can I do for you?'

When I had told him I wanted to cross by ship – any vessel would do – to Samarinda and then to Berau, or even straight to Berau from Makassar, he pursed his lips and frowned as though that might be a problem.

'I don't mind – really don't mind,' I added quickly, 'what sort of vessel it is. Wood, iron, sail, steam – anything.'

'If you say that,' Captain Tomasoa doubtfully smiled, 'I believe you. Of course, one must think of the weather. About now it can rain the whole week. Hard rain, and the wind – always west. At that time the harbour master can announce that all shipping will be moored off the buoys – away from the wharf, you see.'

'The sea is too rough?'

'Well, the *pinisis* can't go to sea. The wind's too strong for them.'

Despite the difficulties Captain Tomasoa would do what he could for me. He recommended me now to wait for him to make a few inquiries. He promised to call the hotel in a day or two, not more. He had an idea that his Paré-Paré office might be helpful.

'We have ships – wooden ones – going regularly up to Berau and back. Via Balik Papan and Samarinda. I doubt if they'll have cabins, though. It's more like sleeping on deck.' He spread his hands, 'Well, it'll be wet.'

'As long as I get to Berau – '

He smiled. 'Yes, I see what you're after.'

While I waited for Captain Tomasoa's message I thought of Wajo and turned to *The Rescue* again. I remembered with what disgust Wilfred Thesiger had laid the novel aside, baffled by Lingard's betrayal of Rajah Hassim and Immada. In his overwhelming infatuation for the white woman on the yacht, he had abandoned his Bugis friends to their deaths.

Hassim had saved Lingard's life in a sudden scrimmage on a Papuan beach not unlike the scrimmage on a remoter island that had ended the life of Captain Cook. In return Lingard had rescued Hassim, surrounded by his enemies, from the shore of Wajo. But that was only part of Lingard's debt. The other half consisted in gathering men and arms ('Look ahere, these Colt pistols I am selling – through and through like a sieve.'), to launch a very lively row to restore Hassim to the throne of Wajo. He had recruited old Jörgenson to help him.

The men were gathered, the arms and powder bought and stored, in the hulk of the *Emma* under Jörgenson's fading eyes on the Shore of Refuge, and then the yacht turned up with the Travers couple aboard, and Lingard's infatuation with Mrs Travers began, ending in his abandonment of his Wajo friends. For while his back was turned, their Malay enemies closed in, and old Jörgenson, seeing the jig was up once Lingard had failed to respond to the SOS of Hassim's emerald ring, did the only thing he could do. He put the lighted cigar into his mouth and blew them all – and himself – to blazes.

What had appealed to Lingard was the complete trust in him of Hassim and Immada. Off the coast of Wajo, in the thunderstorm, Jaffir, Hassim's faithful servant, had swum to Lingard's brig bringing the Rajah Laut his master's ring – 'a thick gold ring set with a fairly good emerald' – as a reminder of his friendship. Lingard had honoured his pledge, and then returned the ring renewing his promise to Hassim, 'Send me this ring again and I will not fail you.'

The next time Hassim had needed Lingard's help on the Shore of Refuge the ring had been confided to Mrs Travers, since she was the only one who could get it to Lingard and she had deliberately withheld it. When it was all over, nothing was left to Lingard but to try to pick up as best he could the broken thread of his life. But by then Rajah Hassim and his sister had no threads left to pick up.

The strange thing was that Conrad himself sympathised with Bugis *pacce*. 'Man is a vicious animal. His viciousness must be organised,' he had told his socialist friend Cunninghame Graham. He did not believe, like Graham, in an international kind of Fraternity, for 'What would you think of an attempt to promote fraternity among people living in the same street? I don't even mention two neighbouring streets.' For Conrad a few simple notions – solidarity, fidelity, belonging, duty – were far more likely to 'knit together the loneliness of souls', and in this part of the world these simple notions could be condensed into one word, Fraternity, in Bugis *pacce*: a limited, tribal fidelity.

Naturally *pacce* did not permit a total disregard of the binding nature of rings. But of course the love-lorn young Lingard of *The Rescue* was not the experienced Rajah Laut of *Almayer's Folly* or *The Outcast of the Islands*. The Lingard of *The Rescue* should have listened to the words of wisdom of the old ghost Jörgenson (lately of the barque *White Rose*) on Cavenagh Bridge: 'Drop it!'

I was paid a brief visit before my departure by the hotel's manager, the diminutive relative of some local big-wig and a charming man.

Knowing that I was interested in the Bugis and their ways, he came up one afternoon to my room followed by a waiter with a present of a box of sweet cakes. Unfolding with difficulty a tightly coiled scroll of stiff paper with many lines and names on it, he said, 'So that you won't forget all the names of the Bugis kings.' He laid it like a crackling cloth on my table.

Noticing two enormous rings on his right hand, that rose up from his knuckles like giant carbuncles, I asked what they were.

'This is white magic,' pointing first to one then the other, 'and this is black magic. I like white magic, yes; black magic, no!' Nevertheless, as he said it, he twisted his plump, pale pixie face into a mischievous grin that led me to think he might be quite happy with one as with the other. His rings were decidedly unusual; and being extraordinarily large for his little fingers, they looked extremely uncomfortable. One stone had flecks of orange in an off-white, milky base, the other was a black stone about the size of a cocktail olive, and both were mounted in heavy gold. They had come to him, the manager told me, from a medium in Cairo: the black stone was 'Solomon's stone', particularly heavy with magic. I asked him to explain this, but Shafaat was not there to translate, and I never fathomed how he had come upon the rings.

He was an amusing man. To explain the democratic principles of Bugis kingship he resorted to vaudeville. With a clown's aplomb, he stuck a paper napkin slightly askew on his head to represent a crown and shouted, 'If a king no good – king goes!' Uttering a loud giggle, he deftly flipped the crown from the side of his head on to the floor and vanished from the room. Only the music hall roll of drums was missing.

I told Shafaat about the manager's rings and he took the magic very seriously.

'Ah, yes,' he said immediately. 'This hotel is full of *hantu*, full of ghosts and spirits. It is well known.'

'Where is not, Shafaat,' I asked, 'in Celebes? Or in the whole of Indonesia for that matter?' Since I had arrived in the country I had heard countless stories of haunted houses and magic groves, love potions, even death spells. Here it seemed that magic made the world go round.

'*Betul*! True. Just don't insult the *hantu* and you don't have to worry about them.'

I did not worry about them. I try never to insult spirits, and I like ghost stories.

Good Captain Tomasoa called me as he had promised he would. The best he could do, he said, was to tell me that a wooden passenger and cargo boat would leave Paré-Paré in a day or two for Samarinda. She would take on passengers there and sail again for Berau. He advised me to join her in Paré-Paré and gave me the address of his office there.

With Shafaat I drove to Paré-Paré without delay. There were three harbours, we discovered, none very big. One of them had a restaurant on the water, and we watched an old steamer being unloaded as we ate asparagus soup, fried fish and white rice. An army of ginger cats crawled under our feet and sometimes over the table while we threw fish bones and tails into distant corners to get rid of them.

In the second harbour – a bigger one in the centre of town – several motor vessels lay tied up alongside, and a number of sailing vessels, none of them looking as if they were preparing to go anywhere. The big bay spread attractively around us, looking like no place I could ever remember visiting before. It had grown since *Fiona*'s time. The agents' offices were hidden in a maze of little streets; some only consisted of a dark wood counter on to the pavement, with boards like those you see outside fishmongers in England but bearing the destinations and departure dates of various craft. The vessels themselves were big and unattractive – more like hulks than ships – with superstructures of unpainted plank, unpainted plank decks, and crude and minute 'cabins' of plank with bare plank bunks. They reminded me of ungainly Noah's Arks of unpainted and disintegrating wood. I wondered how they would manage to stay upright and afloat in the rough seas Captain Tomasoa had predicted. Still, their crews had their Muslim fatalism to comfort them. What is written is written: the Strait might stay as flat as a duck pond for them.

Outside an agent's office a board advertised a sailing to 'Brow' – the old Singaporean way of spelling 'Berau' in the days of Conrad. But it was the wrong office. We found the agent we were looking for at last, and he was a friendly man in a barn-shaped room who looked at me with surprise when I mentioned Captain Tomasoa's message; he seemed to think Shafaat was the one who wanted to sail. Recovering himself, he gestured to two leatherette chairs and came to business.

The ship Captain Tomasoa had told me about was called *Mauru III*. She was a little delayed – he could not be sure just when she would arrive: perhaps in two or three days' time. She was a small wooden ship and could carry about a hundred passengers, all of them on deck. Sometimes the crew were willing to rent their cabins – cubicles really – to passengers. At any rate, the agent assured me, however late she arrived in Paré-Paré, she would be sure to leave on time from Samarinda for Berau. That would be in – let's say – four days from now. Check with the agent in Samarinda.

I told the agent to count on me: I would join the *Mauru III* in Samarinda. I would take the PELNI steamer from Makassar to

Samarinda next day, if I could get a ticket. It was always a problem getting a ticket on PELNI, but with help from Captain Tomasoa . . . .

'Good,' the agent said with satisfaction. 'I shall tell the captain. You will join in Samarinda. Samarinda to Tanjung Redeb.'

Tanjung Redeb! The heart of the Berau. Lingard had built his office there. Almayer had lived for thirty years in Tanjung Redeb and died there. I had not been there for twelve years.

I emphasised to the agent again: 'Yes, I shall most definitely join her at Samarinda.'

I drove back to Makassar with Shafaat to celebrate my last evening in the haunted hotel with what was left of Jacob's Old Genever.

Part Five

Rivers

STEIN: A man that is born falls into a dream like a man who falls into the sea. If he tries to climb out into the air as inexperienced people endeavour to do he drowns – *nicht wahr?* . . . No! The way is . . . to follow the dream, and again to follow the dream – and so – *ewig* – *usque ad finem* –

JOSEPH CONRAD, *Lord Jim*

Twentyone

I caught the *Mauru III* at Samarinda with two days to spare. Thanks to Captain Tomasoa's help I crossed to Balik Papan from Makassar on a PELNI steamer where a German friend drove me to his house up the Mahakam river.

The friend, Johannes von Franz, was working for a government project to do with afforestation. We had met in Jakarta and he suggested that he could be of help to me, not least by providing me with an English-speaking guide in Berau. Also, he said, I had to buy a ticket to board the *Mauru III* and her agents might be difficult to find; he might be able to find them. Did I know, he wondered, that there was a branch of the Al Joofree family, descendants of Syed Abdullah of Berau, living in Samarinda; perhaps I would like to visit them.

The landscape Johannes drove me through, from the oil-port of Balik Papan to Samarinda, bore a certain similarity to one of the most fought over battlefields of World War I; it was lifeless, battered and desolate with occasional trunks of dead trees stretching leafless branches to the sky like despairing arms. If there had been any reafforestation hereabouts, there was no evidence of it. I wondered with alarm if Berau, too, had deteriorated into something like this – a latter-day imitation of Ypres or the Somme.

That first night in Samarinda it rained and thundered without a pause, and the following morning it was the same. 'You're going to get truly drenched on that boat's deck,' said Johannes, and it certainly looked as if he were right. Like a dedicated hero of a rather dated film, I remember boasting that with the Berau in prospect I would swim all the way in a typhoon if I had had to.

The *Mauru III*'s agent had premises in a distant bungalow up a remote back alley, and worked out of what may have been his sitting room. He gave me a strange look to indicate he doubted my sanity but at the sight of my money he produced a ticket without hesitation.

'We don't get foreigners like you in here,' he grinned, pocketing my money. '*Mauru III* leaves after tomorrow at eleven o'clock.' The length of the voyage, he added dryly, would depend on the weather. Two days, perhaps; three days. Who could tell?

'There will be rice on the boat,' he added. 'Can you eat rice?'

I like rice, but nevertheless we stopped at a food stall on the way home, and I bought a knife, fork and spoon, a tin of sardines, Brand's Essence of Chicken and a bar or two of chocolate. On past expeditions I had found it a good idea to take plenty of tea and sugar – and two or three cartons of cigarettes, although I do not smoke myself; cigarettes make good presents. For myself I added a bottle of Gordon's Gin and a small bottle of Angostura Bitters. 'Well,' I shrugged to Johannes, 'you never know.'

Johannes's English-speaking guide turned out to be a cheerful young man called Suparno, himself a native of Tanjung Redeb, the principal township of the Berau. He worked in Samarinda with Johannes's development project, but luckily for me happened to be due for a vacation and wanted to return home to see his family. He would be only too delighted, he assured me, to lead me round Tanjung Redeb and to translate for me.

With that satisfactorily arranged, I found Abdur Rahman Al Joofree's name and address in the telephone directory, and Johannes's driver took me to the house with Suparno on our first expedition together.

The Al Joofrees lived in a pleasant one-storey house in a smart middle-class district. Abdur Rahman Al Joofree was away on business in Jakarta, but when I had explained my interest in the family, his wife invited us in. The sitting room was darkened by drawn curtains and panelled walls and full of heavy and ornately carved furniture enlivened by silky wall hangings showing stags at bay and alpine scenes. Mrs Al Joofree was a pleasant, smiling woman of about thirty. I told her of my impending voyage to the Berau, and the later one I hoped to make to Bulungan. She was glad to hear that because the family's historian, a cousin or an uncle, Saihan Al Joofree, lived in Bulungan. In any case, I should visit her husband's brother, Haji Mohamed, in Tanjung Redeb. But 'Bulungan,' she insisted, 'that's where most of the Al Joofrees are.'

She had told me what I wanted to hear: the simple fact that descendants of Syed Abdullah Al Joofree still lived in Berau and Bulungan.

*

Johannes drove me to the waterfront. It had stopped raining for the time being, although Himalayan walls of dark cloud threatened the sky to the north. Suparno, who would fly to Tanjung Redeb in a small local plane and meet me there, might have the rougher journey.

We found the *Mauru III* with some difficulty; she was a puny thing dwarfed between two wooden Noah's Arks from Surabaya, and her decks were awash with shouting human beings. Her short foredeck was largely occupied by two heavy wooden crates and the rest of it with passengers humping their bags, bundles and children, or just passing the time smoking and chatting. Most of them, I hoped, were friends of passengers saying goodbye; otherwise, I wondered, how on earth would the ship manage to stay afloat in the heavy weather we might run into in the Strait of Makassar? I was glad I had restricted myself to two small zip bags and the plastic one inside which the gin was wrapped securely in a colourful towel with 'Hawaii' embroidered on it. On my arm I carried an old green anorak, a dubious defence against rain but better than nothing.

There was no space for Johannes to wait about in and in any case he had to go to his office, so we said goodbye. Then I took a look round.

The *Mauru III*'s *nakhoda* was a sour-faced, grey and rather weedy man who spoke next to no English, and whose name was Jansen Mosé. He and his officers were all from Menado, the northernmost arm of the swastika-shaped island of Celebes, and all were Christian as their first names proclaimed: David Oroh, Johannes Monintja, John Mandagé – respectively the first officer, first engineer and second engineer. They wore T-shirts and old jeans, and most of them knew minimal English at the most. I cannot remember having any language difficulty on the *Mauru III*, thanks to the second officer, with the familiar name for these parts of Raffles. With him I got on surprisingly well with a mixture of vivid hand signs, pidgin Indonesian and, when all else failed, ballpoint pen sketches in my notebook or even on the palm of my hand.

Where to sit, lie or possibly sleep was a fairly urgent problem. I had a recurring vision of my bag of notebooks being seized in error and never seen again; or of it simply falling overboard. At first I had hopes that one of the ship's motormen, Apson, a tall, powerful young man with a pleasant smile, would be willing – encouraged by the *nakhoda* – to come to some arrangement concerning his bunk. 'Look after me, Apson,' I promised him, 'and perhaps I will rent your bunk when you are not using it.' At which Apson grinned widely and the matter seemed settled. Unfortunately his bunk turned out to be only one of

237

three shelves in a cabin of doll's house proportions. Its ceiling was so low I was unable to stand upright and I cracked my head on the lintel every time I went in or out. It was also suffocatingly hot, and although its bulkheads were prettily decorated with on one side the Italian football team and on the other that of Poland, I could never have slept in it because I was too tall to lie down. Apson was apologetic, swearing to look after me nonetheless and keep my bags from harm, and he swiftly made another arrangement with four Malay passengers, who were short and fat and fitted perfectly into the shoebox-sized cabin. Whenever I looked in, I found them sleeping and snoring, or eating or smoking, so the already stuffy little cabin was made uninhabitable through smoke as much as through stifling fug.

'Apson likes ladies very much,' Raffles confided. 'He want to be your son-in-law, he want to marry your daughter.'

'He's welcome. But there'll be a bride price to pay, you know.' Apson thought my reply the funniest thing he had ever heard and so our good relations and his close watch on my bags became, if anything, closer than before.

I find my notebook quite fails to reflect the excitement I felt to be on *Mauru III*, with the Berau ahead:

> Sail half an hour late – not bad considering the amount of cargo and baggage scattered all over the deck – and push down the Mahakam river, wide here, oily and dirty. I sit in the wheelhouse, chatting in a sort of pidgin. Passengers and crew are equally friendly. Luckily the expected rain fails to materialise and we approach the mouth of the Mahakam river, the coast of Borneo and the Strait of Makassar with a blue sky overhead and in calmer water.
>
> One of the more forthcoming passengers is a portly young Chinese with a pockmarked face who speaks English quite well and looks like an oriental Peter Ustinov. He is a merchant from Solo in Java and is on a mission to Berau, which he knows, to buy *trepang* or sea slugs for export to Singapore. Also *kerapu* fish – by which he means 'grouper fish' – if he can find enough. 'Hong Kong people like sea slugs too much,' he said. 'Maybe I buy prawns, too. Now price of prawn is down.'
>
> We twist and turn, following the last meanderings of the Mahakam. A huge log raft comes towards us – so big it needs one gigantic tug and no less than four smaller ones to control it. 'Maybe three or four hundred logs there,' says Ustinov with his computer mind.

At about 3 p.m. – three hours after sailing – we meet the sea. I feel the first exciting heave under our bows which means the vessel feels the deep water swell and is truly alive. As we begin to chug northward up the Makassar Strait, I take a closer look at the *Mauru III* and her passengers. There is not much to her. She has one deck and two holds, one fore and one aft. Behind the wheelhouse – as with Apson's cabin I can just squeeze into it if I bow like a Japanese kowtowing to his ancestors – are four-bunk cabins, all similar to Apson's cubicle, chicken coops which are all filled now with clucking, steaming passengers.

Aft of the cabins is a reasonably open space under a wooden canopy containing a good many tightly packed iron bunks already full to overflowing with families, children, old men and women lying or crouching between bags and bundles and packages of food.

At meal times enormous containers of rice are placed on this part of the deck and the passengers – have they starved for days before coming aboard? – throw themselves greedily on them, thrashing about dangerously with giant ladles. In other containers is a sort of vegetable soup much of which ends up on deck. Further aft still, from what I can see through a door swinging ajar and from the furtive comings and goings around it, as well as a familiar and pungent smell, I hazard there is a ship's toilet. Looking at it more closely, I see it has a hole in the deck, no flushing, and a good many traces of recent use. I pray for fine weather and a minimum of seasickness.

At sea, as usual, things soon settle down. The younger passengers are evidently students going home to Berau having finished their exams in Samarinda; they listen calmly to their Walkmans on the foredeck, smoke and chat. Occasionally they offer me sweets and cigarettes. Older people sit on the few benches in the bows with their feet tucked under them, discussing the cost of living and poring over crossword puzzles. Others have simply retired to sweat and sleep the voyage away on their airless bunks. The *Mauru III* moves steadily up a coast the headlands of which are low and wooded and evidently quite uninhabited. Behind them high mountain ridges are slowly disappearing beneath pitch-black storm clouds. Quite gently, we begin to dip and roll. We ease course to starboard. From the old charts I have salvaged from *Fiona*, I observe we are about to steer a course into the middle of the Strait that will bring us to the prominent beaklike point of Tanjung Mangkalihat. Rounding this very prominent point of land, I remember, we had a very rough passage indeed in *Fiona*. At 1900 we cross the Equator and as we do so, a shoal of flying fish play ducks and drakes alongside us. I take it as a good sign.

Fiona 1977:
Approaching Tanjung Mangkalihat Mac had a good deal more than flying fish to contend with. A wild squall (they are common here, according to the *Pilot*) sprang up off the shore, taking us unawares. Mac had been looking for Sumbang Bay, which the chart showed just round the corner of the point, intending to anchor for a day or two. But we were so badly pummelled in a wind that rose rapidly to gale force that we could not make it.

Nevertheless, I learned something about *Fiona* that was remarkably comforting. Despite the fact that she was staggering about as though drunk, she took the buffeting well – rather, I thought, like a duchess who has overdone the champagne but manages to stick to her pins. Books skittered across the cabin deck; a bottle toppled and broke; a skylight slammed shut with a noise in that confined space like a rifle shot; the sea gurgled and roared against the old boat's ribs; and yet with a horrific wind blasting away outside, *Fiona* somehow seemed as solid as a rock. The old girl kept her head. She calmly and serenely greeted the light of a new dawn as if nothing had happened. Contributing to the homely atmosphere that morning, Mac's radio gave us news of the fourth Test Match in the plummy, familiar but incongruous tones of Brian Johnston and John Arlott.

We gave *Fiona* and ourselves three days' rest in Sumbang Bay, a perfect horseshoe, backed by a long ridge of forest falling sharply into the beach. Rain forest rose up in a cliff to the north, the beach was sandy and white, the water was as clear and blue as any I have ever seen, and we anchored in about 12 feet of it. We swam, and read and swam again.

A Chinese owned a plantation nearby but he was away, and five workers – two from Timor, two Bugis and a man from West Java lived in two shacks on the edge of the beach and looked after it. One of them was down with a bad attack of malaria and we found him shivering in one of the shacks and gave him pills and an old blanket to help him sweat it out. In return his grateful friends brought us bananas and eggs.

I remember memorable sunsets in Sumbang: one in particular beginning deep purple-black, turning to an oyster-like satin with here

240

and there a small unhurried cloud dyed orange-red by the sun's rays. When with great reluctance we left the bay just before five o'clock on the fourth morning Orion was still sharp overhead. Enchanted by the beauty of that exceptional bay and elated by our nearness to Berau, Mac dug a new Red Ensign from a locker and hoisted it for the occasion.

We sailed from the bay on the engine and the mainsail and the sun came up like an orange disc and in its warm light dolphins once more gathered to dive and gambol round our bows. The strong odour of wood smoke drifted from the shore, and soon *Fiona* – under topsail, staysail, jib and mainsail – picked up speed to a cheerful 5 knots.

It was not plain sailing to Berau. On the contrary, it was dangerous. 'We must go out to sea a bit somewhere here,' said Mac, 'to avoid a reef 6 foot under water opposite Tanjung Klanbu. We had also better miss a big reef called Karang Besar. And the *Pilot* warns us categorically that if we can't see an island called Maninbora, we're in trouble. Well, this looks interesting.'

The *Pilot* comments:

> Tanjung Mangkalihat to Sungai Berau. Remarks. The East coast of Borneo between T. M. and the mouth of the Sungai Berau, about 90 miles north-westward is mostly low and covered with mangroves . . . . Pulau Tanjung Buaya Buaya is a low densely wooded island with one large tree in the middle . . . . It is separated from the coast by a narrow channel much encumbered by reefs . . . .

'Much encumbered by reefs' was a charming official understatement. We spotted Pulau Tanjung Buaya Buaya, the Island of Crocodiles; we wriggled our way safely past the great straggling reef called Karang Besar and a number of smaller ones, and only a blind man could have ignored the mass of Maninbora Island. But, even so, it was not plain sailing. I remember a long and exhausting day's haul, endless changes of course, continuous takings of new bearings, a nonstop watch in sunlight for the telltale turquoise gleam of those innumerable and fearful reefs and when the clouds closed overhead, for their brown backs lurking almost invisible below the surface. I wondered how long it had taken Lingard to negotiate this coastline for the first time.

Mauru III:
When daylight faded, I saw Apson grinning from the wheelhouse

gesturing to me to eat. He himself clutched a bowl of *nasi goreng* that seemed to me to be enough for three. I got myself a bowl of rice from the containers aft, poured some Brands Essence of Chicken on to it, added a spoonful of the ship's vegetable concoction and some red chilli and retired with this curious but satisfying dog's dinner to the foredeck. Apson soon came up with a mug of tea, wiping grains of rice from his lips, and announced between elaborate yawns that he was about to retire to the depths of the boat to sleep. Not a bad idea. I spread my Hawaii towel on a thin plastic-covered mattress, wrapped my anorak round my shoulders and lay down with one of my bags as a pillow. It was quite comfortable; the vessel rolled smoothly. The wind was strong but not cold and kept the mosquitoes away. Orion kept guard overhead among stars as sharp as diamonds and as big as pearls.

Mauru III passed Sumbang at daybreak, and I trained my binoculars eagerly on it. Its familiar horseshoe of white sand stood out in the early sunlight against the dark shelving backdrop of forest. I imagined *Fiona*'s white hull anchored there framed against the long ridge of the coconut palms, and the curved stems of palms in the plantation, and thought of Wilfred and Mac and Murray and myself, wading through the glass-clear water to the lean-to on the beach where the malarial clouds of mosquitoes clustered round the shivering man like flies round a corpse.

That day was sunny from its very beginning. It was a happy return to times past, in a way. The coral islands I had carried in my mind's eye for twelve years reappeared on cue with their enticing white sands and coconut palms, unchanged. Frigate birds lazed in the sky on sharp rigid wings as they had then, and on the coast the forests rose wave after wave three or four deep, running far into the immensity of Borneo. No one could say there were no forests left here. The topmost of these wild ridges was half lost in a heavy, rainy cloud.

The passengers were talkative, relieved that the night's weather had been calm. The gentle rolling and a splash or two of light rain were all they had had to put up with. They sat and lounged on deck watching the forest fray out into coconut plantations, and plumes of small fires rise above the thinning trees.

Apson brought me tea the colour of milkless coffee about once an hour, and the Chinese-looking chief engineer brought me one of his sarongs, saying, 'More better than pants,' and adding reassuringly, 'I wash it before one day.' In exchange I unfolded from my bag the old charts updated from 1864 we had used on *Fiona* – including the one that showed the coast of Kalimantan where we were now.

The *nakhoda* was interested in the map of the Pantai branch of the Berau estuary, the one of the many arms of the delta we would take to join the main river up to Tanjung Redeb which lay 40 miles from the sea. I pointed out Lingard's 'secret passage' – the channel which had given him unique access to the upstream settlements. It was marked 'Oversteek van Lingard' on old Dutch charts: 'Lingard's Crossing'. The *nakhoda* and Raffles trailed greasy fingers following *Fiona*'s course all over my charts. They were impressed that we had visited places they knew so well, but thought the world would know nothing of.

'Oh, Paré-Paré?' Raffles cried. 'Carimata? O-o-h ... so many places.'

I remembered the reefs on the approach to the Berau estuary stretching for miles like glowing green submarine pastures. But I had forgotten how really dangerous it was to be sailing here until a strange thing happened. For some hours a fishing boat had been motoring fast and confidently towards the Berau estuary, well ahead of us, if anything increasing the distance between us. Now she stopped in her tracks as if she had bumped into a brick wall. In a moment, she swung abruptly to face us, her bows held fast. At full speed ahead, she had hit something very suddenly: '*Karang* [reef],' the *nakhoda* said, and we skirted the reef the other vessel had inexplicably failed to avoid. Was she in danger? Evidently not. Nobody waved at us or called. 'She will get herself off at high tide,' the *nakhoda* assured us after a close look through my binoculars, and we rattled on at full speed.

Now I remembered the many headlands that protected the estuary from the south, and how as we advanced mountain ridges kept changing position in a most disconcerting way. A headland I had seen from *Fiona*'s deck, for example, seemed to have a very prominent conical hill growing on it like a clown's hat; but later, when we progressed a mile or two further north, the hill was revealed to be part of quite another headland. For several hours we went on from one false perspective to another.

Some passengers paid no attention to the sea or the land. Ustinov, for example, talked business all the time. 'Birds' nests,' he informed us, 'are very expensive in Berau. One kilo maybe one and a half million rupiahs.' – which is £300 – 'Haji Mohamed Al Joofree in Tanjung Redeb sells them very often.'

'You know Haji Mohamed?'

'Oh, yes. We have business.'

It seemed that Mohamed Al Joofree sold rattans, and a good deal of *kayu gaharu*, a much prized wood which produces a fragrant resin. Evidently he followed a family tradition. His ancestor, Syed Abdullah, had founded his business here on those same rattans and *kayu gaharu*. Birds' nests, too, of course.

Despite his girth, Ustinov was intrepid in pursuit of trade. From Tanjung Redeb, he said, he would go to a much wilder place called Biduk-Biduk. He showed it to me on the chart, just opposite where we were now; a very long way from the Berau and in thick forest. There were no roads here. Ustinov would take a smaller boat – much smaller and slower than *Mauru III* – and stay with a trader there. When I expressed admiration, he said casually, oh, he had done it before. He thought nothing of it.

I slept some of the day on deck and woke with a mild case of sunburn to find we had made a lot of progress; had in fact reached the outer fringe of the muddy Berau estuary. 'Fairly prominent high trees,' Mac had pencilled in on the chart I held in my hands, and now, through my old Leitz glasses, I could see those trees across Tanjung Birai to the north of the mouth of the Pantai channel, which is the southernmost branch of the tangle of mud-blocked waterways that lead deviously to the Berau River proper and then up to Tanjung Redeb.

The *Pilot* describes it thus:

> In the approach to the Sungai Berau is an extensive estuary formed by many uninhabited islands, with various passages between them. The islands are low, monotonously wooded, and without any distinctive features visible from seaward, and the channels through the estuary are only suitable for small vessels with local knowledge . . . . The principal channel of approach leads through the Muara Guntung . . . . There are also navigable approaches through Muara Pantai on the southern side of the estuary . . . . Owing to the muddy water the shoals and banks off the delta are not marked by discoloration; vessels should not, therefore, proceed into a depth of less than 16 fathoms until the buoys off the mouths of the delta have been identified – .

'Caution' – the *Pilot* warns – 'In 1961 a number of beacons and buoys were reported to be missing.' And it adds: 'Muara Pantai, the southern arm of the Sungai Berau, is now seldom used.'

*

Nothing in that respect had changed by 1977. 'Of the five buoys that should have marked the entrance to the Pantai Channel,' Mac wrote in *Fiona*'s log, 'all were missing.' Nonetheless we defied the *Pilot* and began to ascend the delta by the 'seldom used' Muara Pantai.

We were right. There was a deep water channel. With infinite slowness the two arms of the Pantai Channel began to close around *Fiona*, and on a strip of yellow sand to the left a few wooden shacks unexpectedly appeared. Who could live on this exposed lip of the river? It seemed too much to expect that the huts belonged to the great-great-grandchildren of the fishermen Marlow had seen in *Lord Jim*, living in flimsy mat hovels.

But this was the place Conrad had described. Jim, saying goodbye to Marlow for the last time, pointed out these hovels, remarking proudly: 'The trouble is these beggars of fishermen have been considered as the Rajah's personal slaves – and the old rip can't get it into his head that – '

'That you've changed all that.'

'Yes, I've changed all that.'

His liberation of those half-naked fishermen, 'dark brown as if dried in smoke', were to Jim an important part of his final triumph over the shame of the *Jeddah* scandal. Heeding Stein's advice and following his romantic dream – *usque ad finem* – Jim had buried his shame in this completely new world – the world of the 'immense and magnanimous Doramin and his little motherly witch of a wife'; of Tunku Allang, 'wizened and greatly perplexed'; above all of Dain Waris, Doramin's son, 'intelligent and brave, with his faith in Jim and his ironic friendliness', and his total indifference to Jim's scandalous past; his irrelevant white man's past.

No one from that past would have recognised Jim up here; no one in Emmerson's, certainly not Schomberg. Jim by his own efforts, his own courage and goodwill, had become, so to speak, a White Rajah. He had built a fort to house these liberated captives – 'my own people' he called them – and constructed huts for them and little plots of land protected by an earth wall and a palisade defended by guns provided by Doramin. Here he was loved and trusted for a nobility and courage for which his white acquaintances would never have given him credit.

Once Jim received a chatty letter from an even more distant world – from his parson-father. It was full of family chit-chat. It told him a brother had 'taken orders', that a brother-in-law had money problems, that a pony 'which all you boys used to ride' had gone blind with age and had had to be shot. Jim, Conrad believed, never answered it.

Did Austin Williams, who found salvation easier to come by in a ship chandler's in Singapore, answer similar letters? We do not know. Did he receive any? We do not know that either.

Almost the last words Jim spoke to Marlow in *Lord Jim* were spoken here on the mouth of the Pantai.

> I must go on, go on for ever holding up my end, to feel sure that nothing can touch me. I must stick to their belief in me to be safe . . . . I shall be faithful.

Before sending him up here Stein had said: 'Jim is a romantic,' and the old entomologist had been right. In his younger days Jim's thoughts had been full of valorous deeds. They had been the 'best part of life, its secret truth, its hidden reality, passing before him with a heroic thread'. Then, with the guilt of the *Jeddah* affair, he had fallen 'under a cloud' which it seemed would stay with him for ever. Yet at last in this forested world on the brink of the 'ever-undiscovered country over the hill, across the stream, beyond the waves', the cloud had been lifted. Now there was nothing he could not face.

Marlow listened to Jim on this spot and understood. He saw the sea 'stretched with a slight upward tilt' to the horizon on which a low sun was about to set. Over *Mauru III*'s stern the sun was sinking into the same sea, and I, like Marlow, smelled the mud and marsh and sweltered in the same 'stagnant, superheated air'.

1977:
Mac anchored *Fiona* between the nipa-lined banks of the Pantai in 10 feet of water and within about 150 yards of the Lingard Crossing. Two men fishing off a creek in a tiny canoe stopped their paddling to watch us as we poured buckets of Berau water over our heads to cool off.

I pulled out *The Outcast of the Islands* and read what Lingard had confided to Peter Willems about the Crossing,

> I've found out the entrance for a ship like mine. It isn't easy. You'll see. I'll show you . . . . I have no doubt my secret will be safe with you. Keep mum about my river when you get among the traders again . . . . That's where I get all my guttah and rattans. Simply inexhaustible, my boy.

Far from keeping mum, Willems had revealed Lingard's secret to Abdullah.

The water was fresh on the strong incoming tide, We watched the sun go down in a swirl of Turneresque oranges and yellow and whites, while a huge black cloud threw a dark dragon's wing across the pale

246

disc of the dying sun. We sat in the warm near-silence of the river and listened to the breeze gently shaking the 40-foot nipa-palms with the sound of the rattling of a million dried insects' wings. After a while we ate, I remember, the curried remains of a barracuda we had caught after Sumbang, and we all, except Wilfred, celebrated our landfall on the threshold of Sambir in whisky. To be there had been a part of my dream for a long time. It was something worth celebrating.

For Captain Jansen in *Mauru III*, on the contrary, there was to be no loitering. We swept full-ahead into the Pantai like a rabbit bolting into its warren; everyone was on deck chattering and laughing with the smell of home in their nostrils, and the *nakhoda* was smiling at last and put his baseball cap on at a rakish angle for luck. It was a perfect evening, the nipas green and gold in the last almost horizontal rays of sunlight.

So there was no question of *Mauru III* anchoring as we had done in *Fiona*. The *nakhoda* carried a map of the river's depths and shoals in his mind, and we had a schedule. I saw Ustinov's plump face grinning under the wheelhouse – and passengers lining the rails waved to passing canoes, while the heavy boat swung abruptly from one side of the river to the other to skirt the submerged mudbanks.

Darkness fell with unexpected suddenness; a moon with a full and shining face rose over the river as we veered sharply up the side of Sodang Besar Island to Lingard's Crossing, where the *nakhoda* swerved *Mauru III* round the submerged bank that once held the 'secret' to the Berau, brushing the river's verge so that the roar of our engine rebounded back to us like metallic thunder, and our wash swept the bank, driving small tidal waves up half-hidden creeks. The *nakhoda* throttled back only where the fires glowed in the doorways of tumbledown huts on the bank. Passengers shouted to friends – 'Ya, Mohamed!' and 'Ya, Yanto!' – and answering shouts came from the shadows.

A lookout stood in the bows keeping a watch for logs, but Jansen briskly spun the wheel and swept his vessel into branch after branch of this maze of mysterious delta without a qualm. Lingard in the *Coeran*, the *West Indian* and the *Rajah Laut* had done the same; and Conrad, too, in Syed Mohsin's *Vidar*.

I began to think of our arrival; of the junction of the two wide rivers, the ancient palaces of long-gone rajahs, the big tree marking the promontory where Almayer had lived and died. Would Mr Suparno,

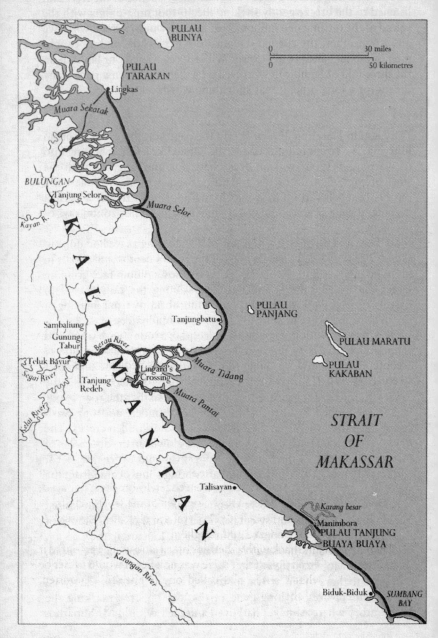

my interpreter from Samarinda, be waiting for me at the wharf at Tanjung Redeb? On that very wharf, meeting for the first time, Almayer had whined to Conrad, 'Didn't expect you in till this evening.' And Conrad had taken pains to explain to him that having picked up the beacon at the mouth of the river just before dark and the tide serving, Captain Craig was able to cross the bar and there was nothing to prevent him bringing the *Vidar* up the river at night.

'"Captain Craig knows this river like his own pocket."

'"Better," said Almayer.'

Evidently Jansen, our *nakhoda*, knew it pretty well, too.

It was dark with a moon like a silver sixpence when we reached the Berau, and we raced up the wide expanse of water where the two rivers come together over a sandbank which had ignominiously grounded *Fiona* for a while under the curious gaze of the local inhabitants. We drew alongside the wharf at Tanjung Redeb with a triumphant thump that threw down some people prone, but soon, unharmed and laughing, passengers poured across the deck, hurling boxes and small bundles ashore from the gunwales of the listing vessel. I leapt across a gap three feet wide, was tripped by an old woman with a plastic bag full of sarongs, and by the time I picked myself up Apson, with an excess of zeal, had thrown himself and one of my two bags into a pedicab and the driver was speeding off to God knows where.

It was lucky that at that moment Suparno appeared. Barely recognisable in a huge motorcycle crash helmet, he loaded me on to his scooter's pillion and we caught up with Apson's pedicab quite soon. Acting for the best, he was not absconding with my bag. He had had an idea I would be staying in one cheap hotel (*losmen*), and Suparno had made arrangements with another. Relieved, we arrived quite shortly at Suparno's choice, the *Losmen* Herlina.

My room was small as rooms in *losmen* usually are – a bed, chairs, a table fan, a bathroom with chipped tiles and a tank of cold water with a plastic scoop – but I was not worried about that. I sat on the bed getting my breath back while Apson went to fetch some tea. Suparno, clutching that gleaming black helmet, grinned at me from a chair.

'Welcome to Tanjung Redeb. I guess you are pleased to be back.'

'Pleased, Suparno? Amazed and delighted.'

Then Apson came back with a thermos of tea, and while he poured it into three mugs, I told myself that there was nowhere I would rather be than here – in what Conrad had called one of the still 'forgotten, unknown places of the earth'.

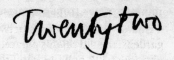

The *losmen* Suparno had taken me to, the Hotel Herlina, was a short stroll from the river and a little above the wharves of Tanjung Redeb.

In the morning I walked to the water's edge and saw on my left the makeshift mosque alongside which years before we had anchored *Fiona* on the orders of the *shahbandar*. I would never forget that mosque. In issuing those orders, this mild, easy-going man, on whose office wall an old map of the Berau quite clearly showed the 'Oversteek van Lingard', the Lingard Crossing, had unintentionally condemned us to nights of mental torture since it was Ramadan and the mosque's loudspeakers were up to Sengkang's raucous standards. Prayers, invocations, sermons continued without a break for hours on end. There had been little sleep for us in Tanjung Redeb.

As usual, a heavy morning mist covered the Berau – almost as bad as a proverbial London fog. It hung like smoke over the river, and poured up out of the trees as if the forest floor was on fire. Later the sun would gobble it up and the heavy heat of the day would settle over the meeting of the rivers.

The Berau – how many times had I seen that name on the old shipping lists of Singapore? How often had Captain Ellis, the Master Attendant, pursed his lips and, looking speculatively out of his window at one or another of Lingard's vessels anchored in the roads, thought, 'Back again, eh? In from "Brow".'

The Berau had been 'Sambir' to Almayer; 'Patusan' to Lord Jim and Marlow. The meeting of the rivers deserved more than one name. For 'the Berau' is the result of the confluence of two rivers, both of which flow down from the vast interior of Borneo, from hills that in Conrad's time had barely been touched by European foot and even at the present time are inhabited by Dayak tribes seldom seen except by mis-

250

sionaries. The northern river is called the Segai and, curving down to Tanjung Redeb, it passes between the town and the string of houses, gardens, the old rajah's palace, and a mosque or two, that lie along the opposite bank and are known as the settlement of Gunung Tabor, or 'the mountain that crumbled away'. The Segai is quite a wide stretch of water, wider than its sister tributary, the Kelai; perhaps as wide as the Thames at London Bridge.

The Kelai comes together with the Segai from the south and divides, in its turn, Tanjung Redeb from a third string of houses with another old palace and another mosque, called Sambaliung. By that time it has wiggled down from the ocean of mountains and forests that rise, wave after wave, to wash over the border of Sarawak.

These two rivers meet and flow, as 'the Berau', commingled through the tidal flats of delta to the sea. And the whole district takes its name from the river Berau.

Tanjung Redeb was – and still is – the old trading post of Berau. On the promontory where the rivers flow together William Lingard set up his office and wharf. In 1870 he installed Almayer (or Olmeijer) to keep his accounts, and had built warehouses on the water's edge, which soon bulged with the rattans, dammar resin and gutta-percha he and Olmeijer bought from the Dayaks, and which waited there for his ships to carry it to the markets of Singapore, Makassar or Palembang. From the verandah Lingard could look over to Sambaliung from his cane chair, and dream out loud of the enormous profits ahead, filling Olmeijer's fat head with visions of a fortune. At first, the business was Lingard's monopoly; the private commercial preserve of a bold English privateer who alone had discovered the only way for big ships to pass through the treacherous shoals of the delta. It would remain his monopoly for about ten years. Then the Arabs arrived and that was that.

With Suparno I walked in sunlight to the wharf, found *Mauru III*, and thanked the *nakhoda*, no longer surly but smiling, for the ride from Samarinda. While Captain Jansen ordered up mugs of tea, Apson and Raffles produced paper and pencils and wrote down the addresses of their families in Menado. 'Come and visit,' they said.

The street that runs by the water – the main street of Tanjung Redeb – is not a long one. It runs about two hundred yards to Almayer's promontory where the Segai and Kelai join to form the Berau.

There had been a few changes. I remembered an unpaved street of

251

stone and earth; now it was asphalted. There had been shops or stalls on both sides of it. On the river side they had gone, since a terrible fire, Suparno explained, about a year after the departure of *Fiona* had devastated the street: a paraffin lamp in a back room had exploded and the wooden buildings had gone up. My favourite *warung* had vanished, too. Perhaps its owner, Mr Lim Jin Sian, had emigrated once again, as he had hinted he might. 'My grandfather came here to make money,' he had confessed to Mac and me when we came to buy paraffin for *Fiona*. 'But business is not good. So few people here to buy things.' He had one hope. He asked us again and again: 'Do you think there's oil here?' Apparently the answer had been no.

Even so, much was unchanged. Pedicabs still scurried along the uneven street, their drivers pumping their stringy legs up and down and rattling their handbrakes to clear the way. The line of narrow front stores facing the road – rebuilt since the fire – still sold just about everything; there were tin kettles, plastic buckets, canned goods, soft drinks, powdered milk – everything from cheap cotton dresses to batik blouses and plastic sandals to mosquito coils. As before, the stalls in the food market displayed blue sea prawns as big as miniature crayfish, shrimps, a kind of freshwater sardine full of bones, three-inch river crabs, and expensive deer meat ferried down the river from far Dayak country. Only the boxes of turtles' eggs, white and round like ping-pong balls were missing. Since *Fiona's* time, their sale had been made illegal.

As before, people would stop dead in the street and stare at me, smiling. It was curious. I did not mind them wondering who I was and what I was doing in this remote place where Europeans were still seldom seen. They had every reason to wonder. Many years before, Mr Lim's daughter – back from school in Surabaya for the Ramadan holiday – had looked at me as if I were a monster, her eyes round with wonder, and asked timidly, 'Are you a globetrotter? What is your name?' Remembering her, I recalled that Mr Lim himself was a refugee from southern China, he had called his *warung* 'Usdekar', which he said meant self-help – 'because I made it alone'. It looked as if he had gone away to make it alone somewhere else.

Mr Lim was gone and I dare say some other inhabitants of Tanjung Redeb, too. There were few if any cars here even now; all I saw were a few jeeps and a minibus or two in back streets, and a good many motorbikes. On the waterfront shops a few television aerials had sprouted – although now I come to think about it, I don't remember seeing a television set, so perhaps the aerials were only for show.

Across the Segai, one scene was certainly unchanged: the little tree-shrouded houses and mosque of Gunung Tabor. Longboats with outboard motors puttered up and down the river and canoes propelled by as many as four paddlers still ran swiftly with the tide from one side of the wide river to the other. On the riverside of Tanjung Redeb's main street, skiffs with makeshift rattan roofs were tied up waiting for hire, and higher up a lesser version of the *Mauru III* was offloading sacks of rice or some other cargo for delivery to one or another of the warehouses that lay behind the line of shops and the *shahbandar*'s office at the end of the street. The *Mauru III* lay even further upstream, taking on cargo for her return to Paré-Paré.

We walked on. At the end of the main street there was a prominent two-storeyed wooden house and between it and the point of the promontory a jumble of trees and wooden roofs. Charles Olmeijer's house and the office of Lingard and Co's had stood here, and where we stopped now by a jetty, Conrad had first set eyes on the extraordinary creature whose name he changed in his novels to 'Kaspar Almayer'.

> That tropical daybreak was chilly . . . wet dripped from the rigging . . . and it was in the middle of a shuddering yawn that I caught sight of Almayer . . . . He stepped upon the jetty. He was clad simply in flapping pyjamas of cretonne pattern (enormous flowers with yellow petals on a disagreeable blue ground) and a thin cotton singlet with short sleeves.
>   He came quite close to the ship's side and raised a harassed countenance, round and fat, with that curl of black hair over the forehead and a heavy, pained glance . . . . In the accents of a man accustomed to the buffets of evil fortune, he asked hardly audibly: 'I suppose you haven't got such a thing as a pony aboard?'

Conrad was never to forget Olmeijer – this unusual man, 'a man who was afraid of his letters' because the *Vidar* had brought him the first mail he had received for ages and he had held it unopened in his hand for one whole morning.

> 'Well, Mr Almayer,' I said. 'You haven't started on your letters yet.'
>   He glanced at it when I spoke and, for a moment, it looked as if he were on the point of opening his fingers and letting the whole lot fall overboard. I believe he was tempted to do so. I shall never forget that man afraid of his mail. . . .
>   'Trade is very bad here.'
>   'Indeed!'
>   'Hopeless! . . . And when one has important interests . . . up the river . . . Well, I must be off. So long!'

With these crazily disjointed sentences Almayer (or Olmeijer) hurried away, throwing a mumbled invitation to dinner over his shoulder.

That unforgettable encounter must have taken place more or less where I stood now by the waterside with Suparno. The pony Almayer was waiting for had been landed in a sling right at Suparno's feet – and the moment Almayer took hold of it it had bolted, disappearing into the morning mist towards the blurred bulk of a house with a high-pitched roof of grass, where now there was a sharp turning to the right off the main street leading, I knew, to the modern brick house belonging to Haji Mohamed Al Joofree. On the corner itself was a big store with a Chinese name board over the door, and I saw the cheerful bulk of Ustinov (of the *Mauru III*) grinning at me from a chair. He gave me a cheerful wave. 'Business good?' I called, and he nodded energetically back, shouting, 'Plenty rattans,' and giving the thumbs up sign.

I asked Suparno to go alone to ring the bell at Haji Mohamed's and see if he was there, while I continued to the tip of Almayer's promontory from where I could see the Berau beginning its eastward flow to the sea. Across the confluence of the Segai and the Kelai the twin breast-shaped hills below Gunung Tabor stood as they always had, on the lookout for strange craft coming from the delta round a sharp bend in the river.

By the big wooden building at the end of the street, I turned left and followed a slippery network of walkways made of rotting planks across an area of mud, grass, and bushes. A few trees with big, dark leaves and a soaring palm towered over a few two-storeyed plank houses with thatched or tin roofs, whose glassless, shuttered windows faced directly on to the Kelai, and whose jetties ran shakily out over the water between rotting logs and mooring-poles to which canoes were attached and an occasional motor boat with wooden awnings.

Across the river I could see the village of Sambaliung – a line of houses and dense trees, with here and there the glint of the metal dome of a mosque. Beyond was a low green hill called Gunung Illanun (Illanun Hill), after the Sulu raiders and slavers, the Illanun from Mindanao, who once infested these parts. Almayer's wife had been rescued from the shambles of a Sulu war-prau Lingard had blown out of the water.

In Sambaliung, in Almayer's time, the Bugis potentate Lakamba had held court among his followers 'with a stolid face, his big, bloodshot eyes blinking solemnly, as if dazzled by the noble vacuity of his thoughts'. His stockade was always full of armed men and watchful

eyes, not the least watchful of which belonged to his crafty one-eyed 'prime minister' and *shahbandar*, Babalatchi.

The Kelai looked as wide and deep as the Nile, but Lingard and Almayer had no trouble spotting Abdullah's ship, *Lord of the Isles*, lying at Lakamba's jetty the fatal day she arrived. Willems, Lingard's protegé, stood on her deck and Almayer had immediately understood that he had ignored Lingard's request to keep mum, and deliberately divulged the 'secret' of the river to his Arab rivals. He had sold out to Syed Abdullah and thanks to his betrayal Abdullah's ship had found the way up the Berau. Lingard's monopoly was ended. Looking at Willems through his telescope, Almayer was so enraged he had shaken his fist at him.

The sombre wooden walls of the houses around me were so sheer and their small windows placed so high in them that they might have been warehouses. But one in particular struck me as very like Almayer's house and office. Had I heard his wife's shrill shriek of 'Kaspar! *Makan!*' the sound even now would not have seemed inappropriate. A strange tumbledown structure, it stood bang on the river and its ramshackle verandah ran out over the water on rotting wooden piles.

> In the middle of the verandah there was a round table. On it a paraffin lamp without a globe shed a hard flare on the three inner sides. The fourth side was open and faced the river . . . . In one of the side walls

there was a doorway. Half obliterated words – 'Office: Lingard & Co.' – were still legible on the dusty door .... A general air of squalid neglect pervaded the place –

A white mast poked above shrubs and trees where a small prau was moored against the bank; a neat little thing, her hull half white, half dark green. A boy washing clothes on her foredeck, left in charge, I suppose, while her crew were ashore, looked up and waved, but with the duckboards under my feet creaking ominously over yellow ooze, I staggered in alarm back to the house that might have been Almayer's. There I stood on its steps and listened to the low mutter of motorboats passing on the Kelai.

I had read and re-read of the decline and fall of Almayer so often that, standing on the site of his home for thirty years, scenes came back as if they had been recreated.

Almayer's lunch – I felt sure – was on that round table on the verandah: a plateful of rice and fish, a jar of water, and a bottle half full of trade gin beside a cracked glass tumbler and a tin spoon. Trying vainly and pathetically to swat one of a dozen bluebottles, Almayer would soon be staggering about, swiping at them, yelling like a madman, 'I wonder what such damned things are made for!'

On this spot Lingard had admitted to Almayer that, after the loss of his brig, he was powerless to halt Abdullah and the Arabs. What a blow that had been. Easy to conjure up the voices from the verandah – one moaning, recriminating, the other deep and infuriatingly calm:

'What? You don't mean to expel Abdulla out of here by force? I tell you, you can't.'

'That's all over, I am afraid .... If I had *Flash* here I would try force. Eh! Why not? However, the poor *Flash* is gone, and there is an end of it – '

'What's going to happen to me and her? [Nina, Almayer's daughter] That's what I want to know. You brought me here, made me your partner, and now, when everything is gone to the devil – through your fault, mind you – you talk about your ship! .... But here. This trade. That's gone now, thanks to Willems .... Your dear Willems!'

Later, Lingard had gone for good, had disappeared utterly in England; and then Almayer, abandoned on this god-forsaken promontory, surely had something to whine about.

'Look at Abdulla now' – Almayer was close to tears – 'He has hundreds of thousands. Has a house in Penang. What did he not have when he stole my trade from me! He knocked everything here into a cocked hat; drove father' [Lingard] 'to gold-hunting – then to Europe where he disappeared. Fancy a man like Captain Lingard disappearing as though he had been a common coolie. Friends of mine wrote to London asking about him. Nobody ever heard of him there! Never heard of Captain Lingard!'

Inside the disintegration of Almayer's house – this house? – had been scattered the dust and very bones of 'a dead and gone business': books with torn pages, account books that looked as if they had never been opened, a big office desk with one leg broken and its drawers on the floor, a revolving chair that no longer revolved. Torn books, broken shelves, and dust. Wreck, ruin and waste – all that was left after half a lifetime of work.

I tried to imagine Almayer's years up here among the mists, the mangrove swamps, the malice, and the disease. One bout of shivering and feverish dreams on *Fiona* had been enough for me. Olmeijer had endured two decades of them. He had lost two sons to disease. He was to lose his wife, too.

No wonder Almayer's howl of despair had reverberated across this stretch of water.

'What's the sense of all this? Where's your Providence? Where's the good for anybody in all this? The world's a swindle! A swindle! Why should I suffer? What have I done to be treated so?'

If tragedy leaves behind its vibrations, how much of Almayer's anguish had been absorbed into the waters of the Kelai, these dilapidated buildings, the lifeless trees, the ooze under the planking? On moonless nights, I wondered, did people living here wake to hear a voice sobbing by the water's edge – '*What have I done to be treated like this?*'?

'He's not there,' a very unspectral voice said in my ear. 'Gone to Surabaya. His nephew will come to see you at the hotel tomorrow morning.' Suparno was looking at me as if I needed bringing back to earth. 'Are you all right?'

'These Al Joofrees are always travelling, Suparno. Will we ever catch up with them?'

We walked back to the main street and took a pedicab back to the Herlina. I wanted to take a look at the other side of the river.

I had read of the existence in Berau of the graves of two of the sons of the real Olmeijer.

Young Suparno had never heard of Conrad, Lingard or Olmeijer, so on his own he could not help me find them. I had no notion where they might be buried. Had they been lost in grass or jungle, obliterated by floods, ploughed up in one of the three villages of the Berau; Tanjung Redeb, Gunung Tabor or Sambaliung? It was a large area to cover; too large. So when Suparno, after pondering the matter, came to me smiling and said, 'Tomorrow, we shall go and see a friend of mine in Gunung Tabor. He might know,' I was not too optimistic, but it was certainly worth a try.

Next day, before the heat had become really troublesome, Suparno and his friend brought a canoe with an outboard motor to the jetty down the lane from the Herlina. From the first I was heartened when the boatman set off confidently down the left bank of the Berau. He seemed to know where he was going. 'My friend thinks he knows the place,' Suparno said encouragingly; and my hopes rose.

Past the string of houses, a mosque and the two breast-like hills of grassy meadow land began, knolls capped with clumps of forest and patches of cultivation. An expensive Chinese tomb designed like a bandstand dominated the edge of the river but, ignoring it, we pulled alongside the bank beyond it and scrambled ashore into long grass.

A man and his dog moving about a makeshift thatched hut – a sort of grassy tool shed – on a hill overlooking a pepper plantation were the only sign of life. The dog, wearing a string of amulets round its neck, began to bark. More men appeared. Suparno's friend talked to them, explaining what we were looking for, and the men nodded as though they understood. Beckoning to us, they led the way through a field of pepper plants, entwined on poles like young vines. Soon a hillside sloped towards the river into a small wilderness of tall grass and bamboos, and there the men began laying about them with parangs, levelling a narrow way through thick undergrowth. I followed them, in air like damp cotton wool down a newly cut tunnel through vegetation 10 feet high.

'Be careful. Snakes,' said Suparno cheerfully. 'Follow the footprints of the men with parangs.'

'That's what I am trying to do.'

Half blinded with sweat, I could not have seen a cobra if it had risen up and hissed in my face.

But at last, there were the graves. Two slabs of stone stood like islands surrounded by flattened undergrowth. The one I leaped on, panting, had been totally defaced; any dedication had been prised off with a crowbar. But the other, a fine upstanding tombstone unblemished, marked with a large and well-defined cross and several lines of writing.

Suparno's friend had had foresight. He fished a few short sticks of chalk from his trouser pocket and began to rub them over the writing, across the shallow indentations; and soon, as if by magic, words and dates appeared. They were Dutch words – but they were decipherable.

Hier rusten onze lievelingen
'Here lie our darlings . . .'

And then the names:

Carel George
29 December 1874   4 February 1875

Albert Eduard
2 July 1878   28 November 1878

I copied down the Dutch inscription and later had it translated. It was simple and sad:

Hun dood betreuren wij destemeer,
Daar wij alhier verlaten eenzaam
En zonder enigen troost gevonden.

'We mourn their deaths, we who remain behind,
lost and lonely . . . inconsolable . . .'

Who had erected the stone? I scraped away the last stray roots of wiry grass and saw the names:

Charles Olmeyer
Johanna Maria Cornelia Lieshout.

Not much over a hundred years before, Olmeijer's servants, similarly sweating, had toiled with spades and crowbars and hoisted this stone into place above the grave of his infant sons. Olmeijer would have read some sort of burial service over it, while the Malays, resting on their spades, watched with interest these curious Christian goings-on.

The stone, if not the inscription, had worn well in this climate of fierce rains and a fiercer sun. Olmeijer's wife, Johanna, a Eurasian –

half Dutch, half Menadonese – had married Olmeijer in 1874. So it must have been their first child – they had eleven in eighteen years – who had died aged only five weeks old. Contemplating one more cruelty of fate, the flabby figure with its round, glistening face, the black hair lank with sweat curled over his forehead, had stood here, had lifted his sun helmet to mop the sweat from his brow and the tears from his puffy cheeks.

Returning to the hotel in the boat, Suparno asked, 'Charles Olmeijer, what was he doing here?'

'Trading. He was the only European trader here for about twenty-five years.'

'Was he successful?'

'At first. Then he was less successful. The Arabs came – the ancestors of Haji Mohamed Al Joofree – and stole his trade and his profits.'

'Haji Mohamed?'

'An ancestor, Abdullah.'

'And the graves?'

'They were two infant sons of Olmeijer. They died of cholera, I expect, or typhoid or malaria or worms. There wasn't much medicine in those days. No air-conditioning, only a few fans and not much ice. And mosquitoes, dirt, heat.'

Suparno looked appalled. I realised he had never seriously thought about the times of, say, his grandfather. He had taken things like medicine for granted; they had been around as long as he had. But he was interested now in these old Europeans who had lived here years ago.

'Was Joseph Conrad a famous writer?'

'Very. Before that he was an officer on a ship owned by Arabs from Singapore, the Al Joofrees. Conrad came here four times.'

'He is dead?'

'He died in England in 1924. A very famous writer.'

'Well, we have no books here.'

'There are books in Jakarta.'

'Jakarta,' Suparno said mournfully, 'is too far.'

'I will send you some of Conrad's books from Singapore,' I told him.

I went next to visit the *kraton* – the former palace – of the Sultans of Gunung Tabor.

'The old *kraton* of Gunung Tabor,' Suparno informed me apologetically, 'was burned in 1945.'

This one was an imposing bungalow in unmistakably Dutch style: high ceilings, floors covered with green-flowered linoleum and cool, breezy rooms. Among the usual yellow ceremonial umbrellas and cases of royal robes, were photographs of the last sultan, in an embroidered morning coat, something like European court dress of about 1910, with a shako and a sword. The palace had a homely atmosphere. A Dutch grandfather clock ticked in one corner and an upright piano stood in another. Large windows looked out across the water to the Tanjung Redeb promontory and the tall palm over Olmeijer's house.

'The royal families of Gunung Tabor and Sambaliung were closely connected,' Suparno said, 'in the old days.' And often deadly rivals in the bad, old days of pirates and slaving.

Sambaliung, too, across the Kelai branch of the Berau, faced directly into Almayer's compound. It was true that Sambaliung and Gunung Tabor were dynastically connected. Both rajahs were Bugis and related to the rulers of Kotai upstream from Samarinda. The Bugis 'mafia' had straddled the east coast of Borneo. In *Almayer's Folly*, Conrad had placed Lakamba's settlement here and in easy view of

Almayer across the river; Lakamba had entertained Syed Abdullah the day his schooner reached the Berau for the first time.

Suparno's family lived there, too, and its palace was rather larger than the one at Gunung Tabor. In an upper room two rusty cannons lay draped in yellow and on a table wrapped in a cloth was something sinister. Mysteriously, it resembled a sandwich. A terrific smell of mothballs pervaded the room like ectoplasm.

When I asked what was concealed in the cloth, an old retainer in horn-rimmed spectacles almost jumped out of his skin. 'Nobody can open it. Nobody can touch it.'

'What is it?'

'All we know is that it is something made of brass. And its name is *Anakbaccing*, the name of an old sultan who was the only one who ever saw it.'

'What if you opened it – or Suparno?'

The old man looked shocked by the suggestion. 'Undoubtedly we would get sick and die.'

The temptation to unravel the sandwich was very strong. Probably it contained nothing but a pistol or a brass cannon ball. But it would cause immense umbrage to open it – and that, with the possibility of a fatal curse, decided me to leave the mystery unsolved.

A pillar covered in Bugis twig language stood outside the *kraton*. Pointing to it, the old man said, 'The sultans came from Boné. This pillar sets out certain rules of society. A man running from his enemies will be given sanctuary here. Adultery is punishable with forty strokes of the rattan on the back.' Other rules emphasised the sultan's supremacy over his subjects.

'If the sultan is resting,' the old man went on, 'anyone passing this gate must go down on his knees. Various misdeeds merit various punishments. A certain bad act might mean a man would have to cut the grass round the *kraton*.' In the kriss-wielding Bugis world, I thought, a man sentenced to grass-cutting might be considered to be getting off lightly.

In a *Narrative of the Voyage of HMS Samarang*, Captain Sir Edward Belcher had written of Gunung Tabor in 1845, twenty-five years before Olmeijer's arrival.

The immediate reason for Belcher's penetration of so remote a river as the Berau (which he spelled 'Brraou') was the following letter:

Goonoong Tabboo, 10 Sept.,1844

To the BRITISH CONSUL or any European Merchant at
Sooloo or Manila

Gentlemen,

I take this opportunity of informing you of the sad state we are now living in. On the 27th of July, 1844, the barque 'Premier' from Hong Kong, bound for the island of Bally, in ballast and Chinese cash, for Rice, was wrecked on Pulo Panjang, and was obliged to take to our boats, but next day after leaving the ship, was taken in tow by a prao, and enticed us to go to Sultan Gooning's, as he would send us to Macassar soon; but when we got there, he put us off from day to day, and made the excuse, that we would get all things from the ship, and send everything to Macassar with us in a proa.

We remained at his house five days, and was sent on board a proa in the river to live, where we had little to eat, and not a mat to lie upon . . . .

The letter signed by the captain of the *Premier*, accused the Sultan of taking all he could remove from the wreck of the *Premier* – mainly iron and cash – and then dividing the prisoners with the neighbouring Rajah of Bulungan. The Sultan apparently had kept six lascars and seven Europeans for himself, and he had lost no time in selling the lascars to the Dayaks. The letter went on to state that the wicked Sultan had been preparing to sell the Europeans similarly into the interior of Borneo (never to be seen again), but that they had made a bolt across the water to Sambaliung to the camp of the Sultan's cousin. Now, the letter warned, 'the Sultan is threatening war against the Rajah'. Help was urgently required.

This alarming story demonstrated two things. First, that such goings-on were quite credible at that epoch; and second, that European officers could be as scurrilously dishonest as any native ruler. For the captain's letter was a pack of lies. The Royal Navy responded to the appeal of this poor shipwrecked British seaman, but when HMS *Samarang* had made her way through the hazardous sandbanks of the Pantai and reached Gunung Tabor, Belcher found quite a different state of affairs.

He was greeted like a hero – by the natives. Ambassadors from the 'wicked' Sultan having greeted him with broad smiles and bade him welcome, Belcher blasted off a salute to the Sultan of twenty-one guns. This must have made the *kraton* rattle, but it started things off on the right foot, for although the guns would have made a terrifying din within the enclosed neighbourhood of the Berau, the main thing was that it pleased the people of Gunung Tabor no end. They clapped their hands in raptures of astonishment, exclaiming, 'Well done, English!

263

English brothers, Gunung Tabor!' In this heady atmosphere, to the sound of squeaking flutes and the excited banging of bass drums, Belcher and the officers of the *Samarang* were helped along an immense log that led into the Sultan's stockade, and shaded from the sun by men carrying huge scarlet silk umbrellas. There the ruler, elegant in scarlet and gold, affectionately embraced them.

Belcher expected a kind of Bugis Bluebeard, but the Sultan proved to be 'a fine, well-shaped young man of about five foot eleven and thirty years of age', only too willing to come to an immediate agreement. For it soon turned out that not he but the master of the *Premier* was the villain of this story. The rogue had given his name as 'Brownrigg' but was in reality called 'Milne', and from that falsehood followed a long succession of others. No one, it turned out, had been sold to the Dayaks; nor had any Europeans escaped to Sambaliung. They had no need to. The Gunung Sultan had placed them on a Dutch vessel which shipped them off to safety. The Sultan waved a receipt from the Dutch captain under Belcher's nose to prove it.

The whole business ended in amiability all round. The jolly Sultan restored every last item his men had taken from the *Premier* – he had taken care to have an inventory made at the time – and expressed his intense eagerness to make an alliance with Great Britain. Accordingly a treaty was drawn up. The Sultan symbolically linked right thumbs with Belcher and declared him a brother; more guns were fired from the *Samarang* with a few Congreve rockets added for luck. ('Fortunately,' wrote Belcher, 'the second rocket entered a large dead tree at about 800 yards distant, and setting it on fire astonished them greatly.') Finally, the Sultan 'conveyed into Belcher's hand, with great mystery,' what he whispered was called the 'Snake Stone'. It was a polished globe of quartz about the size of a musket-ball, said to have been taken from the head of an enchanted snake.

All remaining lascars being accounted for, the treaty was signed, and a paragraph of it declared that 'the Sultan of Gunung Taboor engages, that the subjects of the Queen of Great Britain shall always meet with friendship and protection within his dominions'. The treaty bore the signatures of 'Sultan Maharajah Dinda, Gunung Taboor' and 'Edward Belcher, Captain of Her Majesty's Ship, *Samarang*'. The following day, with a farewell exchange of blessings from all concerned, the *Samarang* dropped down to the mouth of the Pantai.

Belcher had all the evidence he needed to show that Captain Milne of the *Premier* had used gross language to his crew, become hideously drunk and tried to wash his hands of the lascars of his crew, even telling the Sultan, 'Do what you please with them, sell them.' Conduct tending, as much as anything Jim or Austin Williams were guilty of, to bring the reputation of British officers into disrepute.

I told Suparno this story and showed him a photocopy of the wording of the Anglo-Gunung Tabor treaty. He was delighted to see that the Sultan was exonerated from blame; he obviously felt that was one up to Berau.

'Subjects of the Queen of Great Britain,' he cried, 'shall always meet with friendship in Gunung Tabor. That's what it says. You always have my friendship, Mr Young.'

'It also says "protection", Suparno,' I reminded him. 'And you come from Sambaliung. I hope you will not try to sell me to the Dayaks.'

Haunted by the pathetic shade of Olmeijer, I wanted to pay a last visit to the site of his house before I left Tanjung Redeb.

It was nearly sunset when I walked up the main street by the side of the Segai where in the cool twilight men and boys were loading boxes and sacks onto skiffs, and sailors in sarongs scrambled about a prau preparing to take her to sea. On the far bank I could just see the *kraton* of Gunung Tabor and the mosque's metal dome, and the twin hills were still visible in the sun's last rays, but shadows and the sharp bend in the river hid the pepper field and the high grass and bamboo concealing the grave of the Olmeijer babies, Carel and Albert.

In his Chinese friend's store, Ustinov was bustling happily about with an armful of what might have been invoices. When I went to shake his hand, he told me he had done good business and was leaving for Biduk-Biduk next day. 'Nineteen hours by boat – wah!' he shouted gleefully.

I turned off as before between the sides of the old wooden houses. On the shaded promontory, darkness had already fallen. The slippery planks over the mud creaked again under my weight but they did not give way and soon I came to what I thought of as Almayer's house. Shadowy figures moved round lighted doorways. There was a smell of cooking fish and the tinkle of kitchen utensils. The sunset call to prayer floated across the dark shapes of boats scurrying home on the Kelai, over the palm trees and the white mast of the prau that the low tide had lolled at an angle against the sky, as if she had decided to doze there for the night.

> The main branch of the Pantai was lost in complete darkness, for the fire
> at the Rajah's compound had gone out altogether; but up the Sambir

[Almayer's] reach, his eye could follow the long line of Malay houses crowding the bank, with here and there a dim light twinkling through bamboo walls, or a smoky torch burning on the platforms built out over the river ....

Almayer's final humiliation had come with the desertion of his only daughter, Nina, with Dain, her lover-prince from Bali. 'I shall never forgive you, Nina!' Almayer had shouted in the extremity of his fear and loneliness. He watched the sail of their prau disappear over the horizon, then fell to his knees and, 'creeping along the sand, erased carefully with his hand all traces of Nina's footsteps', piling up small heaps of sand in 'a line of miniature graves down to the water'. His face had been like the face of 'a man that has died struck from behind'.

For Almayer what was there left? Nothing that he could see. After that, he took to opium, lying half-senseless on his back on the floor, his head on a wooden pillow, and in the end he was found like that by his servant, dead in the house that had stood on this spot. Syed Abdullah, hearing the news, came to confirm it.

The crowd massed in a semicircle . . . opened out before the group of white-robed and turbaned men advancing through the grass towards the house. Abdulla walked first . . . .
  He made a few paces forward and found himself for the last time face to face with his old enemy . . . not dangerous now, lying stiff and lifeless

in the tender light of early day. The only white man on the east coast was dead . . . .

  Abdulla looked down sadly . . . took in his hand the beads that hung at his waist . . . glanced coldly once more at the serene face.

  . . . The beads in Abdulla's hand clicked while in a solemn whisper he breathed out piously the name of Allah! The Merciful! The Compassionate!

Abdullah looked down on poor dead Almayer as I was soon to look down on Abdullah.

Olmeijer's end was sad, too: not the result of opium in his case, but cancer.

Some time before I had found him lying beneath the long grass of a long abandoned cemetery in Surabaya. An old caretaker opened its flimsy iron gates after I had rattled them for some time, while a child peered out at me from an old gatehouse, screaming '*Orang belanda, orang belanda*! Dutchman! Dutchman!' as if I was some kind of bogeyman.

The old man, suspicious at first, was helpful when I told him I was looking for an old Dutch grave of about 1900. He unlocked a cupboard in the gatehouse and took out an index of burials, and with skinny arms heaved it on to a table so that I could consult it.

There were several Olmeijer graves named and numbered. The first was Carolina Dorothea, died 1874, aged thirty-five years old; she was a bit early for me. There was a Carel Olmeyer, spelled with a 'y', born in 1799; he had died in 1877, the book said, so he could not have met Conrad in Tanjung Redeb. There was a Frans Olmeijer, and a Frederika Olmeijer (oddly enough, *née* Coenraad) who died in 1941, and she was the last Olmeijer listed here.

Except that with a final turn of a page there was 'Almayer'. Charles Olmeijer – died 2 September 1900 – and a number.

The cemetery was a grim place. The sun beat down like fire from heaven on horribly decaying vaults and acres of palsied headstones among sombre trees, lapped by dead brown leaves and coated with moss and creepers. Many seemed to have been deliberately prised apart by grave robbers, or perhaps they had simply fallen to pieces with age. '*Hier rust . . .*' – on many of the barely decipherable inscriptions these were the only legible words. There were broken crosses, headless angels and a vault dated July 1807 shattered by the roots of a tree; there was something indecent in the way time had disclosed cheap, badly-laid bricks behind the pompous marble and the stone cladding. Peering deep into a half-open private vault, you expected to see someone's bones and perhaps a skull; but there was only scummy water, rubble and, in one tomb, a plastic sandal. The hot wind hissed through stiff grass, and I thought once more of snakes. On a horizontal slab with an elaborate inscription, a man in jeans lay face-down with a towel over his head – drugged, dead or merely sleeping, it was impossible to say.

'*Tuan! di-sini, di-sini!*' The old man had found Olmeijer's grave now. He swept leaves from a corner of a stone and I brushed the sweat from my eyes and bent to check the number on it. I saw a slab of dirty grey, raddled and pitted like the skin of a man who has spent too much time drinking too much in the tropics; like Olmeijer. The name had been vandalised, but this was his tomb all right – as undistinguished as one would have expected, faceless and nameless, too, abandoned to rot in a forgotten cemetery.

Poor Olmeijer. Wherever he is now I hope he knows that Conrad has made him immortal.

Haji Mohamed's son, Ahmad, came to call at the *losmen* as he had promised. His father, he said apologetically, was still away. He travelled often to Samarinda or Bulungan, north of Berau, which is where he was born.

Ahmad told me, 'Many Arabs still live in Bulungan – in Kampong Arab, as they call it. Many, too, in Samarinda. Quite a few of them are Al Joofrees.' He smiled. 'If you want to meet Al Joofrees, go to Bulungan.'

'I do want to meet them,' I assured him. 'And I am going to Bulungan.'

twenty three

To get to Bulungan I had to fly to Balik Papan, the oil town below Samarinda, and from there take a steamer, called the *Kerinci*, to Tarakan island.

Suparno would be in Tarakan to meet me; at least he hoped to – he was not certain he could arrive there in time, so there was a possibility that I would find myself without a translator in a place where it would be most important for me to be able to communicate with the local population; particularly with the Al Joofree family.

But I was lucky.

Shortly after the *Kerinci* sailed from Donggala I was contemplating sadly from her rail the increasing evidence of the damage that timber companies were doing to the already threadbare landscape of northern Celebes, when a polite voice at my elbow said in English,

'Where are you going to?'

I saw a smiling face, a plump, round, rather Chinese face: a student, I thought.

'Tarakan,' I said, and then for accuracy's sake, 'Really a place called Tanjung Selor.' Tanjung Selor was the town on the Bulungan; according to Suparno, it was a smaller version of Tanjung Redeb. It was unlikely that this young man would know of it.

But he surprised me. 'I *live* in Tanjung Selor,' he said with a broad grin. He was studying 'oil' in East Java and was returning to his home in Bulungan for a holiday. When I told him why I was going there and mentioned the Al Joofrees, he burst out laughing. 'I know many Al Joofrees in Tanjung Selor. I know all of them.'

The young man's name was Alfred Baya and his mother came from Menado, but there was not a drop of Chinese blood in his body. His father was pure Kenyah Dayak, and his grandfather, who, he said, had

270

just died at a great age, had been the head of the Kenyah Dayaks, the *'Kepala Adat'*.

'King?'

'Not king. King is very rich, we are not rich. Maybe chief.' Then, he asked, 'Mr Young, will you please stay in my father's house?'

'With pleasure, Alfred. What better place to stay.'

I soon began to wonder if he had thought better of his offer because for the rest of the short voyage I did not set eyes on him again. I need not have worried. When the steamer tied up at Tarakan and the passengers were tumbling down the gangway on to the wharf in the usual turmoil, Alfred bobbed up at my elbow, taking control, marshalling porters to collect his baggage (he seemed to have been on a shopping spree in Java), grabbing my bag, loading everything on to a metal tumbril, and trotting along beside it to keep an eye on everything as the porters wheeled it off to the harbour gate. A churlish driver in a pick-up truck bundled a mass of passengers aboard and dropped them off one at a time at various points in the town, taking me to the hotel Suparno had recommended. Of Suparno there was no sign. 'Never mind,' said Alfred reassuringly. He made a note of the hotel's name, and promised he would pick me up there next day in time for the boat to Bulungan.

When we arrived at the Bulungan boat, the first thing I saw was a huge rat sitting on the pier, blocking our way. It faced us so calmly I wondered if it was diseased. Alfred took a reasonable view: 'No, it is a nice day. It is sunning itself.' And in its own good time the rat casually squeezed between the planks, and vanished.

The boat was certainly not a large one; and later I saw why. Inside under a canvas awning there were only seats for about seven or eight people ranged round its sides facing inwards. Or would have been. One young man lying full length blocked half of one side and, although with one open eye he saw the other passengers looking for somewhere to sit, he showed no sign of moving. Alfred boldly tapped his knee and to my surprise said to him, 'This gentleman' – indicating me – 'is looking for Al Joofrees. He's a writer, a historian.' The young man sat up sharply when he heard that. Alfred introduced him to me as a member of the Al Joofrees, and we shook hands.

My first Bulungan Al Joofree was a tall, extremely slender young man with a noticeably long sallow face and wide eyes that tilted upwards at the outer corners. His nose was the distinctive feature about him – it was much longer and straighter than the ordinary Malay nose and certainly much longer than Alfred's Dayak snub. It was undoubtedly an Arab nose. The young man was unusually well dressed for a day on a steamy river on the equator; in a long-sleeved pink shirt, dark blue trousers, purple socks, and highly polished loafers with pointed toes – shoes that once were known as 'winkle-pickers' – he might have been a model for natty gentlemen's clothing. Remembering the name I had been given in Samarinda of the family 'historian', I asked this dandy of the islands, 'Do you know Saihan Al Joofree?'

He smiled. 'He's my uncle,' he replied and, I think through shyness, he only addressed five other words to me on the boat.

Our progress up the channel was slow and frequently interrupted by groundings. The water was often low to the point of vanishing and once the mangroves closed round us in a series of twists and turns, the mudbanks were all too obvious. Sometimes we stopped completely, grinding the boat's flat bottom on a bank while the two men who made up the crew ran to the bows and prodded the mud with long poles to get us off. The navigator, although he was a local man, had misjudged the depth of the water, and I could see it was easy enough to do so. The Berau delta had required careful navigation, but this tentacle of the Bulungan estuary was far narrower and trickier even for this tiny craft.

I had looked up 'Bulungan' in the *Kerinci*'s copy of the *Pilot* and it made no bones about the hazards it posed at low water.

> The islands and land forming the delta are low, monotonously wooded and marshy, and almost covered at high water . . . . Of the numerous arms of the delta of Sungai Bulungan only two are of any importance for shipping . . . . The minimum depth of low water level in the main entrance 2.5 ft. (0.8 metres).
> . . . As local knowledge is necessary for proceeding up them, none of the marks for these rivers will be described and no direction given.

Those entries have sounds of 'you-have-been-warned' about them, and undoubtedly it was true that local knowledge was absolutely necessary. One twist of the estuary was so blocked with silt that the flow of water was reduced to a rivulet of little more than 10 feet wide; we had to press into the bank of an island as spindly branches of emaciated trees rattled on the awning and the long-haired youth at the wheel had to duck to avoid being swept away. Mud was visible close below the surface and when we grounded for an instant it was as if a hand had snatched our keel – before we hauled off with the water, a rich brown soup, gurgling below us. *Fiona* would never have made it; *Mauru III* would have stuck fast on the first bend. Lingard and

Abdullah forced a way up here, but how long it took them is not recorded.

The passengers talked or drank cola or beer, slept and snored. Young Al Joofree smoked incessantly, giving a new meaning to the expression 'chain-smoking'. He could join two cigarettes together, thrusting their combined lengths into a holder to make a wand of tobacco over six inches long. 'Sorry, mister,' he said to me, as people choked in the confined space under the awning. 'I like to smoke.' I was glad I was sitting in the stern with my head in the open air, and wondered why the other passengers did not throw him overboard.

Nipa palms on both sides of the river grew into a palisade 15 feet high, which was interrupted now and again by stretches of dense trees. Here proboscis monkeys agitated the branches, thrusting their absurd banana-shaped noses through the leaves and observing us with disapproving eyes rather as grumpy clubmen peer at intruders over the top of their newspapers.

The river opened up at last and ran straight and deep to the little town of Tanjung Selor, which was mostly hidden in trees with a wharf and an hotel and a few low houses immediately visible. Across the

273

river was a similar strip of low dwellings, and this was Tanjung Plas, where the former rajahs of Bulungan had built their stockades and palaces. A wall of wooded hills ringed Tanjung Plas and its houses, like those of Tanjung Selor were half-buried in mist-shrouded foliage. Behind the wharf at Tanjung Selor narrow lanes led away towards bungalows enclosed by patches of green, or the spire of a church, the dome of a mosque, football posts on the playing field of a primary school. We had arrived at a sprawling village rather than a town – or toy-town – since neither the churches nor the mosques looked much larger than big doll's houses.

At Alfred's house his mother – a slim, attractive lady with the fair skin of Menado – greeted me, showing some surprise, but at least she showed no alarm. The house was one storeyed like all its neighbours, but for Bulungan it was modern; simply and comfortably furnished with sofas in grey leatherette and grey wall-to-wall carpets. Two or three huge Chinese jars of the sort in which Dayaks in the jungle store their *tuak* stood in corners.

Air conditioning had not reached Bulungan and in the bedroom that Alfred, who now was begging me to call him Eddy as his family did, had generously given up to me I sweltered in the humidity of an approaching thunderstorm. Eddy had thoughtfully brought me a portable electric fan, but it barely managed to stir the air. In the night thunder broke overhead, the town's electricity failed, the fan stopped, and then all I could feel was the sweat cascading off me and I only hoped that the mosquitoes would not penetrate the thick screen of insecticide I had squirted with abandon round the room.

By day all was well. In the early hours the cool weather came and turned the sweaty night into unreality. Eddy's mother served eggs and bread and rice and tea. The house was pleasantly decorated in a part Dayak, part Christian way: garishly painted Kenyan Dayak shields, a framed needlework reproduction of the Lord as Shepherd, crook in hand, a lamb in his arms; large prints of vividly coloured hornbills and one of a giant woodpecker; and a wall mat woven in some silky material showing the scene on Calvary with the text 'Yesu mati untuk kita', Jesus died for us. There was enough breeze to keep things moderately cool when we sat on the terrace under a mynah in a wicker cage – perhaps the only member of the species I have come across that had nothing to say for itself.

*

To my surprise and pleasure Suparno appeared next morning by the first boat from Tarakan, grinning with satisfaction that he had caught me. He had been slightly delayed by pressure of work in Berau, but he hoped he was not too late. Suparno took everything in his stride; he was always cheerful. He might have merely bicycled round the corner for our rendezvous; but in fact he had flown to Tarakan in a tiny bumpy plane on which he had barely managed after a struggle and a small bribe or two to find a seat. From Tarakan he had had to hurl himself on to the boat as it was pulling away from the wharf and in doing so had lightly bruised his shoulder.

After his breakfast in a *warung* by the jetty, Suparno came with Eddy and me by canoe to see the Sultan's former palace across the river at Telok Plas.

Communists, according to Suparno, had burnt most of it in 1963 – a turbulent time in Indonesia – and the new palace, a museum of sorts, was extraordinarily elaborate, sumptuous compared to those at Gowa or even in Berau. 'Thick carpets,' I wrote in my notebook, 'fine Chinese vases and carved bureaux, tables and high-backed chairs inlaid with mother-of-pearl. The last Sultan, Jalaluddin, who died in 1958, looks down from a wall in a gold braided coat and a plumed hat and sword.'

'The Sultan seems to have been richer than your Sultan in Gunung Tabor,' I remarked to Suparno.

'Oh, yes. Much richer.'

The Sultan of Bulungan had made a treaty of friendship with Belcher, identical to the one signed by the genial ruler of Gunung Tabor. Belcher was under no illusions about the close ties between Bulungan and the Illanun pirates of Sulu and Mindanao who sallied out annually in fleets of 90-foot boats with a hundred oarsmen each and armed with 20-pound brass cannon to raid, burn and collect slaves. Slaves captured along the coast of north Borneo, or snatched from the coastal villages of Sarawak and Brunei, or kidnapped in raids on one of the undefended islands of the Eastern Archipelago, were regularly sold to the Bugis Sultans of Bulungan and of Koti on the Mahakam river above, and they in turn sold them to Dayak tribes further inland. If you add the Sultan's legitimate income from virtually limitless supplies of rattans, birds' nests, dammar and gutta-percha to the ransom or sale of slaves, no wonder the rulers of old Bulungan were rich men. A treaty meant British citizens were less likely to be held for colossal ransoms.

*

There was a cosiness about Bulungan that had been missing in Berau. It had to do with its smaller size and the narrowness of the river, although its remoteness, too, encouraged the feeling of intimacy in isolation. The Berau at Tanjung Redeb was a far bigger stretch of water, being the commingling of the Segai and the Kelai which divided the riverine settlements of Tanjung Redeb, Gunung Tabor and Sambaliung; whereas here the single river actually seemed to unite Tanjung Selor and Tanjung Plas.

What was Eddy's life here? Secondary school in Tanjung Redeb; followed by exile to college in another up-river town, Samarinda; the annual family holiday – boat to Tarakan and steamer to Surabaya; irregular shopping expeditions to Tarakan – three hours down and up the familiar muddy stream with its silted tidal channels, its proboscis monkeys, its eagles patrolling the rustling nipas, and tiny kingfishers flashing like jewels from bank to bank: the equatorial sun and the crushing tropical downpours.

If you had known nothing else you got used to the wet heat in this oven of a place, and the inescapable insects, the fluctuating electricity, the telephones that could barely make a connection beyond the next river down the coast. You had to reconcile yourself to the isolation; the forests and limestone mountains shaped like vast organ stops were only the visible tip of the tens of thousands of square miles of wilderness at one's back. Up there, the Dayak villages lay isolated in patches of cultivation hemmed in by trees with tangled roots where evil spirits lurked. They could only be reached in longboats with reliable engines, for a sudden loss of power among rapids plunging over half-visible rocks guaranteed a boat dashed to pieces and no hope of survival.

Suparno's life in Berau had not been so different from Eddy's; it was just that Bulungan was smaller and remoter. In both of these young men, Malay and Dayak, remoteness and a simple life had bred good nature.

The thin, well dressed, chain-smoking toff on the boat from Tarakan had been the first Al Joofree I met; a second member of the family came the next afternoon to meet me at Eddy's. This was Mohsin (spelled 'Muchsin' in the Indonesian way), a plump, youngish man who spoke a little English in a soft, friendly voice and who, to my surprise, arrived at the door in a brand-new air-conditioned Toyota jeep.

Mohsin, I later discovered, was the most successful businessman in the Al Joofree family. Not only did he own the only air-conditioned jeep on the river, his house was air-conditioned, too, though even he was the victim of the frequent power failures. He had prestige; he owned the only petrol station in Bulungan.

Mohsin had come to take me to Kampong Arab where the Al Joofrees were gathering to offer me tea and talk of the great Syed Abdullah. They had had, Mohsin confided, word from Samarinda and Berau that I was coming.

A series of old wooden buildings lined the riverbank, most of them two-storeyed with colonnades supporting upstairs balconies. It was impossible to tell their age. Some of them had been elegant houses and some were now used as warehouses. Where the road ended with a sign warning that to proceed further would mean an abrupt plunge into the water, a sharp left turn took us to a lane of bungalows of similar modest design with louvred glass windows and green-framed lintels. A tall, beefy, smiling man stood on the verandah in a white skullcap and a checkered red and white sarong. 'Haji Al Hud,' said Mohsin, introducing us, and he gave my hand a powerful squeeze.

The interior of Hud's house was somewhat smaller than Eddy's, and instead of Calvary and the Lord posing as a shepherd on its walls the pictures showed the Kaaba at Mecca and turbaned men on camels riding between palms in the silvery light of a full moon.

Other Al Joofrees soon joined us, kicking off their sandals at the door and hitching up their sarongs before arranging themselves around me on the sofa and chairs. There were about a dozen of them between the ages of about thirty and seventy.

The first of them, Saihan, in a large white skullcap, a sallow-faced man with unusually large ears and a gloomy face, the family historian, was the eldest. He was the father of Mohsin and also Syed Abdullah's grandson. Like the rest of them he was helpful, but I seldom, if ever, saw him smile. Next there was Saleh Al Joofree; younger than Saihan yet older than Hud and remarkable for his height. The others I cannot now put names to – I was not there long enough and they were so many – although I see from my notes there was a Hassan Al Joofree and an Abu Bakr. They all welcomed me, though none as kindly as Hud or (above all) Mohsin, who – apart from Eddy and Suparno – was one of the most endearing individuals I met in Kalimantan. Without exception, the Al Joofrees had one thing in common – the long Arab nose.

Saihan calculated that as many as two hundred Arabs lived in Berau and Bulungan; but few, if any, spoke Arabic. Everyone spoke *bahasa Indonesia*; no Arabic was taught in schools.

About their illustrious ancestor Syed Abdullah, son of old Syed Mohsin, late of 36 Raffles Place, Singapore, they knew quite a lot. After all, we were sitting a short stone's throw from the site of his house, his warehouses and his wharf. 'The Sultan of Bulungan welcomed Syed Abdullah here,' smiled Saleh, 'because he thought he would bring him much money.'

When one of them asked if there had been a German in Tanjung Redeb at the time of Abdullah, I told them about Olmeijer and Captain Lingard, and how Syed Abdullah had managed to run them out of the Berau thanks to his father's foresight in buying steamers.

I thought they would be interested in the reference to Syed Mohsin in the *Singapore and Straits Directory* for 1883 and I read it to them: 'Syed Mohsin bin Salleh, merchant and shipowner of 36 Raffles Place, with branch houses in Brow and Bulungan and agencies in Samaran, Soerabaya, Bally, Macassar, Pulo Laut, Saigon, Penang, Galle, Karical, Aden, Jeddah, Suez.'

At this point they seemed to forget about their tea, and having got their attention, I told them one or two things they were unlikely to have known; the names, for example, of four steamers Syed Mohsin had owned – the *Emily I*, the *Tiang Wat Seng*, the *Eastern Isles*, and the *Vidar*. I ripped out a page of my notebook and drew a sketch for them, based on Conrad's description of the Al Joofree house-flag – a white crescent on a red ground in a green border. I told them of Joseph Conrad's arrival in Berau as first officer of Syed Mohsin's *Vidar*, and Lingard's trade with Berau and Bulungan, but neither the name Conrad nor Lingard meant anything to them.

I read to them, slowly, with Eddy translating as best he could, the obituary of Syed Mohsin in the *Singapore Free Press* on 22 May 1894.

Another of the old faces of Singapore has passed away today in Syed Massim [Mohsin] bin Sallie Al Jeoffrie, an Arab merchant who twenty or thirty years ago had a large business and owned several steamers in this place. He first came to Singapore about 1840, as the Nakodah, or master, of an Arabian trading vessel, and having then saved a few dollars he opened a small shop in Arab Street. In time he amassed a good deal of money and bought some steamers, and was a rich man; but his business did not continue to prosper, for times changed and the old systems of thirty or forty years before were no longer successful after the many changes which the opening of the Suez Canal and speedy steamer communication to all the native countries round Singapore brought about. In 1891 he was compelled to place his affairs in the hands of trustees for his creditors, and about that time his eye-sight, which had been failing for some time, failed almost completely. His

office for many years was in the building next to the former Oriental Bank premises which are just being pulled down. There was, perhaps, no native merchant better known in Singapore in the old days than Syed Massim was, but of late years, in his misfortune, he has been little known except to the older residents. He has been very ill for some weeks and his death was expected. The funeral took place this afternoon at 2 o'clock and there was a very large crowd of persons. All the principal Arabs, and many of the old European residents were present. He was close upon 80 years of age.

The competitive world of modern maritime trade with its international ramifications had become in the end too much for Syed Mohsin, as well as for Lingard. A pity for the people of this region for, according to Conrad, Syed Mohsin's extensive almsgiving covered almost the whole Archipelago.

A silence fell while the Al Joofrees contemplated all that.

In the silence Saleh said, 'Syed Abdullah is buried here.'

I was astonished. Buried here? I had never dreamed I might find Abdullah *here*. In Penang, perhaps, or Singapore. But not in Bulungan.

'He died of a tumour of the brain in Tarakan. He died in 1911.'

'May I see his grave?'

'Of course,' cried Hud. 'We thought you would like to. Saleh and Mohsin will take us tomorrow.'

I was impatient to go straightaway – why lose a second? But the sun was beginning to go down. We had sat here longer than I thought. I wondered about the character of Abdullah. In Conrad's novels he is a formidable and pious grandee. Had he been loved as well as revered?

Saihan, his grandson, answered. 'To tell you the truth – he wasn't a very loving man as far as his children were concerned. He had always told them one thing, only one thing – "Make money!" He drove them on to sell rattans, and then more rattans. Money, he said, money! And the more money he made, the more he made them work.' Saihan's picture of Abdullah was of a stern, exacting patriarch.

Leaving Hud's house we walked back to Eddy's through the twilit lanes of Kampong Arab, between village houses not much different from those Abdullah had seen. One old house in particular seemed to harbour Al Joofree bric-a-brac from a much older time. Out of it one of the Al Joofrees brought an old oil-lamp for me to look at; a relic of the turn of the century, I was told. 'Ross Patent Sunlight Lamp' was embossed on its ornate glass globe which was supported by a pair of ornamental gryphons.

'Antique,' said Hud nodding sagely. But how antique I could not tell. Nor could I judge the age of a dilapidated strongbox – 'Abdullah's' – which might have been there for twenty, fifty or a hundred and fifty years, judging from the rust, dirt and its broken locks.

On the riverbank the site of Abdullah's wharf was marked by a massive iron ring half sunk in the earth: one of the mooring rings Abdullah tied his father's ships to, Hud said. Any one of the ancient planked buildings facing the water looked old enough to have been there in Abdullah's time. So did an old jetty rotting in the water – only a few dead piles by now, decaying under a grove of mangosteen trees. How on earth had *Emily I* or the *Eastern Isles*, or Lingard's *Rajah Laut* managed to arrive at this remote reach of the river? The water was deep here, but how had they negotiated that impossible delta?

Back in Eddy's house I dug a battered copy of *An Outcast of the Islands* from my bag and read about Syed Abdullah, this 'stern and exacting' man, whose grave I was going to see next day.

> For upwards of forty years Abdulla had walked in the way of his Lord. Son of the rich Syed [Mohsin], the great Mohamedan trader of the Straits, he went forth at the age of seventeen on his first commercial expedition, as his father's representative on board a pilgrim ship chartered by a wealthy Arab to convey a crowd of pious Malays to the Holy Shrine. That was in the days when steam was not in those seas .... The voyage was long, and the young man's eyes were opened to the wonders of many lands. Allah had made it his fate to become a pilgrim

very early in life .... Later on it became clear that the book of his destiny contained the programme of a wandering life. He visited Bombay and Calcutta, looked in at the Persian Gulf, beheld in due course the high and barren coast of the Gulf of Suez, and this was the limit of his wanderings westward. He was then twenty-seven, and the writing on his forehead decreed that the time had come for him to return to the Straits and take from his dying father's hand the many threads of a business that was spread all over the Archipelago: from Sumátra to New Guinea, from Batavia to Palawan ....

That explained how Abdullah became the controller of a great commercial network.

Owner of ships, he was often on board one or another of them. In every port he had a household – his own or that of a relation – to hail his advent .... In every port there were rich and influential men eager to see him, there was business to talk over, there were important letters to read: an immense correspondence, enclosed in silk envelopes –

What had Abdullah *looked* like? Conrad may have invented his looks even though it is possible he actually saw him:

He was very handsome, and carried his small head high with meek gravity. His lofty brow, straight nose, narrow dark face with its chiselled delicacy of feature, gave him an aristocratic appearance which proclaimed his pure descent. His beard was trimmed close and to a round point. His large brown eyes looked out steadily with a sweetness that was belied by the expression of his thin-lipped mouth. His aspect was serene. He had a belief in his own prosperity which nothing could shake ....

Whether that description fitted Abdullah or not, Conrad had certainly conveyed the essence of an Al Joofree face.

I had expected Abdullah's grave to be elaborate, befitting his fame and his fortune; an affair of marble canopies, cupolas, domes and labyrinthine eulogies in the Arab script. But it was nothing like that. It was as unassuming as any Muslim grave could be, its site indicated only by an unremarkable wooden *nisan* – the usual peg-like Muslim equivalent of a headstone – among a collection of similarly unremarkable headboards, flat-faced or cylindrical, scattered about a wide expanse of bedraggled grass.

One of Abdullah's daughters was buried in his plot – 'she died in 1902,' according to Saihan – and two of his wives, one a Sulu lady, the other from Malinau, a village which is on a river to the north of Bulungan.

We wandered about in the calf-deep grass, the Al Joofrees fanning out to inspect other Arab graves to the point where the undergrowth faded into foliage and trees.

To Saihan I said, 'Is it surprising that Syed Abdullah doesn't have a more elaborate tomb?'

'He was not one for a big display.'

Conrad had written of the 'meek gravity' that was a product of Abdullah's 'belief in his own prosperity'. As a descendant of the Prophet, he had, of course, another belief – that his prosperity came not from his brilliance but uniquely from Allah's favour. It was only in Europe that successful businessmen had themselves expensively cast in bronze and stuck on pedestals in city squares.

One of the Al Joofrees had heard of a European grave in the undergrowth, and we scattered through the even thicker grass with parangs to clear pathways among fallen branches and piles of dead leaves.

Suddenly Mohsin cried, 'Here! There's a *belanda*, a Dutchman. Here!' And Saleh, hacking at the undergrowth, called out, 'Here's another.'

I looked over Mohsin's shoulder and read with difficulty on the face of badly mildewed stone a name: 'G. Hune'. It meant nothing to me, and I doubted that the other grave was more interesting. I was wrong. A few minutes of scraping at a thick layer of moss and creepers revealed a surprisingly well-preserved headstone, on the top half of which an inscription was clearly visible:

Sacred
To the Memory of
JAMES KENNEDY
of Arran, Buteshire, Scotland
Died 16 August 1870
Aged 39

There was an outline of more writing; grass and moss obscured it, and we scraped and hacked until two more lines were gradually revealed –

This stone is inscribed
by his sincere friend

'Let's find out who the sincere friend is!'

Mohsin and I were kneeling now, scraping at the stone face with our fingers and the point of a parang; at last the creepers fell away and a name began to appear. 'It says "Adrian",' Eddy said, his nose close to the stone. But it was not 'Adrian' – it was 'William'. And with a final tug the last word was exposed:

'LINGARD'

I sat back and stared at it. We had almost missed the stone William Lingard had erected to his friend James Kennedy in the year he had installed Olmeijer in Berau. Syed Abdullah had died forty-one years later. Had he known that a Christian grave would be so close to his own before that last journey to Tarakan? Would he have cared?

Mohsin Al Joofree, who seemed to think of everything, brought some chalk from his Toyota and smeared it over the tomb's inscription. The stone was well preserved and erect on the edge of the jungle. Now the moss was gone the words 'WILLIAM LINGARD' stood out boldly in sturdy capitals.

One question remained: who was James Kennedy?

Later, from the shipping list of the *Makassarsch Handelsblad*, I found a sort of answer: a Captain Kennedy, the master of an English sailing ship called the *Fanny*, had sailed from Makassar for Bulungan on 21 June 1868, and on 24 November that same year he had returned in the same vessel to Makassar from a voyage to Berau. The *Fanny* was again reported in Makassar from Berau in 1873, and by then the Master had become a certain J. D. Voll. If the grave in Bulungan was that of Captain Kennedy of the *Fanny*, who died between the last two dates, the presence of a new master was accounted for. As master of the *Fanny*, Kennedy would have known Lingard well. As a fellow British captain, following the same trade to places like Bulungan and Berau, it was extremely likely that he was 'his sincere friend'. As for the *Fanny*, a look through the records of shipping in Singapore showed that a two-masted sailing vessel of that name was registered there in 1863; the entry under 'Owners' reads, 'Francis Thomas McDougall, Lord Bishop of Labuan'.

But another theory is possible. I have recently read a reference to a letter supposedly written in 1875 by Lingard himself, in which he refers to 'my schooner *Fanny* outward bound to Boelengan'. In which

284

case James Kennedy was the master of a ship belonging to William Lingard. 'A sincere friend', indeed.

I have a photograph in front of me as I write of the Al Joofrees of Bulungan. They stand awkwardly, unused to posing for cameras, in white short-sleeved shirts; one or two wear songkoks, and Saihan his extra-large white skullcap. They all wear sandals on their bare feet. They are standing on the steps of Saleh's bungalow in the sunlight. On the left is Mohsin, one of Syed Abdullah's great-grandsons, whose full name is Mohsin bin Saihan bin Salim bin Abdullah.

I had much to thank them for. They were friendly to a foreign writer arriving up the river out of the blue with an interest in their family that no one had shown before. Above all, Mohsin became, I hope, a true friend. He was a man with flair – his house was the only air-conditioned residence in Bulungan, the only one with a front lawn, though an artificial one, he admitted, because lawns are out of the question in Bulungan's tropical sun and rain. Inside the house an artificial waterfall splashed noisily over an arrangement of stones in the floor of his wood-panelled living room where he kept a collection of bulbous Chinese jars big enough to hide Ali Baba's forty thieves.

When the time came for me and Suparno to catch the boat back to Tarakan, Mohsin found a pretext to sneak ahead of us to buy our tickets and a couple of cans of beer for the hot three-hour trip. And he waited on the wharf in the sun until it was time for the boat to cast off and rattle away down the river.

One of the last things he did was to mention the photograph of Syed Abdullah.

'Photograph?' I asked him, astonished. 'Were there photographs in those days?'

'Oh, yes. It is not a first-class picture, but it is there. Go to Johore Bahru. Ask for Ali bin Abdullah al Joofree. He has it.'

'Ali bin Abdullah? There is a son – he is Syed Abdullah's *son?*'

'Yes,' replied Mohsin, smiling. 'He is very old, of course. But he has the photograph.'

Twenty four

Back in Singapore, I drove one afternoon to Johore Bahru, on the brink, I hoped, of a discovery. It was difficult to believe I would meet Abdullah's son and see the old Syed's picture all in one afternoon, as Mohsin Al Joofree had said. It was not that he would have lied to me. It was simply that things did not happen like that.

I passed the address Mohsin had given me to the driver of my taxi, but when we reached it I saw to my dismay it was a school. Tiny children were tearing round a playground, laughing and shouting. When I managed at last to detach a reluctant teacher from the infantile bedlam, he misunderstood me and thought I wanted to buy the building.

'No, no,' I told him, 'I am looking for Syed Ali Al Joofree.'

'I don't think he is selling this place,' the man repeated doubtfully.

He had no idea in any case where Syed Ali lived. This, I thought in despair, is the end of the trail.

But it was the driver – a Malay from Singapore, God lengthen his life – who after a long and rowdy palaver extracted, heaven knows how, a new address, and this proved to be the correct one. To my intense relief, almost at once an attractive woman in early middle age answered the bell and said in perfect English and with a charming smile, 'Al Joofree? I am an Al Joofree. Come in, come in.'

I know now that Sharifah Zaina binti Mohamed has a habitually sunny disposition. A teacher until recently, which was why her English was so good, she confirmed that Ali bin Abdullah was the son of the great Syed Abdullah; he was her grandfather, her mother's father. Unfortunately he had recently died. When I told her why I had wanted to meet him – about my search – and who had told me where I might find him, she threw up her hands in dismay.

'Oh, what a shame,' she cried, 'and you've come all the way from Borneo. He was such a dear old man. I called him "Aba". I was his daughter's eldest child, you see.' She smiled at her recollection of her grandfather, and repeated, 'Oh, what a shame. You should have met him. He was eighty-six when he died but he loved to recall those old days. We should have made a recording of his memories, really.'

At least she had Abdullah's photograph. In fact she brought me two photographs. One, taken in 1924, showed her grandfather as a young man in a white suit that might have been a college uniform. He had glossy black hair then, the unmistakable prominent Al Joofree nose, large gentle eyes and a humorous mouth that made him look as if he were about to smile. He had ended up in Johore's Public Works Department.

The other photograph was what I had been waiting for. There was Syed Abdullah. The photograph showed a well-shaped head sur-mounted by a high white skullcap with ears slightly larger than the average (though not as large as Saihan's). His eyes were disquieting. Focused off-camera they gazed under straight dark eyebrows steadily into the studio wall with an icily appraising expression from under drooping lids that made you glad he was not looking you in the eye. Of course, his nose was the straight, long nose of the Al Joofrees and the lower part of his face – far from being well-trimmed as Conrad said – was sparsely covered with a nondescript beard that sprouted raggedly from the line of his jaw bone. The picture showed a mouth that was decidedly full-lipped and sensual, contradicting Conrad's 'severe' and 'thin-lipped'. In the photograph any sweetness was in the mouth, not in the bleak, searching look of those cold eyes.

When I spread photographs of the Bulungan Al Joofrees on the table the Sharifah was entranced. She had never seen them; she did not know Al Joofrees lived there.

'I must write to them,' she cried excitedly. 'But to which one? Mohsin? Oh, he looks nice.' She laughed.

Then she added, 'It's funny, it takes a total stranger – an Englishman – to bring back the family history.'

'I hope you don't resent the total stranger.'

'Certainly not,' she laughed again. 'I am glad to hear all this.'

After looking at them a bit longer, she said, 'You know, there are no Al Joofree women in your pictures.'

'No,' I told her, 'I didn't see any.'

'Do they keep them hidden?' She hooted with laughter. 'They can't have eaten them surely. By the way, you say the family in Bulungan told you Abdullah was severe. Well, so was his son – I mean my grandfather. He was a strict Muslim. He was always shooing young men away from my door. But at least – no – we didn't have to wear a veil. It wasn't as bad as that.'

On my way back to Singapore I sat with Abdullah's photograph in my hand. It was not as well-defined as a modern camera and a modern film would have made it. But the main thing was that it was Syed Abdullah. I divested him of his skullcap and imagined him in the turban and long white robe Conrad said he wore as he pushed through the crowd round Almayer's shabby house to look down on his dead enemy. The only white man on the east coast, the sad, dismal man he had bested so many times, lay there lifeless and quite harmless now. Was there in Abdullah's ageing heart, as Conrad had surmised, a feeling of regret for that thing gone out of his life? Could the cold eyes in the picture I held in my hand ever have registered regret? I could see him, this proud Arab, on that promontory of the distant Berau, clicking his beads and piously whispering the name of the Merciful, the Compassionate. Then in my imagination I saw him stalking away, solemn and implacable.

I did not go straight back to my hotel. I stopped the taxi in one of the oldest parts of Singapore, off Beach Road, at the corner of Arab Street. Abdullah's father, Syed Mohsin, had started life in this humble lane. The chrysalis had grown here; the proud butterfly had flapped its wings at 36 Raffles Place.

I walked down the street of narrow-fronted shops, running back, bigger than they appeared. These shops had been here a long time and the street names reflected the population of Straits Arabs that once had congregated here: Jeddah Street, Bussorah Street, Muscat Street, Baghdad Street, Haji Street, Arab Street itself. 'The House of Batik' was still owned by an Arab family called Al Juneid. I had told Abdullah Al Juneid that I was going to Celebes and he had been interested because he imported silk sarongs and sandalwood, *kayu gaharu*, from Paré-Paré and Samarinda. I wanted to tell him about Berau and Bulungan, and how there was *kayu gaharu* to be bought there from Arabs. The Juneids were an old Singapore family; like the Al Joofrees and the Alsagoffs, they had arrived here in the 1820s or 1830s soon after the city's founder, Stamford Raffles himself. Like

288

most of the Arabs they came originally from the Hadhramaut in southern Arabia, and one Al Juneid had stopped off in Palembang in Sumatra to make his first fortune before coming here.

Abdullah Al Juneid was away so I gave Mohsin Al Joofree's card to his eldest son. I had not the remotest business interest in any deal they might come to. It just seemed a good gesture to put two pioneering Straits Arab families in touch.

By chance, the House of Batik had recently received a new shipment of silk Bugis sarongs. Inspecting counters stacked with the checkered sarongs from Sengkang and Paré-Paré was an odd experience, and I saw again quite clearly the road north to Paré-Paré from Makassar, the coast road past Tomisa reef, then the climb to Lake Tempé, sombre and mysterious, within mountains where thunder rumbled like old cannons of squabbling rajahs. Even so, Princess What-for, the old *kratons* with their jewelled krisses, and Bugis rings with magic stones seemed a long way from the rumble of traffic in Beach Road.

Leaving Arab Street, I began to stroll west down North Bridge Road, past street after narrow street where for years Javanese, Bugis, Arabs, Malays and Indians had lived and traded side by side. The Old Singapore of the Europeans began at Stamford Road. I crossed it opposite the Capitol cinema, the old site of the Sailors' Home and then branched off down the path that runs diagonally across the shaded grounds of St Andrew's Cathedral. A service was in progress that evening, although it was not a Sunday. A choir, accompanied by a piano, was singing 'The King of Love my Shepherd is'. In the thirty years and more that he lived in Singapore, Austin Williams must have listened to similar hymns Ancient and Modern on this very spot. Had they brought back to him memories of an English church by the sea, of his parson-father, of his brothers and sisters, of that pony 'which all you boys used to ride'?

It was getting dark by the time I reached the long façade of City Hall and the Supreme Court. The lights were going on in the Cricket Club and in some of the high floors of the skyscrapers over the river. Beyond the green stretch of the Padang, the gnarled rain trees interlaced their branches to spread a screen of leaves over the huge hotels that these days blocked the view of ships in the Anchorage.

Passing the Victoria Memorial Hall and the stately Empress Building I came to the Cavenagh Bridge. A plaque overhead said simply: 'Major General Orfeur Cavenagh, Governor Straits Settlements from 1859 to 1867'. And a reassuring motto under the coat of arms read, '*Pax et Copia*', Peace and Plenty.

I leaned over the water. The river was dark and green and empty; the sampans and *tongkangs* had long since been cleared away, the godowns closed, its access to the sea blocked by the new artificial islands created by reclamation. Captain Henry Ellis, the Master Attendant, would not have believed his eyes. A bank, all marble cladding and plate glass, stood white as a sepulchre on the site of Charlie Emmerson's, and only the General Post Office survived as a reminder of the past, a monument to old-fashioned dignity with its huge columns, its massive stone porches, its sheer solidity.

There was still a quiver, a whisper from the past on this bridge. 'There is a lot of discontent in Wajo,' an old used-up voice seemed to breathe in my ear. 'Drop it, Captain Lingard!'

'Lingard never dropped anything in his life, Jörgenson,' I said out loud to the water below. But he had. Lingard had dropped Hassim and Immada, and Jörgenson himself. He had left Almayer to cope all alone up the Berau.

The Berau: how far was it from where I stood on Cavenagh Bridge? It seemed a question to be answered no longer in miles or kilometres but in years.

The Singapore river was not a bad place to consider the different destinies of Jim and Austin. Austin Williams had grown old in his ship chandlers office; his face inexorably sagging and coarsening, his watch chain year by year stretching across an ever more grossly swelling paunch, the folds of three or four chins burying the firm jawline of the *Jeddah*'s young and handsome first officer.

Jim had died young as befitted his romantic notion of himself. He had taken old Stein's advice and followed the romantic dream, literally, *ad finem*. At the mouth of the Pantai Marlow had parted from a man who had transcended his shame and become a hero in the world of the Berau.

Of course, the triumphant dream was brought crashing down, ironically enough, by one of the few white men out here who had never heard of the mate of the *Jeddah*: Gentleman Brown. With a murderous crowd of ruffians he had come from Sulu on the scrounge for provisions and loot,

> They were sixteen in all: two runaway blue-jackets, a lanky deserter from a Yankee man-of-war, a couple of simple, blond Scandinavians, a mulatto of sorts, one bland Chinaman who cooked – and the rest of the nondescript spawn of the South Seas. None of them cared; Brown bent them to his will, and Brown, indifferent to gallows, was running away from the spectre of a Spanish prison.

This ill-assorted gang of murderers failed to overpower Jim's Bugis friends in Berau, and Jim – the last sort of person they had expected to meet in that godforsaken hole – was able to persuade them to go back in peace to wherever they had come from.

The Eurasian, Cornelius, was the traitor of Berau. Cornelius, eaten up by jealousy of Jim, guided Brown down the river by a secret way, and his gang of ruffians was able to surprise Dain Waris's inoffensive Bugis, waiting to make sure they actually left the delta. It was a cold-blooded act of revenge. Three volleys of shots decimated the Bugis almost to a man. Doramin's son, Dain Waris, Jim's best friend, jumped up just in time to receive a bullet in his forehead. That was the end of Jim.

When the news of his son's death reached Doramin, Jim saw at once that his destiny had run out. Doramin could only see what had happened as white man's treachery: Jim had arranged the surprise attack with his compatriot Brown; white men were always white men. Nothing would convince Doramin of any other truth. Dain Waris had been killed by his best friend. So Jim must die.

By the time Jim's canoe reached Doramin's side of the river, the old man's courtyard was full of armed Bugis.

Doramin, alone, immense and desolate, sat in his armchair with a pair of flintlock pistols on his knees . . . 'He came! He came!' was running from lip to lip. 'He hath taken it upon his own head,' a voice said aloud . . . [Jim] heard this and turned to the crowd. 'Yes. Upon my head . . . .' He waited awhile before Doramin, and then said gently, 'I am come in sorrow.' He waited again. 'I am come ready and unarmed . . . .'

The unwieldy old man made an effort to rise, clutching the flintlock pistols . . . while Jim stood stiffened and with bared head in the light of the torches, looking him straight in the face . . . Doramin, struggling to keep his feet . . . clung heavily with his left arm round the neck of a bowed youth and deliberately lifting his right, shot his son's friend through the chest.

'Not in the wildest days of his boyish dreams could he have seen the alluring shape of such an extraordinary success,' said Marlow of Jim's last moment. 'A pitiless wedding with a shadowy ideal of conduct.'

Is it better to die of bulbar paralysis, aged sixty-four, still 'under a cloud' – for even Austin's obituary mentioned his part in the *Jeddah* scandal – and be buried in the snake-ridden Bidadari Cemetery – or, like Jim, to go out in a flash, still young, on a bank of the Berau?

An impossible question.

On this bridge in Singapore I could imagine the twisting muddy coils of the Berau and hear the echo of Doramin's shot – it must have resounded up to Tanjung Redeb and down the river to shatter the silence that hangs over the tangle of nipas, mangroves and mud flats of the delta. I could see the fishermen at the mouth of the Pantai raising their heads in sudden curiosity, and the sea birds rising in alarm, screaming and wheeling on the green reef-bound islands I had passed through in *Fiona* and *Mauru III*.

Crack! A deafening report seemed to jolt the iron struts of Cavenagh Bridge. The air quivered; one of Singapore's sudden evening storms had arrived overhead. In the Anchorage lightning forked down from heavy black clouds silhouetting the dark outlines of the waiting ships. The first heavy spots of rain were making rings in the river beneath Cavenagh Bridge. I turned towards the Cricket Club to see if I could find a taxi, the lightning-clap of Doramin's shot reverberating in my ears.

It would take too long to explain the intimate alliance of contradictions in human nature which makes love itself wear at times the desperate shape of betrayal.

JOSEPH CONRAD, A Personal Record

Part Six
Home

Oswald's

twentyfive

I drove down to Porthleven on a summer's day, to Austin Williams's birthplace in that farthest part of Cornwall that seems like a foreign country because it is so unlike any other region of the West. Surrounded on three sides by wild ocean, its foreignness emphasised by place names ending in 'a' and 'o', the echo of the defeat of the great Spanish Armada still lives in the memory of generations of local-born seamen.

Across the treeless plains of Bodmin Moor, the road runs well inland from an Atlantic seaboard on whose huge cliffs the gales have bent the trees almost parallel to the ground.

' "Let him creep 20 feet underground and stay there!" ' – I quoted Captain Montague Brierly of the *Ossa* on the subject of Jim to a tangle-maned pony on the edge of the Moor. ' "Frankly I don't care a snap for all the pilgrims that ever came out of Asia, but a decent man should not behave like this to a full cargo of old rags in bales." '

Past Jamaica Inn, surrounded by cars and buses, I followed the road southeast towards Falmouth where Conrad had kicked his heels for nine months in 1882 while the *Palestine* was undergoing repairs enough to enable her to survive as far as the Bangka Strait and there blow up. Then I went wiggling down narrow lanes to a place which even in this old county seems unfathomably old: a little horseshoe-shaped fishing port near the very toe of Cornwall: Porthleven, where Austin Podmore Williams had been baptised by his own father on 30 May 1852.

' "My dad," ' Jim (and no doubt Austin Williams) had said when it was suggested he should go home after his disgrace, ' "has seen it all in the home papers by this time. I can never face the poor old chap." '

'Poor old chap'! – Austin Williams's father was hardly that, not by a very long chalk. An Anglo-Catholic ayatollah – that is what I would call him. Norman Sherry's expert homework had dug out a photograph of the Reverend Williams and his family that more than bears me out, and I too have discovered one or two additional things about the 'poor old chap' that put things in perspective.

No wonder Austin chose not to go home. Of course, he was right that his 'dad' had certainly seen it all in the papers – the talk of the *Jeddah* scandal must have swirled disconcertingly about the draughty parsonage of Porthleven like the dour midwinter gales that frequently torment that small and distant port. How did Mr Williams cope with it? Did he turn the scandal of his son's shame to advantage, preaching spirit-searing sermons from his seaside pulpit contrasting merchant navy officers who fail in their duty with the inability of the unerring power of God to abandon any ship of souls however lost they might seem to be? Or did he face out the shame of it in grim, Jehovah-like silence, his God-fearing eye gazing at his parishioners, daring – *daring* – all comers to connect *him* with such distant dereliction of Christian duty by a son of whom he now made it plain he had washed his hands?

The photograph of the Williams family shows them in the garden of the parsonage at Porthleven long before anyone had dreamed of a ship called the *Jeddah* – twelve years before, to be precise. 'Dad' – the Reverend Thomas Lockyer Williams – is seated, cross-legged and unsmiling under his mortarboard; his cassock buttoned severely up to a chin hidden under a chest-length beard. The beard itself, thick, dark and forbidding like deep tropical scrub, meets a similarly thick, dark moustache and sideburns that frame cold, sunken eyes, high cheekbones, and a turned-down mouth that looks as if it had never smiled. A

small girl leans against him – one of his fifteen children no doubt – and his wife seated beside him clasps two others. Two teenage boys, a young man, a young woman and an older man holding a wide hat complete the picture. Except for a figure on the extreme right. This is of a very young man in a distinctly naval or mercantile marine sort of uniform with an official-looking peaked cap leaning against the back of a chair. Hands in pockets, ankles casually crossed, handsome in a proud, self-assured way that could indicate an attitude ripe to develop into what someone writing a report might brand with the damning word 'officious'. It seemed to me that it might very well do so. There was no doubt in my mind who that brass-buttoned, well-built youth was staring unsmiling and warily self-satisfied at the camera. August 1868, someone had written on the photograph. The Bidadari Cemetery was forty-eight years away.

The road as it enters Porthleven dips steeply between low houses and shops. Below me I could see the pale blue sweep of the English Channel. Just before the harbour I turned sharp right, as I had been told, and there was the parish church. I drove through the gate and braked at the door. I was more or less on time. The Reverend Father Stephen Jones, who had arranged to be here, came out to meet me saying, 'Welcome, welcome.' No one could have looked less like Thomas Lockyer Williams, the bearded ayatollah. Stephen Jones was youngish and beefy, with an upright and active sort of build, a brick red, smiling face, and smart black sandals under his long, black cassock. When, later, he told me he owned a dog which he called 'Monstrance' – explaining, 'I have to have a sense of humour in this business' – I knew that there must have been quite a few changes up at the Parsonage since Williams's time.

From the outside, the church of St Bartholomew the Apostle has little to recommend it: no tower, long grim windows set in grey stone and a black tiled roof. 'All the goodies are inside,' was how Jones put it, leading me in; and there things were indeed very different. Past the spacious porch containing appeals on behalf of hostages in Beirut, I suddenly found myself in a high, wide building with white walls into which the sun streamed so that it was hard to imagine that the depressing exterior was part of the same building. There were beautiful things in that church, and Porthleven's vicar was proud of them.

'Dedicated in 1842, you'll find. See our alabaster altar and the panelled wood behind it. The first person buried here was a poor boy who fell into a plump – that's what they call a well in this part of Cornwall.' The most eye-catching feature of the church was the great wooden representation of an anchor that dominated the nave – as tall as a man, with a carved Christ draped from it, his hands nailed to the cross-bar.

'Thomas Lockyer Williams became vicar of Porthleven in August 1851,' the Rev. Jones was going on. 'He had been an undergraduate at Cambridge, but because he was a friend of John Keble he was responsible for putting the Oxford Movement into practice in this place. This was a pioneer Oxford Movement church under Williams. Anglo-Catholics – the greats, of course, were Newman and Pusey – and the quiet, saintly Keble. Porthleven was the first church in Cornwall to have vestments.' He smiled. 'I suppose when many people think of High Church, they think of "bells and smells". I am not sure if Williams introduced "bells and smells" here. Probably, but not necessarily.'

He handed me a booklet. 'History. It might interest you.' It did. When Parson Williams arrived in Porthleven the church was very drab, the booklet told me. There was no drain to the font so that after baptisms water had to be ladled out of it, to be scattered over the pews and floor to lay the dust. A sinister black bottle contained the communion wine. The porch was so miserably small, it was almost impossible to get coffins through it. Apart from that, Porthleven was a Nonconformist stronghold. Williams had to struggle to put things to rights – and he was obviously a born struggler. Six foot tall, the booklet said, and a 'stone-hard man who brought his family up with typical Victorian discipline, and taught his eldest sons to swim by throwing them off the rocks', giving one of them a nasty gash on the head. He was a scholar, a great chess-player, and a hellfire preacher. 'A very powerful preacher, oh yes,' said the Reverend Father Stephen Jones. 'He was even invited to speak in the London Docks. A great honour.'

Yes, no wonder poor Austin had preferred to stay in Singapore. Well, his self-made plan had worked in its way. He had earned forgiveness the hard way, but there wouldn't have been much mercy here. The bearded old man in Porthleven no doubt heard of his decision somehow; heard by roundabout means, and probably with a shiver of distaste, of Austin's marriage to a Eurasian woman. Perhaps he even heard of his death from bulbar paralysis, because Thomas Lockyer Williams died three years after his son – in 1919, aged ninety-seven. But for Austin to have come back here as a world-famous failure aged twenty-eight – no one could be expected to do that.

In the churchyard near the porch a clump of gravestones caught my eye, the first one marking the last resting place of Emma, Parson Williams's wife ('of Your Charity Pray for the Repose of her Soul'). Beside her were a fourteen-year-old daughter, Augusta, and Hilda, 'an infant sister who sleeps with her in Jesus. 1868'.

With the Reverend Stephen Jones I drove to the old Parsonage in the garden of which that family group had stood and sat and lounged so long ago. It stood on a hill above the town. It had ceased to be the vicar's home, Mr Jones said, in 1980. His parishioners spoke of lovely parties in the garden. It was too big for him: nineteen rooms. 'I moved to a little place right on the sea by the harbour mouth.' It was a handsome house, though: Cornish stone and warm red brick round the windows and doors; a small, elaborate stone cross on a gable. Its lawn was neatly mown and you could see under the trees the wall that had stood at the back of the group in the photograph. We rang the front door bell and a dog barked. But whoever lived there now was out.

'Many commanders of fine merchant ships came from these abodes of piety and peace,' Conrad wrote of places like Porthleven. And in *Lord Jim* he had thought of Jim's family 'peopling this quiet corner of the world as free of danger and strife as a tomb; never taken unawares; never called upon to grapple with fate.' Of all those brothers and sisters posed on this lawn, 'bone of his bone, flesh of his flesh, gazing with clear unconscious eyes', I imagined most clearly Jim himself as he might have been, 'returned at last – full of stature, standing disregarded amongst their untroubled shapes, with a stern and romantic aspect, but always mute, dark – under a cloud'.

The Reverend Father Stephen Jones gave me a hefty handshake outside the former parsonage. 'Drop by again,' he said. 'Any time.' Then I drove down the steep hill to the little harbour. It was shaped like an elongated stone horseshoe, surrounded along its rim by cosy two-storey houses. A storm more violent than most had struck Porthleven the winter before; Mr Jones had told me how half the church roof had been whipped off in the gale and 50-foot waves had battered the houses round the harbour so that they had to be evacuated. I could see the vicar now across the narrow harbour, bareheaded and ruddy, plump in his cassock, talking genially to a parishioner outside the Harbour Inn. I leaned my elbows on the ancient seawall that young Austin must have known and looked at the pale blue sea dancing at the harbour mouth, stretching away into the deep water of the Channel. The fitful sunlight came and went on its surface.

The subdued voice of old Stein among his butterflies came to me: 'A man that is born falls into a dream like a man who falls into the sea. To follow the dream, and again to follow the dream – and so – *ewig* – *usque ad finem*.' For ever. To the very end.

Huge, grey-eyed seagulls strutted among the stones or took to a sky clear and bright in a wind that was light and cool. A tanker began to pass very slowly left to right far out to sea. People were coming out of a waterside pub down the road and settling with their beer in the sun to look at the horizon.

> The good old time – the good old time. Glamour and the sea! . . . Tell me, wasn't that the best time, that time when we were young at sea . . . ?

I remained a few minutes longer leaning on the seawall. Then I went and joined the drinkers in the sun.

Kent, at the extreme opposite end of southern England, is where I ended my journey. With none of the bleakness of Cornwall, out of sight and sound of sea, its interior has nonetheless a calm, rolling remoteness that can remind one of slow ocean swells. Some friends took me to Oswald's, the house in which Joseph Conrad died in Bishopsbourne, my last port of call. It was a good-looking house with big windows, an elegant porch, a high sloping roof and tall, well-proportioned chimneys. The fair-sized garden and house were overlooked by the square, solid church tower and magnificent copper beech tree behind them. Conrad's study, with a bow window almost from floor to ceiling, looked out to a stream where a pair of kingfishers lived. How different were these gentle Kentish willows from the spreading trees that marked the site of Almayer's pathetic wooden house on the Berau, or those creepered giants that stood in mist-shrouded ranks over the grave of Syed Abdullah at Bulungan. Conrad's bedroom over the front door had once in its austerity reminded his son John of a captain's cabin – linoleum on the floor, a plain mahogany chest of drawers with a small mirror on it, an iron bedstead rather higher than is usual, with at its foot books by W. W. Jacobs and his old friends John Galsworthy and Cunninghame Graham; but the new occupants of Oswald's had given it over to billiards and darts. There had been tea in a small 'den' about as big as a

302

rabbit hole – strong China tea for Conrad and a slice of seed cake – and a whisky and soda before dinner. Conrad was abstemious. There had been no schooners of sherry and bitters in recollection of Emmerson's in Singapore; no pink gins in remembrance of the rascally Schomberg at Surabaya.

And so in this pleasant house 'the heat of life in the handful of dust, the glow in the heart that with every year grows dim, grows cold, grows small' had expired at last with life itself.

I crossed from Bishopsbourne through the rolling landscape sparsely dotted with little red-brick villages, by lanes sometimes too narrow for two cars abreast and roofed with canopies of leaves – a very English countryside, I thought – to Canterbury. It had been cricket week when Conrad was buried in the cemetery of St Thomas's Roman Catholic Church. That was just over by the time I got there. But it was still summer and the sun illuminated the grave that stood out quite plainly among other peoples' crosses.

Conrad's grave had no cross. It was unexpectedly and unusually beautiful – a thrusting, heavy, wedge-shaped, irregular slab of white rock. It stood as though immovable in the sunshine and something in the texture of the rock made it sparkle, so that it seemed immeasurably strong and alive. The inscription was black, clear and bold.

Joseph Teador Conrad
Korzeniowski
Born December 3rd 1857
Died August 3rd 1924

and then the inscription:

Sleep After Toyle, Port After Stormie Seas,
Ease After Warre, Death After Life Does Greatly Please

I laid my hand on its wonderfully uneven surface – on this seemingly imperishable rock. It was strange. I had set out to follow Conrad from his first escape from death as Second Officer Korzeniowski – I could hear Captain Henry Ellis: 'Polish? Russian? God knows' – in the Bangka Strait, to malarial Borneo where he had found Almayer, and to the Gulf of Siam where he had become master of the *Otago*. There had been storms and cholera and pirates on the way, but in the end it had come to this – a peaceful grave in a sunny cemetery in Canterbury in Kent.

In *Youth*, Marlow drank and said – 'Wasn't that the best time when we were young at sea?' His listeners nodded – the man of finance, the man of accounts, the man of law, all of whom had begun life in the merchant service – leaning on their elbows round the mahogany table, the bottles and the claret glasses. The polished table, reminding Conrad of a still sheet of brown water, reflected their faces 'marked by toil, by deceptions, by success, and by love'; and weary eyes that still looked anxiously for something out of life – an elusive something 'that while it is expected has already passed unseen, in a sigh, in a flash'.

After all these years, I have no recollection of the expressions on my school friends' faces or what they said when our Headmaster closed the covers of his anthology on 'the glow in the heart . . . that expires . . . before life itself', and the rest of it. Personally I might as well have been struck blind and deaf. And when years later I read out the same passage myself, how many of my listeners found in the words of Joseph Conrad something to inspire them? One would have made it worthwhile. I hope there was one.

Discover more about our forthcoming books through Penguin's FREE newspaper...

Penguin Quarterly

It's packed with:

- exciting features
- author interviews
- previews & reviews
- books from your favourite films & TV series
- exclusive competitions & much, much more...

Write off for your free copy today to:
Dept JC
Penguin Books Ltd
FREEPOST
West Drayton
Middlesex
UB7 0BR
NO STAMP REQUIRED

FOR THE BEST IN PAPERBACKS, LOOK FOR THE 🐧

In every corner of the world, on every subject under the sun, Penguin represents quality and variety – the very best in publishing today.

For complete information about books available from Penguin – including Puffins, Penguin Classics and Arkana – and how to order them, write to us at the appropriate address below. Please note that for copyright reasons the selection of books varies from country to country.

In the United Kingdom: Please write to *Dept JC, Penguin Books Ltd, FREEPOST, West Drayton, Middlesex, UB7 0BR.*

If you have any difficulty in obtaining a title, please send your order with the correct money, plus ten per cent for postage and packaging, to *PO Box No 11, West Drayton, Middlesex*

In the United States: Please write to *Dept BA, Penguin, 299 Murray Hill Parkway, East Rutherford, New Jersey 07073*

In Canada: Please write to *Penguin Books Canada Ltd, 2801 John Street, Markham, Ontario L3R 1B4*

In Australia: Please write to the *Marketing Department, Penguin Books Australia Ltd, P.O. Box 257, Ringwood, Victoria 3134*

In New Zealand: Please write to the *Marketing Department, Penguin Books (NZ) Ltd, Private Bag, Takapuna, Auckland 9*

In India: Please write to *Penguin Overseas Ltd, 706 Eros Apartments, 56 Nehru Place, New Delhi, 110019*

In the Netherlands: Please write to *Penguin Books Netherlands B.V., Postbus 3507, NL–1001 AH, Amsterdam*

In West Germany: Please write to *Penguin Books Ltd, Friedrichstrasse 10–12, D–6000 Frankfurt/Main 1*

In Spain: Please write to *Alhambra Longman S.A., Fernandez de la Hoz 9, E–28010 Madrid*

In Italy: Please write to *Penguin Italia s.r.l., Via Como 4, I-20096 Pioltello (Milano)*

In France: Please write to *Penguin France S.A., 17 rue Lejeune, F-31000 Toulouse*

In Japan: Please write to *Longman Penguin Japan Co Ltd, Yamaguchi Building, 2–12–9 Kanda Jimbocho, Chiyoda-Ku, Tokyo 101*

'Intrepid, reflective and gregarious ... plainly a man in a million and a writer in two' – Bernard Levin in the *Observer*

Return to the Marshes

A remarkable portrait of the remote and beautiful world of the Marsh Arabs. 'A superbly written essay which combines warmth of personal tone, a good deal of easy historical scholarship and a talent for vivid description rarely found outside good fiction' – Jonathan Raban in the *Sunday Times*

Slow Boats to China

Gavin Young's bestselling account of his extraordinary journey in small boats through the Mediterranean, the Red Sea, the Indian Ocean and the Malaya and China Seas to China.

Slow Boats Home

'I am decidedly envious of Gavin Young and his *Slow Boats Home*, successor to his highly entertaining *Slow Boats to China* ... a fascinating, memorable book' – Eric Newby in the *Guardian*. 'Like *Slow Boats to China* this is likely to become a classic of travel' – Francis King in the *Spectator*

Worlds Apart

A collection of journalistic pieces that are elegant, vivid and compassionate and show Gavin Young's acute understanding of the varied worlds in which we live. 'Some have to travel dangerously and it had better be Gavin Young to tell us about it' – Anthony Blond in the *Spectator*

and

Beyond Lion Rock: The Story of Cathay Pacific Airways